Yonder One World

By Frank Moraes

Report on Mao's China
Jawaharlal Nehru: A Biography
Yonder One World: A Study of Asia and the West

Yonder One World

A Study of Asia and the West

FRANK MORAES

The Macmillan Company 1958
New York   Toronto   London   Manila

First Printing
Printed in the United States of America

Library of Congress catalog card number: 58–6962

for
Rashid and Tara

Foreword

SINCE 1942 I have had occasion to travel a great deal through almost the whole of Asia. My travels include two visits to China under Kuomintang and Communist rule, and journeys to Japan, Indonesia, Indo-China, the Philippines, Burma, Thailand, Malaya, Pakistan and Ceylon. In between I have returned more than once to Europe where as a student I spent seven uninterrupted years, and I have also visited the United States, Australia and New Zealand. In the course of these travels I have had the good fortune to meet many of the leading personalities in the countries I visited, and some of their conversations are retailed in this book.

The relations between Asia and the West depend as much on an understanding of personalities as of principles. This book attempts to explain both and to present the Asian outlook on many of the problems which beset the world today, such as Communism, the future of democracy, State planning and free enterprise, military pacts, the Eisenhower doctrine and co-existence. If as a result the area of understanding and co-operation between Asia and the West is strengthened and extended, I shall feel that the effort was worth while.

Many friends have helped me in various ways. I am indebted particularly to Donald Thomas who read the manuscript and gave me the benefit of his judgement and advice. I am grateful also to B. Krishnaswamy who cheerfully typed the many drafts.

FRANK MORAES

Contents

1   Means and Ends

HE SAT on the floor in the flickering light of a kerosene lamp, and grouped around him were the shadowy white-clad figures of his disciples. A shawl draped his bare brown shoulders, the only other garment he wore being a white loincloth tied neatly around his waist. His legs, thin as a heron's stilts, were drawn under him. He spoke in a soft low voice which sank at times almost to a whisper, but there was something compelling in the meekness and majesty of the man and in the intense earnestness of his manner and tone.

I had come that night to see Gandhi on behalf of a British newspaper which I then represented. It was the last time I was to see him, for shortly after the interview I left India for Ceylon where I stayed for two years, and Gandhi was dead before I returned.

The talk that night was political, but in an aside which was prompted by something I cannot now recollect the Mahatma spoke on his favourite doctrine of means and ends.

"The means matter," he insisted. "Bad means make for bad ends."

There was nothing novel or remarkable in what he said, for I was familiar with his writings on that theme, but this was the first time I had heard him expound it. The memory lingers, and I can recall being struck particularly by the earnestness which crept simultaneously into his voice and eyes.

His eyes were wonderfully eloquent, and mirrored his mood —thoughtful, gay, candid, wary, persuasive, shrewd and stern. How vividly one remembers the gaiety which lit them when an incident or remark amused him and moved him to a cackle of reedy laughter! But sometimes they could be stony.

Means and ends. The insistence on right means and right ends, on the belief that when men use evil methods to defeat evil it is evil that wins, is as old as humanity, and common to all religions. Gandhi made the principle distinctive by projecting it from the moral to the material plane and by applying a maxim of daily life to the political life of a whole people. His means were often ends; therefore a method, non-violence (*ahimsa*), became with him a mission. Alongside *ahimsa* he advocated *satya,* or truth, and together these formed the twin stars of his teaching.

How far he succeeded in impressing his people with his teaching only posterity can say. The cynical might point to the manner of the Mahatma's death by assassination and hold it up as a warning that not only those who wield the sword shall perish by it. But Gandhi himself, as his writings and speeches reveal, was conscious of the fact that his countrymen were neither prepared nor willing to practise completely the gospel he preached. "If India," he once wrote, "adopted the doctrine of love as an active part of her religion and introduced it in her politics, *swaraj* (freedom) would descend upon India from heaven. But I am painfully aware that that event is far off."

He wrote this in 1921 in an introduction to his little brochure *Hind Swaraj* (Indian Home Rule) which was first published in 1908 and which contains the gist of his philosophy. The rebuke was to recur through the years until almost the eve of his death in January 1948.

On January 18th the Mahatma broke what was to be his last fast. He had undertaken it, following the terrible bloodshed of the partition riots and killings, in an effort to induce all Indians —Hindus, Muslims, Sikhs and others—"to live like brothers." The fast ended with a verse from a Vedic hymn:

> "Lead me from untruth to truth,
> From darkness to light,
> From death to immortality."

Gandhi was to die twelve days later, felled by an assassin's bullets.

The partition killings which descended on the subcontinent with its cleavage into India and Pakistan had shocked and grieved Gandhi profoundly, and his utterances on the day he broke his fast reflect the sorrow and shame which overwhelmed him.

"I embarked," he said, "on the fast in the name of Truth whose familiar name is God. Without living Truth, God is nowhere. In the name of God we have indulged in lies, massacres of people, without caring whether they were innocent or guilty, men or women, children or infants. We have indulged in abductions and forcible conversions, and we have done all this shamelessly. I am not aware if anybody has done these things in the name of Truth. With that same name on my lips I have broken the fast."

And having rebuked his people, he once again pointed the way: "We should shed all fear. Every Muslim child should feel safe among Hindus and Sikhs. Up till now our face was turned towards Satan; now I hope it will be turned Godward. If we do so, India will lead the way to world peace. I do not wish to live for any other purpose."

When shortly after his fast he was assassinated, the drama and horror of his killing stunned India into sobriety. Does the sobriety persist? It is too early to tell. In national life as in international politics truth and non-violence are among the first casualties. And of India it would be pharisaical, more especially of an Indian, to pretend that it was otherwise and that we are not as other men.

The point of Gandhi's teaching was that we are. The world, he insisted, was kin, and only when a people employed the right means, which in his vocabulary were truth and non-violence, could they achieve the right ends. Truth made for honesty and fair dealing. Instinct in non-violence was an appeal to the better nature of man to find through conciliation, not conflict, a common way of endeavour and achievement.

Gandhism is founded on respect for the human personality, and to the Mahatma the individual mattered more than the State. He respected and cared passionately for the personality of the individual. Here Gandhism differs sharply from Marxism with its stress on the omnipotence of the State and its identification of the individual's weal with the State's will. Respect for the human personality led to the doctrine of good means and good ends. As inevitably, the denigration of the individual led Marxism to proclaim that the ends justify the means. Communism is not concerned with means and ends. Its entire philosophy is built on the devising of ways and means. Hence its opportunism.

Gandhi was by no means a simple person, but there was nothing devious in him or in his teaching. To many his political and economic tenets seemed elementary because they were fundamental; and, believing in first principles, the Mahatma characteristically refused to compromise with them. Herein lay his ruthlessness. There was no room for manœuvre within the four corners of his beliefs.

To pretend that India has imbibed all of the Mahatma's teachings and is faithful to his tenets would be disingenuous and dishonest. In Gandhi's own lifetime Nehru, along with many other Congress followers, found it difficult to accept non-violence as a principle but was prepared to adopt it as a practical weapon. "It attracted me more and more," Nehru wrote, "and the belief grew upon me that, situated as we were in India and with our background and traditions, it was the right policy for us." Similarly Nehru rebelled against the Mahatma's frequent stress on the religious and spiritual aspects of the civil-disobedience movement. Religion had nothing to do with politics. With his modern rational, scientific outlook he disagreed with Gandhi's views on machinery and contemporary civilisation, with his idealisation of poverty and with his belief that private wealth constituted a trust.

Nehru shares none of Gandhi's spirituality; he is, if anything, adverse to this quality. He would put goodness above holiness, works above faith. He is moral, not spiritual—in the sense that his perception of right and wrong leads him to insist on right means and right ends, though even here he is fond of clothing a moral precept in a practical attire. "The means," he once explained, "that are not good often defeat the end in view and raise new problems and difficulties."

Helped by the signpost of means and ends which Gandhi

above all men taught him to observe, Nehru follows within his own and India's limitations the path which his master trod and travelled. If in the process he is apt to pontificate, it must be remembered that he does so more for the benefit of his own people than for the outside world, employing a verbal idiom which might sound sententious and morally highfalutin to Western ears but one to which Eastern, more especially Indian, ears have long been attuned. Nehru, even when using English, talks on an Eastern, not a Western, wave length.

The paradox of Nehru consists in the fact that while representing in his own personality a synthesis of East and West he also embodies the contrast and clash between Asia and Europe. Gandhi, further away from the West, was in a sense nearer it. He was a humanist more than a politician, and no man in our time blended more successfully the temporal and the spiritual without injury to either. Yet in a curious way his retreat from industrialisation and the big machine intensified the gap between the East and the West, for the divisive factor lay there and not in any differences of religion, culture, social habits or outlook. The march of science and technology marks the dividing line between Asia and Europe.

In the last half of the fifteenth century the Renaissance reached its culmination in Europe, and from then until the twentieth century Europe forged ahead of Asia. For the next two hundred years scientific discoveries and inventions such as movable type, the magnetic compass, the telescope and gunpowder enlarged the frontiers of European knowledge and extended its area of action. The second half of the eighteenth century ushered in the Industrial Revolution with its marvels of science and technology, and the frontiers between Asia and Europe, already divided by science, were hardened by the political domination and racial exclusiveness which Europe was enabled to impose on Asia by the power resulting from scientific knowledge and industrial progress.

Thus in the cleavage between the East and the West, science, not religion, is the divisive and decisive factor. Of the Asian nations Japan was the first to realise that science spelt strength and that in technology and industrialisation lay the key to progress. In achieving this, Japan had the advantage, unlike other Asian countries, of being politically independent. Its downfall is a sad illustration of the maxim of means and ends. The means were right but deployed for the wrong ends.

There is nothing to substantiate the claim, often heard in India and in other countries of the Orient, that the East is more spiritual than the West. If the claim rests on the spiritual motif which inspires the voluntary renunciation of wealth, this is by no means peculiar to India or to Hinduism; for in the West, too, men have been known to renounce wealth for the service of their fellowmen or in the pursuit of an inner spiritual peace. Materialism and the worship of Mammon exist equally in the East and in the West; but alongside these manifestations there also exists in both spheres a life of the spirit and of the mind.

The intensification of the spiritual motif in Indian thought and writings springs not only from the religious traditions which animate Hindu society but from the tendency to identify a life of action with a life of the spirit. Therefore society, according to the orthodox Hindu, should conform to a religious or spiritual mould. The Hindu sees a kinship between the human and the divine, an attitude exemplified by the story of Socrates and the Indian philosophers.

"With what is Greek philosophy concerned?" they asked Socrates.

"With the study of all things human," said the Greek.

The Indians were puzzled. "But how," they asked, "can you study anything human until you know what is divine?"

Thousands of years later the same idea was expressed by Gandhi, and finds an echo today in the Bhoodan* movement of Vinoba Bhave and in the interpretation of socialism by the American-educated Jayaprakash Narayan who sees the roots of Indian socialism in Gandhi, not Marx.

Gandhi interpreted religion as self-realisation, and therefore the spiritual, he argued, was bound to permeate every sphere of human activity. "You cannot," he said, "divide social, political and purely religious work into water-tight compartments. I do not know any religion apart from human activity."

Between religions there subsist concord and conflict. The kinship between Hinduism and Buddhism is often contrasted with

---

* Movement for the voluntary surrender of land.

that between Islam and Christianity. The two latter creeds are distinguished by a common belief in monotheism, by the possession of a sacred book (the Muslim Koran and the Christian Bible), by the acceptance of the principle of divine reward and punishment, by a belief in the brotherhood of men, and by an active, often aggressive, tendency to proselytise.

Neither Buddhism nor Hinduism indulges in organised proselytising, though of late Hindu institutions such as the Arya Samaj have adopted a militantly missionary attitude. Some see a touch of poetic justice in the so-called untouchables of India shedding the stigma attaching to them by mass conversions to Buddhism. Hinduism has no sacred book nor has Buddhism. Both represent a way of life more than a religion; each is inspired by conduct more than by faith; and neither demands belief in a divine being or God.

"A man," Gandhi remarked, "may not believe in God and still call himself a Hindu. Hinduism is a relentless pursuit of truth. Truth is God."

Such religious alignments with some approximation between Hinduism and Buddhism on the one hand and Christianity and Islam on the other have influenced national outlook and political history. They have affected inter-State relations within Asia and between Asia and the West. But the historian and the sociologist would do well not to read too much into a seeming pattern of "likes" and "unlikes," for the pattern is crisscrossed, often confused and contradictory, bearing in practice little relationship to religious alignments, such as they are. Buddhism, born in India, was edged out of the country by another religion of indigenous growth, Hinduism. In their common adherence to monotheism and in their possession of a sacred book the religions of Islam and Christianity have certain philosophical links. But politically it was the land power of Islam in the Middle East, based on Egypt and on North Africa, which from the twelfth to the fifteenth century barred Europe's way to Asia. The discovery of the Cape route to India turned the flank of Islam and took Christianity to the Indian Ocean.

Islam and Christianity came to India as conquering faiths, for both were proselytising creeds. Though intrinsically flexible, Hinduism has a habit of ossifying in self-defence; and the pres-

ervation over centuries of institutions such as caste, untouchability and the joint family derives from this protective habit and
crust. It had two results. On the one hand it hardened the social
core of Hinduism and on the other it made the internal reorgan-
isation of Hindu society difficult. Because Hinduism is a national
religion confined to the boundaries of a single country, unlike
Islam and Christianity with their international ramifications,
these developments had a direct impact on the political structure and progress of India.

That an affinity in religious thought, even as between two
separate creeds, creates a certain affinity of mind and outlook is
illustrated by the fact that the average Briton in India (before
and after independence) was and is generally closer and more
sympathetic to the Muslim than to the Hindu. None the less,
certain paradoxes and contradictions persist. Although Islam believes fervently in social democracy, holding all men equal,
Islam as a whole leans politically towards an authoritarian system of government, as the Middle East States demonstrate. On
the other hand India with its vast Hindu population adheres
scrupulously to parliamentary democracy. Can it be that political democracy is not a necessary adjunct of social democracy?
The caste-ridden Hindu, like the class-conscious Englishman,
has no difficulty in accepting the concept of political democracy.
But the Muslim, steeped in social democracy, appears averse to
the political form.

Why? Benevolence, it would seem, does not automatically
cancel out autocracy. The two are reconcilable. Moreover habit
and environment condition outlook; and the early followers of
Islam, being of nomadic habits, accepted the principle of leadership with its concomitant of undivided authority. Hence possibly the authoritarian strain in Islam's political thinking.

A story is told of the late King ibn-Saud of Saudi Arabia that
on one occasion he asked a British visitor to explain to him the
system of government in Britain. The visitor described the party
system as the basis of parliamentary democracy.

"Strange," mused the king. "And does it not lead them to
war?"

Environment does much to influence thought. The Buddhism

which the Chinese pilgrims such as Hsuen-Tsang took back with them to their country was of the Mahayana school, which, like Hinduism, is both polytheistic and metaphysical. Over the years it has been blended with Confucianism, which contains a strong practical and authoritarian strain. Confucius seldom spoke of spiritual beings. "When you cannot serve men," he once observed to an inquisitive disciple, "how can you serve spirits?" Confucius also visualised society as an ordinance of Heaven which decreed that the ruler, symbol of benevolence and righteousness, was entitled to his subjects' submission. Is it altogether a coincidence that the Chinese has always been more practical than the Indian? Hinduism places great stress on religion as experience of reality. Yet the Hindu mind is essentially more metaphysical than the severely practical mind of the Chinese. A fact or system such as Marxism or Fascism interests the average Hindu as an idea more than as a reality. The metaphysical bent of his mind has given the Hindu the spurious reputation of being spiritual.

In my journeyings through Asia, Europe and the New World I have often encountered these paradoxes, conflicts and contradictions which at once unite and divide, the cleavages running at times along religious boundaries but on other occasions cutting across frontiers to unite nations politically or to create similar patterns of political outlook and thought in lands with widely contrasting religious systems. President Nasser of Egypt, a devout Muslim, when I met him in Cairo a few weeks before the Anglo-French aggression of October 1956, was openly contemptuous of Pakistan and its policies. Some years earlier I had been interested to hear President Sukarno of Indonesia insist that on the basis of population Indonesia, not Pakistan, was the largest Islamic State in the world.

"But we're not theocratic," he added hastily. The keen edge of rivalry showed through his talk.

Therefore religion in itself, while it might colour or influence a country's outlook on moral, social and spiritual matters, is not necessarily a cohesive political force. Even the international solidarity of Islam, which a common religion makes compact, reveals chinks in its political armour.

The same is true of Europe. In his monumental *A Study of History** Dr. Arnold Toynbee traces the course of English history through seven stages, beginning with the conversion of the English from the religion of the so-called Heroic Age to Western Christianity which took place in the last years of the sixth century, and ending with the establishment of the Industrial System of economy which occurred in the last quarter of the eighteenth century. The Christian metropolis, originally at Jerusalem, moved to Rome in the middle of the first century, but the Emperor Constantine, before his death in A.D. 337, established a second, or Eastern, Rome at Constantinople. The resultant Christian cleavage between the Catholic form of the West and the Orthodox form of the East was not repaired until the Crusades, which, beginning in the closing years of the eleventh century, were waged for another two hundred years, leaving Egypt and the coast line in Muslim hands. Materially Christianity lost, for the Crusades, launched to save Eastern Christendom from Islamic rule, ended with the establishment of Muslim dominion over the whole of Eastern Christendom. But the followers of the Cross benefited in other ways.

Brought into contact with the Moors, the Christian Crusaders imbibed something of the arts and sciences of the Arab people, their medicine, chemistry and accountancy, their zoology and mathematics. Within a hundred years of the Prophet's Hegira † (A.D. 622) the Arabs had wrested Spain from the Visigoths, and by the tenth century the university of Cordoba was acknowledged as a great seat of Muslim learning. Thus in a way science entered the West from the East.

Not only science but religion, for from Asia emerged the world's great religions—Christianity, Hinduism, Buddhism, Islam, Judaism, Zoroastrianism and Taoism. It is an odd fact that while Christianity came from the East, Communism came from the West. The roots of Marxism go back to Plato's ideal society and to Thomas More's Utopia, to Ricardo, Adam Smith and Hegel. Lenin, writing of Marx, upholds him as the genius who

---

* Published by the Oxford University Press under the auspices of the Royal Institute of International Affairs, London.

† The Hegira, marking the Prophet Mohammed's withdrawal from Mecca to Yathrib, or Medina, has been adopted as the inaugural date of the Islamic era.

continued and completed the three chief ideological currents of the nineteenth century—the classical philosophy of Germany, the political economy of England and the socialism and revolutionary fervour of France.

Through the Spanish Moors Europe was imbued with the Greek spirit of inquiry and intellectual adventure; and the Crusades had revived a sense of the religious unity of Christianity. Under this combined impact European thought quickened in the fields of science and philosophy as Western thinking explored new spheres, studying the working of physical forces and inventing scientific instruments. From here begins the great cleavage between Asia and Europe.

Printing was introduced into Europe around 1440,* and later gunpowder and the magnetic compass. Anatomy began to be studied. Advances in navigation brought the names of Columbus and Copernicus to the fore, the latter improving on the observational astronomy of Johannes Müller. Galileo and Newton followed this trail. In the seventeenth century came the development of instruments such as the thermometer, telescope, microscope, barometer, air pump and pendulum clock.

The harnessing of steam power in the latter half of the eighteenth century signalised the Industrial Revolution in England. The scientific age had begun. Progress in mechanical engineering induced the manufacture of the first textile machinery in wood. Nasmyth invented the steam hammer, and the Siemens brothers, with Bessemer and Snelus, foreshadowed the making of modern steel. Meanwhile, Faraday's chemical discoveries had stimulated the metal industries; earlier, coal had begun to replace charcoal in blast furnaces and forges. With the invention of the flying shuttle, the spinning jenny, the mule and a roller spinning frame the textile industries were revolutionised. Before the nineteenth century had closed, electricity was discovered. England became the world's workshop.

Just as Europe following the Crusades developed a sense of the religious unity of Christianity, so also the major religions of Asia, particularly Hinduism and Islam, acquired a protective rigidity in the four decisive centuries following 1500. Until then

* Printing was known to China as far back as the tenth century, in the epoch of the Sung dynasty.

the political and scientific progress of the East and the West
was approximately similar. The discovery of the Cape route to
India enabled Vasco da Gama to reach Calicut in the closing
years of the fifteenth century; and Christendom, bypassing the
land power of Islam, reached out into Indian waters. Commerce, Christianity and Conquest marched hand in hand into
the Orient. The expansion of the Christian Church was accompanied by an expansion of European empire.

By identifying political dominion with the pervasive power of
Christianity, Europe and Asia created an artificial division between themselves which was also false. Not Christianity but its
concomitants of scientific and technological achievements had
made the Western triumph possible. Science reared the dividing
line between East and West, creating between them an abyss of
backwardness, illiteracy, poverty and ignorance in which Asia,
left behind in the race for industrial and scientific progress,
now wallowed. For not only Islam but Hinduism had earlier
played its part in the development of science and technology.
The symbol for zero is a Hindu contribution, as are also the nine
Hindu numerals with their methods of computation and calculation which preceded the Greeks. Surgery was taught at Kasi and
Banaras in the days of the Buddha. Incidentally, the alphabet
came from Syria and Palestine, being transmitted to Rome and
the Western world by way of Greece and Etruria.

A sudden tiredness overcame the spirit of Asia as Europe revived under the stimulus of the Renaissance. Inertia descended
on the East; and though the battle for political supremacy was
waged intermittently for another two hundred years, until
around 1750, it was clear by the seventeenth century that Europe was winning the race for dominion in the East. The half-
century between 1450 and 1500 roughly marks the culminating
point of the Renaissance, for this period saw the discovery of
America, the exploration of the Indian seas and the consolidation of Spain. The Moors, a race of enlightened rulers, were ex-
pelled from Europe when the little state of Granada was conquered by the Spanish crown which was united in the persons
of Ferdinand of Aragon and Isabella of Castile. Islam retreated
from Europe as Europe in turn crossed a Rubicon which divided
the medieval from the modern order. There was no going back.

Today the political wheel has turned full cycle as the greater part of Asia sheds Western domination following the two world wars in the first half of the twentieth century. But Asia is still far behind in the scientific and technological race, and with Africa constitutes a drag on global progress. Despite the sharpness of international conflicts and the mounting horrors of nuclear warfare, the world is moving to be one. As the jet age finds fulfilment, distances will cease to divide; and if mankind is to march in step to new and shining goals of human achievement, Asia and Africa cannot lag behind. Neither they nor the West can afford to do so.

A backward Asia or Africa is a danger to democracy but a gift to totalitarianism, for Communism thrives on discontent. The paradox of a politically independent country being economically backward because of lack of scientific and technological development and because of unorganised resources intensifies frustration. Democracy loses its leitmotiv in a world of hunger and chaos. Unless democracy can offer not only individual freedom but economic security, based as this increasingly is on technological processes, its appeal to the masses of Asia will be slight as against Communism which offers a proletarian heaven on earth. A hungry man thinks through his stomach rather than through his mind, and prefers a loaf of bread to a political or an economic principle.

In Europe the first flowering of democratic ideas coincided with the Industrial Revolution, and this has not gone unnoticed by discerning Asians. Both the French Revolution, with its principles of liberty, equality and fraternity, and the harnessing of steam power, which signalised a revolution in technological development, belong to the latter half of the eighteenth century.

"It is to him who masters our minds by the force of truth and not to those who enslave them by violence that we owe our reverence," wrote Voltaire, who with Rousseau inspired the ideas and ideals of revolutionary France. Strange that Voltaire should find an echo in Gandhi! But the rebel in both men was strong.

Yet it was precisely here that the West, while adopting the principle of democracy, did violence to the truths it enshrined, and the juxtaposition of the two ideas of democracy and industrialisation, while tarring one, vitiated both in the eyes of the East.

The hundred-odd years between 1750 and 1858 are described
by Asian historians as the Age of Conquest, while the succeeding half-century and more, from 1858 to the outbreak of the
First World War in 1914, is known as the Age of Empire. The
ideas of liberty, fraternity and equality, while applicable at
home, were not meant for export abroad.

As Europe grew industrialised, its need for cheap labour and
cheap raw materials became increasingly urgent. The growth of
capitalism encouraged the growth of colonialism, leading many
in Asia to identify one with the other. The Asian intellectual's
antipathy to capitalism or to private enterprise arose largely
from this situation. It led to some strange attitudes, for it made
him as susceptible to Gandhi's condemnation of the big machine
(another term for technology) as to Lenin's dream of electrification in what seemed to the Asian the socialist paradise of Russia.
The Gandhian view of democracy recoiled from the big machine. Communism, which stood ostensibly for the freedom of
oppressed peoples, had use for it. True, Communism was the
negation of democracy. But electrification meant the difference
between one crop a year and three. Given certain circumstances, it could mean the difference between life and death.

"Perhaps," as an Indian farmer remarked to an American
newspaper correspondent, "we must sacrifice democracy for
electricity."

From this predicament Asia must salvage itself.

I think back over the years to what Gandhi told me that hot
night in June. Right means lead to the right ends. Bad means defeat and vitiate the ends. Though Gandhi was right in saying so,
he was wrong in believing that India's moral salvation lay in
withdrawing from the big machine, from industrialisation, and in
going back to the spinning wheel and plough. Individual freedom can be reconciled with industrialisation. They are two faces
of the same coin which is democracy, but the right means must
be employed to lead to the right ends.

2   Between Two Worlds

SINCE Japan's dramatic victory over Russia in 1905, Nippon has loomed large in Asia's national consciousness. In his autobiography Nehru relates how as a schoolboy in England, while travelling in a train from Dover to London, he read in a newspaper a report of Admiral Togo's defeat of the Russian fleet in the Straits of Tsushima. "I was in high good humour," he notes.

Forty years after their victory over the Russians, the Japanese were to suffer a crushing military defeat at the hands of the Western powers who counted Soviet Russia as their ally. Yet Japan by its intervention in the Second World War undoubtedly accelerated the freedom of many Asian countries.

When I was in Japan for the first time in 1954, a prominent Japanese businessman discussing the reparations then demanded by Burma, Indonesia and the Philippines remarked: "Why should these countries be so exacting? After all they owe their freedom very largely to us."

As a point of view it interested me, since India was an obvious beneficiary; and India was the only Asian nation to write off its reparations claim against Japan.

Together India, China and Japan constitute the core of Asia, for they contain nearly 1,100 million inhabitants, which is almost half the total population of the world. These are Asia's most industrious peoples, and number in their ranks some of the world's best soldiers. Of the three, China is politically the most ancient, having existed as a State as early as the twelfth century B.C.; while Japan, the first to adopt Western science and technology, is industrially the most advanced. Distinct from the other two in its racial pattern, India is culturally the oldest, for its civilisation goes back to the Indus Valley culture which flourished at Mohenjo-Daro and Harappa around 3000 B.C. Because of its own representative institutions and its long tutelage under the British, India has shown itself the most receptive to Western political ideas and forms. The democratic tradition is stronger and longer here than in China or in Japan.

My journeys have taken me twice to Japan—in November 1954 and again in 1956. The Japanese are akin to the British in many ways. Like the British they are an island race combining the hardihood, initiative and industry which geographical isolation and proximity to the sea bring. Britain stole an economic march on Europe with the Industrial Revolution. So did Japan over Asia. As in Britain, the urge for raw materials and markets was to lead Nippon to expansionism abroad with the additional advantage of controlling cheap labour at home and in its foreign territories. The wedge which science and technology drove between Europe and Asia was reproduced inside Asia as between Japan and China. Therein lay the clue to the "differentness" of Japan as compared with other Asian countries. Science spelt the differential.

To an Indian the Chinese and Japanese are perhaps almost as puzzling as they are to a European because, except for a few races inhabiting the northeast fringes of India, there is little, if any, of the Mongoloid strain in the overwhelming majority of Indians. The Aryo-Dravidian synthesis from which Indian civilisation developed found its cohesive focus in Hinduism as it emerged in the later Vedic period from between the tenth and the seventh centuries B.C. Hinduism gave the Indian mind its metaphysical mould.

Little of the metaphysical exists in the mental outlook of the Chinese or the Japanese. Buddhism, born in India, secured a firmer foothold abroad, percolating through China and Korea to Japan, whose people from the latter half of the sixth century after Christ to the early years of the ninth century, a period which coincided with the T'ang dynasty in China, were influenced greatly by the religion, culture, arts and skills of their continental neighbour. In China Buddhism came in contact with the teachings of Confucius and Lao-tse, acquiring in the process a distinctive form, while in Japan the religion was superimposed on the nature worship of Shinto.

Like the Chinese, the Japanese are more absorbed in earth than in heaven; and while both peoples, like all civilised races, are interested in ideas, they are more concerned with the ordinary business of living than with metaphysical exercises. With both, thought is harnessed to a utilitarian end, and in both countries Buddhism has expressed itself as a practical creed.

I have also had the good fortune of having travelled in China, and to an Indian the mental climate and outlook of other Asian peoples have a compelling interest and fascination. Of the Japanese and Chinese, I think the Chinese is closer to the Indian mentally and temperamentally. An Indian finds it easier to talk to a Chinese and understand his cerebral processes than to do so with a Japanese. The Chinese is essentially an individualist. He likes to express his opinions, and did so with considerable freedom in Kuomintang days; although when I met some of the same individuals in later years under the Communist régime I realised for the first time with a sense of shocked dismay that a man's mind could be imprisoned as effectively as his body. Freed, however, from Communist or other forms of totalitarian tyranny and trammels the Chinese delights in the stimulant of words.

His mind is more nimble than the Indian's, gayer, more sensitive and practical. Without being fanciful it likes to express itself in imagery and illustration, and the habit of building up an argument through suggestion rather than statement gives conversation with a Chinese a curiously evanescent, will-o'-the-wisp quality. One thinks of Huang Ch'uan who painted in the "boneless way," disdaining to imprison his landscapes, flowers and birds within a drawn outline.

Whereas the Chinese is inclined to express himself allusively, the Japanese is often accused of presenting an opaque front. My own experience belies this view. Admittedly the average Japanese takes time to thaw, but with few exceptions—and I think I can claim to have met a representative cross section—the Japanese, far from being evasive, is often disconcertingly frank. I remember talking at Osaka with a group of four businessmen who disagreed with India's policy of non-alignment. Their manner was frank but friendly.

"Your policy is due to your long subjection to the British," one of them remarked. "Naturally your bias is against the West. We can understand it but we don't agree with it."

Yet the same industrialist at the close of our conversation said with evident sincerity: "We took fifty years to industrialise Japan. You must do it in twenty-five."

I doubt if a Chinese would have been so direct. Evasiveness, of course, is no Oriental monopoly, for Occidental records of commerce, diplomacy and war reveal that the European, when occasion demands, can be both taciturnly and volubly evasive. The Indian, too, can be both devious and brutally frank, a trait which has led many to accuse him of intellectual arrogance. Men are much the same everywhere.

Meticulous regard for an ordered pattern of social conduct characterises the Japanese in his relations to individuals, and this has given him the reputation of being insincere. He is difficult to get to know. Although he is cordial, one has the feeling that he is never really friendly. In company he laughs often and easily, but again the impression lingers that this at most is a surface emotion. Good manners require a Japanese at times to refrain from expressing an opinion, which sometimes misleads a foreigner into inferring that he is in agreement with the visitor's views, only to discover later that he is not. Yet these are manifestations dictated by a code imbued with a high sense of social decorum and courtesy. Behaviour is governed by rules which all are expected to observe.

Years of authoritarian rule have disciplined the Japanese to the point of docility, and obedience comes easily to him. He likes and expects to be led. If General Tojo said war, it was war. If General MacArthur wanted democracy, democracy it was. Yet the Japanese have not always been docile. In the tenth and eleventh centuries Nippon broke loose from the cultural apron strings of China at a time when the Fujiwara family, which dominated the imperial court from the middle of the ninth century, exercised an uneasy sway. The Shogun, established in the twelfth century, led to the development of a feudal society, and this expressed itself religiously in various forms of Buddhism. In the late twelfth and early thirteenth centuries the new sect of Zen came into being, offering salvation through faith and promising the solace of an afterlife to the warrior and to the steadfast of heart and mind. Japan's fibre was being toughened.

By the time the first European merchant-adventurers led by Antônio Galvano, Portuguese governor of Malacca, reached Nippon's shores in 1542 the Japanese had emerged as a vigorous maritime race. For the next three hundred years Nippon was ruled by the powerful Tokugawa clan, and by the nineteenth century the Japanese had settled down into the disciplined cast of today. With the arrival of a United States naval force under Commodore Matthew C. Perry, Nippon was compelled to open its doors in 1853 to foreign infiltration.

Forced to turn its face to the West, Japan flattered the European intruders by imitation. The Tokugawa régime suddenly collapsed in 1868, giving way to the Meiji restoration. Five years earlier the nation had stirred to the cry, "Honour the emperor—expel the barbarians!" During the Meiji era, which lasted until 1912, Japan built itself into a modern State by adopting the industrial and commercial techniques of the West, creating a strong army and navy and setting up a stable political system adapted from Western models. It also enforced universal education and the Western calendar.

"We chose wisely and well," said an Osaka businessman. "We went to England for our naval and mercantile services. We took our law from France, our business and banking methods from America, our science and medicine from Germany on whom we also modelled our army. Within twenty-five years we were independent of Europe. Within another twenty-five we ranked as a great power."

The rest is recent history. Prosperity brought with it a thirst for power accentuated by the growing pressure of population on a soil which, owing to the country's mountainous terrain, was only 20 per cent cultivable. With higher standards of economic production and health, Japan's population grew from 30 million in the middle of the nineteenth century to 70 million by 1940. Its boundaries threatened to burst. A weak China invited attack.

Japan's rise to power coincided with the disintegration of the Chinese empire as the rule of the Manchu dynasty, entrenched in authority since 1645, yielded to a republican régime in 1912. The Manchus, who had displaced the Mings, gave China two hundred years of firm rule. But from the nineteenth century their political power underwent a sad decline.

By 1895 China had ceded Formosa, the Pescadores and the Liaotung Peninsula to Nippon and recognised the independence of Korea, which became part of the Japanese empire in 1910. The "Chinese melon" was being sliced up. In 1904 came the Russo-Japanese War which ended in Russia's defeat a year later and in the emergence of Japan as a power to be reckoned with. The First World War (1914-1918) left Japan in possession of certain German territories which included Tsingtao in the Far East and the Pacific group of islands comprising the Marianas, Carolines and Marshalls.

Beginning with a politically liberal trend after the First World War, Japan swung to extreme militarism in the early 1930's. By then its population was 60 million, and growing at the rate of about one million a year. In 1931 Manchuria was overrun, being converted into the puppet State of Manchukuo a year later. Six years afterwards, seizing on the pretext of the Marco Polo Bridge incident, the Japanese mounted another offensive on China. Big business joined hands with the militarists in an unholy adventure which was to end in the Second World War with Japan's shattering military defeat and economic prostration.

Four months before I visited Japan in November 1954 I had toured West Germany, and the contrast between the two defeated countries was indicative of their background and outlook. While there was less consciousness and admission of war guilt in Japan, the antipathy to militarism seemed more acute in the Eastern than in the European country. External evidence of damage and devastation was greater in Germany. But then stone, steel and brick survive as ruins, whereas paper and wood, easily inflammable, are also easily replaceable. The devastation in Japan had been prodigious, for the empire of Hirohito had taken a bigger beating than the Reich of Hitler.

When on August 11, 1945, the emperor announced the surrender of Japan, as many as eighty-eight cities and ports had been burned out by incendiaries. The atomic bomb had laid low Hiroshima and Nagasaki. On V-J Day Tokyo was a mass of four million tons of rubble.

The Germans, one felt, had made a far quicker recovery—psychologically and economically. The Japanese still appeared bewildered and confused. Does a continental people react less sharply to defeat or victory than an island race in whom isolation breeds a sense of emotional and economic insecurity? This very sense of insecurity had led Japan to seek an empire abroad, with a foothold primarily in continental China. Aeons of authoritarian rule had inured the Japanese to the leader principle, fused in their minds not only with their dictatorial traditions but with the economic growth which was part of their peculiar political pattern. Science and perverse politics had conspired to lead them into costly and awful adventures. Now, like children in the dark, they groped for a guiding and reassuring hand.

"Having no leader, no one really to look up to, the Japanese are confused," said a Dutch woman correspondent who has been resident for many years in the country.

"They seem to be more anti-militaristic than the post-war Germans."

"Ah, that," she explained, "is because war came to Japan itself, and the civilians suffered casualties for the first time. In Japan, as in China, a soldier has always been regarded as legitimate cannon fodder. But not a civilian. The Japanese have always thought of themselves as a divinely protected race immune to defeat."

Confirmation of this came curiously enough from a Japanese to whom I had observed that the Germans appeared to be recovering their spirit and their economic capacity very fast.

"Yes," he remarked reflectively. "But you forget one thing. The Japanese were not defeated once in 2,600 years. The Germans were defeated twice in twenty-six years."

It was true, of course. But not the whole truth. No *kamikaze*, or divine wind, swept the American forces from the sea or air as it had swept the Mongols when they landed at Hakata Bay in 1281. Six and a half years of foreign occupation superimposed on four years of war had changed the face and mind of Japan.

Defeat had led to the loss of over 45 per cent of territory. This included Manchuria with its rich natural resources such as coking coal, iron ore and soya beans and a cheap labour reservoir of some 30 million industrious Chinese. Cotton had come from the Chinese mainland, salt and food grains from Korea and Formosa. All these had gone, and huddled in the four main islands of Hokkaido, Honshu, Shikoku and Kyushu with a few minor adjacent islets was a population—then* numbering some 88 million—now over 90 million, and growing at the rate of a million a year. The islands have coal, and the mountainous topography of the country, combined with rivers, streams and a heavy rainfall, has given Japan one precious asset—water power.

"We have lost our raw-material sources," said an executive of the Sumitomo Electric Industries—formerly one of the Zaibatsu empire—which I visited at Osaka. "But we still have our water power. That makes Sumitomo possible."

I visited other works, big and small. The Yawata Iron and Steel Company, Ltd., not far from Fukuoka, is the largest of its kind in Japan, having a potential output of over two million tons, but it was working at the time to a smaller capacity. Also in Kyushu Island, which contains 40 per cent of Japan's coal, are the Asahi Glass Works. Besides manufacturing glass, they produce caustic soda, soda bicarbonate, ammonium sulphate and soda ash. At Yamazaki, not far from Osaka, I went round the Dai Nippon Spinning Company Mill, which had 1,700 women among its 2,000 employees. Female labour is cheaper than male, and the mill, which manufactures silk cloth, bleached cotton and printed cotton textiles, was not working to maximum output. At Yokohama I was taken to the Nissan Motor Company, which produces trucks and the indigenous Datsun car.

The comparison with West Germany was irresistible but in some respects unfair. One obvious and overwhelming advantage which the Federal Republic enjoyed was its possession of vital raw materials such as coal, lignite, salt and potash along with

* 1956.

considerable water power. Moreover the pressure of population, though high in West Germany (200 per square kilometre) is lower than in Japan (230 per square kilometre). Like Japan, the Federal Republic had suffered heavily from the devastation of war, but the Industrial Revolution had reached Germany far earlier than Japan. "It reached us too early," I had heard Dr. Adenauer remark.

Experience counts for much in the story of human progress, and the feel of science and industry came to Germany long before it reached Japan. How could one possibly compare the massive Mercedes-Benz organisation near Stuttgart or even Das Kleine Wunder works at Düsseldorf with the Nissan Motor Company at Yokohama? Krupps seemed overpowering beside the Yawata Iron and Steel Works. And the great chemical organisation of Bayer Werke at Leverkusen near Cologne reduced the Asahi Glass Works to miniature proportions.

Technologically Japan is still at least twenty years behind its wartime Western ally. The Japanese work like beavers, with prodigious industry and concentration, and the physique of their workers is better than our own in India. But, looking at them, I thought of the huge big-boned, muscular giants I had seen in the factories and workshops of Germany, and realised that men count as much as, if not more than, machines. Asia, I recognised, had a long way to go industrially and scientifically.

Therein lay the answer to my doubts and queries. The progress of industry depends on much more than men and machines, for the output of factories is linked closely with the work of laboratories and of research students in the back rooms of science. Fast as Japan has moved, it has still much leeway to make up. And Japan is the industrial leader of Asia. To overtake the West, Asia will need the seven-league boots and stride of a giant killer. We in Asia talk much of our cultural traditions. But there is also the vital tradition of science which we lack and sorely need.

By fertilising the mind, science has invigorated the world's living standards. It has opened out new dimensions in human thought and endeavour. Precision and meticulous attention to detail have created a Western habit of mind which expresses itself in a way often different from that of the East. The Occidental belief that the Oriental is devious and elusive arises from this difference in mental approach. Truth, like love, is a many-splendoured thing. And an Oriental often sees the same thing differently from an Occidental. This explains why the East and the West so often find themselves talking at cross purposes. Their mental touchstones are different.

To the Oriental a work of art must be a complete and finished product, but this meticulousness does not extend to a utilitarian object such as a saw, a saucepan or a sewing machine. In Oriental eyes the former has permanent value; the latter is ephemeral. Hence the highly stylised and mannered motif in Oriental art. Hence also the lack of attention to detail which characterises much Asian handiwork in the realm of industry. What we Asians tend to overlook is that this outlook influences and infects not only doing but thinking. "The Indian mind," writes Nehru, "was uncritical where fact was concerned perhaps because it did not attach much importance to fact as such." With the exception of the Chinese, Asians generally have not shown an aptitude for writing exact history. The Chinese are probably more historically minded because the writing of history has always been a function of government in that country.

What is true of Asia is generally true of Japan—with a difference. By adopting the habiliments of science and industry earlier than any other Asian country, Japan has become the industrial leader of Asia. But in doing so it has developed a national schizophrenia which partly explains the emotional and economic insecurity or imbalance which oppresses it. Industrially Japan turned its face towards the West; but the deep-rooted Asian consciousness which makes it difficult for any Asian to abandon indigenous concepts of the mind and the spirit led it simultaneously to turn its back spiritually on the West. As a result Japan has never belonged completely to the East or to the West. In reaching out for the science of the West, and striving simultaneously to retain its spiritual soul, it achieved neither fully. Japan fell between two stools.

I do not thereby mean to suggest that the way out is a choice between the two. Obviously the solution lies in a balanced synthesis, and here the duty of achieving it does not devolve solely on the Orient. The Occident must play its part. There must be an adjustment on each side, and a mutual adjustment between both. To probe ways and means of realising this is primarily the purpose of this book.

Economically and technologically the problems of the West are far different from those of the East. The problem of the West is largely to save labour, while that of the East is to absorb it. Japan is the fifth most populous country in the world, its population having grown by 15 million since 1940, while another seven million of post-war repatriates have added to the burden. Were it not for the casualties of war, the explosive point of 100 million, which is likely to be achieved before 1970, would have been reached earlier.

Because of this, Japan, like China and India, must lean heavily for its industrial development on small-scale industries and handicrafts, with the emphasis on modernisation rather than on mechanisation. A feature of the Japanese economy is the so-called medium and small-scale industries, a small industry including anything from one to twenty-nine workers, while a medium industry employs from thirty to under two hundred workers. These industries are largely unorganised in terms of labour and capital and are resented by the big industrialists much as the hand-loom industry in India is looked at askance by the textile mills. Yet so long as over-population with consequent unemployment exists, there can be no widespread automation or rationalisation. Reluctance to break your neighbour's rice bowl is common in a poor continent such as Asia where the emphasis is more on co-operation than on competition.

I saw a number of these industries in the neighbourhood of Kyoto and Hiroshima. Near Hiroshima was a medium industry manufacturing rice-polishing machines which were exported mainly to Pakistan, Afghanistan, Thailand, Iran and the Congo. It had two factories with sixty-four workers at one and fifty-three at the other with seven executives divided between both. I also visited a small hand-loom factory of eight workers all in a single room atop a small house. Payment was for piecework, and the average earning per month was 15,000 yen (about $40). A small bamboo factory at Kyoto manufacturing handmade screens for shrines and houses entranced me. The proprietor, a fifty-three-year-old man with seven children, took pride in his craft.

The factory was founded by his grandfather. They manufactured about 1,500 screens a month, and there were twenty-eight workers. The highest priced screen was around $20.

Nearly every big industrialist I spoke to was critical of his small-scale and medium competitors largely on the ground that they were difficult to control and that they brought about an element of disorganisation in the industry as a whole.

"They clog the channels of trade," complained Hisakira Kano when I met him at the Industries Club at Tokyo. Mr. Kano, a big businessman, had associations with India.

Others, while also critical, accepted them as a necessary evil. "What can one do?" asked Ichiro Ishikawa, who was then president of the Federation of Economic Organisations. "Their number is very large and one can neither eliminate nor absorb them."

A veteran British journalist who knows Japan well put it somewhat differently. Commenting on the criticism of the bigger entrepreneurs, he said with a laugh, "It isn't Indian, British or American competition they fear—but Japanese."

Like West Germany, Japan had the sustenance of American dollars with the added stimulus of the Korean War boom, but by 1955 the sum of 710 million dollars which the United States was spending annually in Japan was beginning to taper off and had declined to around 600 million. Since then the figure has decreased still more, and any diminution in the number of United States forces should decrease it further. At one time the American troops stationed in Japan spelt a windfall of over 300 million dollars a year, at a spending rate approximately of one million dollars a day. The off-shore procurement purchases of the United States Government, which reached their peak during the Korean War, were on the decline.

"We spent money like drunken sailors," remarked an American friend in talking of the Korean boom. So, unfortunately, did the Japanese.

Instead of ploughing back profits into new machinery and factory buildings, and instead of consolidating the country's export trade, the government and industry went on a "spending spree." No order of priorities was observed, and money was lavished upon enterprises such as television plants, *pachinko* parlours, music halls and theatres. It seemed as if every man and his brother went into the import-export trade after easy money.

The contrast with West Germany recurred to me again. Travelling through the Ruhr to places like Düsseldorf, Duisberg and Essen, one could not help noting the prosperity which overwhelmed the Germans. They had made good use of their money —American aid *et al*. Japan was recovering from the debauch. But it still had a headache.

Why the difference? It could not be accounted for entirely by Germany's greater recuperative powers and resilience which stemmed from its longer scientific traditions and larger reservoir of industrial and commercial techniques and know-how. The human factor counted. As a people the Germans had been able to organise their country and themselves, rebuild their shattered economy, put spring in their spirit and muscle, activate themselves and make their country again the entrepôt of Western Europe and large areas of the world. Machines mattered. But also men—and the Spirit of Man.

Like the Germans, the Japanese had a strong will and purpose, capable of being dedicated to a supreme task. Both countries were responsive to the stimuli of single-minded leadership. But whereas Germany, prostrated equally with Japan by military defeat, was quick to seize the opportunities offered, and not merely to rehabilitate but to regalvanise its economy, Japan showed itself curiously irresponsive, even irresponsible. Was it because there was no one to think for Japan and show it the way? "Turn the people and the money loose and they'll make the country strong," was the slogan of Dr. Ludwig Erhard, Federal Minister of Economics. The Germans had made their country strong. But precisely the same tactics in Japan had led to a state of economic and financial near anarchy, a free-for-all in which each man fended for himself.

Did the Japanese regard economic discipline, along with democracy, as a cloak to be worn and doffed at their leaders' behest? In June 1950, when the Korean War broke out, Japan was still under American tutelage and occupation, the Treaty of San Francisco being signed only a year later, on September 8, 1951. The beginning of the truce talks at Panmunjom in July 1953 ended the war, perhaps earlier than Japan had calculated. But it also brought the "spending spree" to an abrupt halt and forced a re-examination of conscience. I was exposed to some of this during my visit in 1954 and again in 1956; but the sense of bewilderment and confusion, of not knowing where to look for guidance, was evident even in high business and political circles.

Men can be like machines.

3   Shrouded Sun

THE tragedy of modern Japan, I think, is that from ancient days life in almost every sphere of activity has moved to an ordered pattern, whose design has been ordained and regulated from above. Rules govern conduct within the country.

The Japanese at home is elaborately courteous and polite not only within his own circle but to strangers. Yet as a conqueror in the last war the Japanese abroad was notorious for his cruelty and quite irrational excesses, thereby alienating many millions in the Asian lands he occupied. Belonging to an island race, the Japanese is insular and self-conscious. He is romantic, even sentimental, as the saccharine quality of his music and songs reveals, but the repressive quality of his discipline makes him emotionally excitable and apt to erupt violently in an unfamiliar environment. The world outside Japan is peopled by foreigners whose code of behaviour is alien to his, and to which in the absence of specified rules of conduct he reacts abnormally.

The same rigid pattern extends to his public life and has made him politically servile. Unlike other countries revolutions in Japan have not occurred from below but have been imposed from above. The rule and influence of individuals such as the *daimio,** the *shogun*† and the *samurai*‡ testify to it, as do the

* Feudal lord.
† Generalissimo.
‡ Feudal retainer.

periods named after historic figures such as Fujiwara Motosune and Iyeasatu Tokugawa. The Meiji era brought parliamentary forms, but power was in the hands of an oligarchy with the emperor as the fountainhead of all authority in the State. Interesting to an Indian is the creation by the Tokugawa of a hierarchy of four social classes which are analogous to Hinduism's four castes but set to a different gradation. While the priestly teacher, the warrior, the merchant and the serf constitute Hinduism's four main castes, the Tokugawa hierarchy consisted of the warrior-ruler, the peasant, the artisan and the merchant. *Bushido,* or "the way of the warrior," was the code of the samurai.

A feature of the Teuton character like that of the Japanese is discipline carried to the point of regimentation. But the parallel can be overstated. Not all of Germany's revolutions have been superimposed, as the country's history even before the events of 1848 proves. On the contrary, the rebel and creative elements in the German mind have expressed themselves forcefully over a wide field from politics to philosophy, and from music to religion. Germany imbibed the Renaissance spirit from Italy at the end of the fifteenth century, but the Reformation began in Germany with the protestant cry of Luther.

Without Hitler, Germany was numbed but not neutralised. With Hirohito, Japan, defeated and denuded of its empire, was dazed almost into immobility. The natural industry of its hardworking people asserted itself; but, significantly, the country as a whole, deprived of political leadership, looked for someone to impose another revolution on it. MacArthur was the man. In his more messianic moments he personified Jefferson plus the New Deal. He imposed democracy.

I remember asking Hessell Tiltman, who represents the *Manchester Guardian* in Tokyo and who had then been in Japan for fourteen years, how the Japanese had reacted to MacArthur's reforms.

"They don't really understand democracy," said Tiltman. "Some of them are protesting against the tyranny of the majority."

A few days later I called on the Speaker of the House of

Representatives and heard him complain that the members often indulged in fisticuffs.

"But I'll soon put a stop to that," he remarked.

The irascible Shigeru Yoshida, then in the closing months of his seven-year-old premiership, had done little to induce respect for parliamentary traditions. Some weeks previously he had provoked an uproar in the Diet by roundly denouncing the opposition in the chamber as "idiots." Yoshida, his opponents alleged, had stayed in power by the simple expedient of farming out Cabinet posts by rotation. Nearly one hundred members of the Diet had at one time or another served in his government.

Three men destined to succeed Yoshida in rapid order were Ichiro Hatoyama, Tanzan Ishibashi and Nobusuke Kishi. They had seceded recently from the Liberal party which Yoshida led and had joined hands with the Progressive party headed by Mamoru Shigemitsu, to form a new group known as the Japan Democratic party. I saw them separately, and separately they protested against Yoshida's dictatorial methods. Kishi was especially bitter.

"He never consults party members," he complained.

According to a story going the rounds in Tokyo at the time, Yoshida on hearing of the rebel trio's plans to secede from his party and form a new group had threatened to join their group! It was probably an apocryphal tale but characteristic of that wily politician.

MacArthur's plan to give Japan what America wanted was a mistake which many State Department officials are, strangely enough, still prone to make. To impose democracy from above is a contradiction in terms if Lincoln's phrase describing it as the rule of the people, by the people, for the people signifies anything. Democracy is not a coat to be put on and taken off at another's behest.

Not that MacArthur's reforms were doomed to be ephemeral, for some of them have stable value and virtue, and will probably survive. What puzzled the Japanese and confused them was his quick-change artistry. He began, for instance, by decreeing that the Communists should be released, and thus made them respectable. On the outbreak of the Korean War in June 1950, he peremptorily ordered that the Reds should be rounded up and their party outlawed. This made them untouchable. Even for the Japanese such sleight of hand was dazzling in its sudden deviations.

By the time I was in Japan the Reds' two most prominent leaders, Kyuichi Tokuda and Yoshio Shiga, who earlier were invited to SCAP headquarters for consultation shortly after MacArthur took over, had vanished underground. One dismal rainy afternoon I visited a dingy office in Tokyo to interview three Communists, one of whom was Shoichi Kasuga, a machine-tool worker, then chief of the Central Direction Committee, or Politbureau.

The Japanese Communist party, they said, was organised in July 1921.

"What was its peak membership?"

Kasuga replied: "Around 200,000. That was in 1949 when we commanded three million votes and had thirty-five members in the Diet."

"And now?" It was November 1954.

Kasuga blinked. "We have only two parliamentary members now, one in the upper house and one in the lower."

The public rating of the Reds had changed noticeably as MacArthur smiled or frowned on them, and it amused me to see that the Supreme Commander's abrupt change of front seemed to puzzle, even pain, the Reds.

Kasuga looked melancholy and plunged into a prolonged discourse.

"Since June 1950," he wailed, "the Communist party has been purged. We are semi-outlawed, and about a thousand Communists have been dismissed from their jobs. Nearly 2,400 of our weeklies and dailies have been suspended."

It sounded like a grandiloquent figure, and I said so.

"Some of the papers were very small," Kasuga conceded. I had the impression that his omnibus figure included leaflets, posters and propaganda sheets, as on inquiry I discovered it did.

They were not an impressive trio; and, like Communists the world over, their patter ran in a groove. But they had their moments of frankness, and one of them wryly confessed that the

Reds' influence over Japan's six million trade-union members was slight. It showed that the Communists had lost caste not only with the general public but with the workers. Yet labour operating under an umbrella of trade unions was still aggressive, or so the businessmen alleged.

MacArthur's eagerness to democratise Japan had led him in the early years to initiate a purge based largely on categories rather than on individual records, which meant that some 200,000 persons active in the central and local governments and in the economic, financial, social and scientific life of the country were arbitrarily excluded from public office. This blanket ban had resulted in placing the country's leadership in the hands of comparatively minor persons who were prepared to bow to every behest of the new ruler. Schoolteachers, university professors and labour leaders who were associated with the war effort were similarly purged, thus leaving the field open for the activities of so-called progressive groups. Consequently, there developed a militant labour movement entrenched behind enlightened labour laws which guaranteed the principle of collective bargaining and which regularised working conditions. All this was to the good, provided labour leadership was responsible. Unfortunately, this was exceptional.

"It will be difficult to change the labour laws," a prominent businessman confessed. "Labour will not part easily with what it has won."

He was right, as subsequent conversations with the Socialist leaders proved. Japan's Socialists were then divided into two groups—the left-wingers led by Mosaburo Suzuki and the right-wingers headed by Jotaro Kawakami. The split came with the signing of the San Francisco Treaty, the two wings dividing on the issue of foreign policy and rearmament. On foreign policy the right favoured co-operation with the West, while the left believed in a Third Force or the extension of the "area of peace." The left was opposed on principle to rearmament; the right favoured rearmament but, as Kawakami remarked, "only in the distant future." When I was there the two wings were negotiating for unity, which they have since achieved, the left compromising on rearmament and the right on foreign policy.

Both leaders, however, were even then agreed that the labour

laws had come to stay, despite the efforts of the bigger industrialists to have the strike rules and the regulations on picket lines
amended.

From the industrialists I heard bitter complaints of labour's
aggressive attitude. They were between the devil and the deep
sea, for simultaneously they were critical of the banks, which
virtually controlled them by advancing money at a rate of interest averaging about 10 to 11 per cent. Industry had no alternative to acceptance because the wartime destruction of capital
resources had left it at the mercy of the banks. Their dilemma
called to mind the younger Alexander Dumas' reflection: "Business? It's quite simple. It's other people's money." Evidently it
wasn't that simple.

If costs were to be reduced, said the industrialists, not only
the wages of labour but the interest rate of the banks had to
come down. Meanwhile commodity prices in Japan ranged
about 20 to 30 per cent above the international level, and despite various measures they continue to be uneconomic. The
more extreme business elements were hostile to the Yoshida
government.

"They are a government run by bureaucrats," cried Hisakira
Kano. "They know everything and understand nothing."

Although well intentioned, MacArthur's streamlined rule was
in reality a despotic variant of democracy, a type of administrative dealing with which the Japanese were familiar, but which
in the invidious post-war situation intensified their basic sense of
imbalance and insecurity. If the idea was to make the Japanese
democratic-minded it failed dismally, for its effect was to bring
democracy into disrepute. To resurrect themselves the Japanese
in the Meiji era had deliberately but with some cynicism
adopted the West's industrial and commercial techniques, even
its parliamentary forms. Now, after a devastating military defeat, they were being groomed for democracy and the American
way of life. On the principle that man is born in the image of
his Creator, the Japanese were being moulded in the image of
their conquerors.

Japan's prime need was to rehabilitate herself. And the American way of life, with the Americans in control, was as good as
any other—for the time being. This reservation was present in

the mind of almost every Japanese I spoke to, for quite obviously and understandably they were biding their time. As an Indian I knew the demoralising influence which foreign rule exercises on the character and fibre of a people. What I did not realise so clearly until I went to Japan was the almost equally distressing effect of unrestricted foreign aid on a people, particularly a people defeated in war. It seemed to sap initiative and morale.

Germany also had been defeated; but the Federal Republic of West Germany, as I had witnessed, had staged a breathtaking recovery. The Germans admittedly had certain advantages over the Japanese, particularly in the availability of rawmaterial resources. Though their massive industrial background had been destroyed by the war, their knowledge of industrial processes and techniques was left intact. They had a vast reservoir of highly skilled labour. The Germans too had received aid —Marshall Aid—which with Dr. Erhard's courageous currency reform of 1948 had breathed new life into their crippled economy; and, as they claimed, "every Marshall dollar spent in Germany had resulted in ten to twenty dollars' worth of goods produced and services rendered." They could show something for aid received, and hold their heads high.

The Japanese could show very little. Even the windfall brought by the Korean War boom had been dissipated, and both the government and industry had squandered their substance.

I saw Hisato Ichimada, then governor of the Bank of Japan,* a shrewd, cautious, impressively able man, who admitted that industry had been improvident; but he implied that the government was by no means blameless.

"The government," he said, "must also cut down its expenditure. People talk of fiscal reform. But how is fiscal reform possible unless the government supports it with an over-all economic policy?"

Ichimada conceded that Japan's economic position was serious. "To sustain our growing population," he explained, "we have to import annually two billion dollars' worth of goods, commodities and food grains. It follows that, if we are to maintain a favourable balance of trade, we must export above this figure. Our exports now total roughly one billion and 240 million dol-

* He became finance minister shortly afterwards.

lars. This leaves us with a deficit of 760 million dollars a year."

Through American aid, which was then 700 million dollars a year, the government was able to show a trade balance on paper.

Ichimada was realistic. "Until our exports exceed our intake of two billion dollars, we shall have to continue to take American aid," he observed.

In his earnest, quiet way he pleaded for Asia's understanding of Japan's difficulties.

"India," he remarked, "needs trained technical and managerial personnel. We have the technological know-how. We have also capital equipment and goods which Asia can absorb."

I was to hear the same plea raised elsewhere, by businessmen and politicians.

Hatano Okazaki, who was foreign minister at the time, had served as Japanese consul general in Calcutta. Bland and persuasive, he deployed a skilful line of talk.

"Japan," he observed, "must be careful not to be regarded as militaristic. All that belongs to the past. We have no desire for colonies, but there are two things we can offer Asia. Over 98 per cent of our people are literate; many of them are scientifically educated and technically trained. We are also an industrious people. Given the chance, Japan can contribute to the technical and industrial progress of Asia."

Like Britain in 1949, Japan had to step up its exports in order to survive. Kuichi Aichi, who was Minister of International Trade and Industry, planned to reduce commodity prices and simultaneously to increase the volume of annual exports by at least 50 per cent. Despite the expansion of Japan's trade in the past three or four years, exports are still only about three-quarters of their pre-war volume. The need for markets in Asia and Europe persists.

As in West Germany, where the commercial community was anxious for trade with eastern Europe, I discovered that most businessmen in Japan were eager to trade with Red China. They wanted China's commerce but not its Communism. In pre-war days Japan's trade with the Chinese mainland totalled about 30 per cent of its overseas trade, principal imports being coal, iron

ore, cotton, salt and soya beans. In return Japan could give
China machine tools, machinery and capital equipment.

While in Germany I had talked with Hitler's financial wizard,
Dr. Hjalmar Schacht, who recalled the *Drang nach Osten* and
the trade drive he had stimulated in pre-war days between the
Reich and eastern Europe. He favoured the same arrangement
again.

"That is how I built the old Reich economy," said Schacht.
"Germany's pre-war trade with Russia and Russia's present satellites was 20 to 25 per cent of our total trade."

Japan's pre-war trade with China had been slightly higher,
but in the interval much had happened to change the alignment
on the political and economic planes. Politically, Japan no longer
dominated the Chinese mainland, while economically Communist China was more industrialised than it was before the war
and had less need of manufactured goods. Moreover Peking
might only trade in such commodities as it chose. It might, for
instance, refuse to supply Japan with coal and iron ore, or it
might arbitrarily and unilaterally cut off trade at any time.
Again, it might be reluctant to supply adequate quantities at
economic prices. The effect of such trading on the Kuomintang
government in Formosa had also to be taken into account.

To these considerations the Japanese businessmen were by no
means blind, but the urgent need for higher exports and the
unexplored possibilities of a post-war market on the mainland
led them to regard the reopening of trade as a calculated risk.

"At least, a beginning should be made," said a prominent industrialist. "After that we can see how it works."

During my first visit to Japan in 1954, Yoshida was away in
Washington engaged in a bid to interest the United States in a
four billion dollar Marshall Plan for Southeast Asia which was
designed to stimulate Japanese exports to these regions. He
failed, getting instead 100 million dollars' worth of agricultural
commodities. Three years later, in the summer of 1957,
Nobusuke Kishi was to venture out to America on a similar
mission, canvassing the creation of a Southeast Asia Development Fund of about 800 million dollars, the financing to be done
largely by the United States, with Japan supplying capital

goods and technology, and the countries of Southeast Asia providing the raw materials. Such an arrangement would undoubtedly help Japan vis-à-vis Britain and the sterling area. A subsidiary argument in its favour in Washington was that it would
relieve pressure on the Japanese government for trade with Red
China. But Washington preferred to wait and see.

As between Japan's efforts to step up its exports and Britain's
increasingly sensitive susceptibilities, political and economic,
Washington's choice seemed obvious. The Anglo-American alliance takes priority. But with China Communist and India resolutely wedded to non-alignment, the temptation to build up
Japan as the bastion of democracy in Asia must grow in Western
quarters. Why should Japan not be the industrial and political
leader of free Asia?

The Japanese, I noted, while nervous about Communist
China's increasing industrialisation, were also apprehensive of
any advance in the same direction in India. This was natural
and understandable. The reaction was particularly noticeable in
two competitive fields—steel and textiles—and while visiting the
Yawata Iron and Steel plant at Fukuoka I noted with interest
the studied efforts to compare its production and achievements
with Tata's. The Yawata plant is larger than Tata's, and the
executives who showed me around were at some pains to point
out that Tata's, though smaller, had more workers on its payrolls.
Such justifiable essays in comparison could not fairly be resented.

At the Dai Nippon Spinning Company Mill at Yamazaki, I was
told that a single worker handled nearly 500 spindles as against
400 spindles in India. On the other hand, both machinery and
buildings in almost every plant in Japan wore a dilapidated look
contrasting dismally with the new buildings and plants in West
Germany. They did not appear to have been as ruthlessly demolished by Allied bombers as their counterparts in the Reich.
At the Mercedes-Benz works near Stuttgart I had heard an executive exclaim: "This plant was demolished 82 per cent during the
war. I wish it had been 100 per cent. Then all my machinery
would have been new." In contrast with Germany, the Japanese
still operated on a shoestring—and an old one at that.

China and India, unlike Japan, are continental territories able
in a crisis, whether of war or of peace, to trade space for time.

Japan, cribbed within the confines of its four main islands, is more vulnerable, economically and militarily; from the point of view of both territory and population, and their reaction one on the other, the country strains at the seams. If it is to maintain an ordered tempo of progress, industrial development demands abroad the assurance of political dominion or of a profitable market. By depriving Japan of the former, the war has cut it off from the latter. The dilemma which faces Nippon is thus more acute than that confronting either India or China.

It is a crisis primarily of the spirit and of the mind, for the body politic of Japan could not hope to emerge unscathed from the ordeal. Japan has paid a terrible price for its effort to equate itself with the West by adopting its scientific and technological methods, its parliamentary forms and military apparel. It took the means discriminatingly but the ends blindly. This was bound to lead it into conflict and perhaps disaster.

As long as tsarist Russia posed a threat to Britain in the Eastern Hemisphere, Britain's interests lay in giving Japan a free hand in the Far East to allow Nippon ultimately to become embroiled in a war with Russia. Though the Anglo-Japanese alliance of 1902 set the stage, Japan surprised the West by its shattering onslaught on the Russian colossus and by the swiftness of its military and naval triumphs. American intervention led to the Treaty of Portsmouth, which ended a war in which Japan had the moral support of Britain. As a result Russia was virtually excluded from Manchuria and Japan's paramount interests in Korea were acknowledged.

When Japan set about modernising itself on Western lines, it calculated on achieving the mastery of Asia and on contending with the West on equal terms. It overlooked one fact. By modernising itself, Japan did not merely take on the West: it took on the world. Western apprehension of Japan's increasing power was revealed in 1922 at the Washington conference which recognised China's territorial integrity and through the Five Power Naval Treaty set the ratio of capital ships at five for Britain and the United States and three for Japan. The Anglo-Japanese alliance was not renewed, and Japan's naval fleet as a result of the Five Power Treaty was confined to the western Pacific. Nippon was diplomatically isolated, and the command of the Pacific passed to American hands. Japan's subsequent efforts at expansionism on the Chinese mainland, though described as part of a Co-Prosperity Sphere for Asia, alienated Asia and intensified Nippon's isolation.

The early years of the Second World War, by diverting Western attention from the Far East, enabled Japan to probe possibilities in French Indo-China. Japan was reaching out to Southeast Asia. But the West, particularly America, soon woke up to the danger of Japanese freebooting in the Pacific. Japan's assets were frozen, and exports of oil and iron ore to Nippon were stopped. Had the Japanese militarists permitted it, big business, which had profited by the Manchurian adventure, would have favoured the liquidation of the war with China, and would have urged Japan's concentration on economic consolidation in Asia. But the militarists were not so minded. They preferred to go to war with the West.

Many of the businessmen I met in Japan seemed eager to dissociate themselves from the militarists. They laboured under no sense of war guilt, for in the opinion of most of them the economic embargoes were unjustified and provocative. "The Americans edged us into war," was a common accusation in business circles.

Perhaps as fellow Asians they spoke more freely before me than they would before a Western stranger. It interested me to note how much their judgement of men and events was influenced by results, and there seemed to be an adolescent opportunistic streak in their worship of success. I asked a group of highly intelligent, alert businessmen what their opinion was of General Tojo. The reply was revealing: "He doesn't count. He dragged us into a war we lost."

Although many of the businessmen had co-operated with the militarists, the majority of them were bitter, and resentful of them. I felt they were so mainly for two reasons. First, the militarists had destroyed the industrialists' golden dream of quick and easy profits and trade. In the second place, they seemed to be chafing under the domination which the militarists once exercised. MacArthur had decreed the break-up of *zaibatsu*, but there now appeared to be a move to revive it in a milder form.

I asked Ichiro Ishikawa, President of the Federation of Economic Organisations, whether that was so.

"Of course, industry inclines to group itself," he observed. "But there will be no return to the old form of *zaibatsu* where the militarists could order industry and industrialists about."

Because of the Japanese talent for assimilation many mistakenly assume that their culture and institutions are imitative. Adaptation goes with assimilation and gives their borrowed garb a distinctive look. MacArthur's mistake lay in ignoring this, and in believing that he could remould Japan's outlook by imposing a democratic constitution on the country. The Japanese are willing to have revolutions imposed upon them, but these must be by their own people who know the spirit of their national system and way of life.

Some of MacArthur's reforms will survive. I believe that the suffrage and freedom granted to women have come to stay and will ultimately make for national progress. This reform is not so contrary to Japanese tradition, for until the middle half of the eighth century the ancient custom of rule by women prevailed. Although empresses recurred several centuries later, the status of women in Japan thereafter gradually declined, and was demeaned to that of social and intellectual handmaids.

Among educated Japanese women, I encountered an outlook generally more independent and frank than that of many men. They have been quick to capitalise on their right to vote, and in 1954 they counted fifteen women in the House of Councillors and nine in the House of Representatives. Of all the reforms enforced by MacArthur, few have been more wise and perceptive than the greater freedom granted to Japanese women. India too has benefited by the emancipation of her women.

Outside Japan, interest has concentrated largely on the alteration in the emperor's status; but in Japan itself I found little, if any, resentment over the emperor's new status, which many Japanese pointed out was in fact though not in theory in accord with past practice. The emperor was not always autocratic; indeed, he was very often powerless, being led by an oligarchy, and being only the centre of reverence by the people. Constitutionally the emperor even in the past had less power than the

British monarch, who enjoys certain prerogatives which the mikado does not possess.

Article 1 of the new constitution stipulates that "the Emperor shall be the symbol of the State and of the unity of the people, deriving his position from the will of the people with whom resides sovereign power." Since this in no way circumscribes the emperor's position as the centre of the people's reverence, the Japanese by and large have accepted it without surprise or disapproval. True, the mikado is no longer sacred, but the emperor himself in a message on New Year's Day 1946 denied his own divinity.

"The only people who would want the emperor as head of the State again are those who, like the old militarists, want to use him for their own purposes," remarked a shrewd foreign observer who knows Japan well.

What the Japanese would willingly take from their own people they are naturally unwilling to take from a foreigner. MacArthur's imposition of a democratic constitution was widely resented, particularly in so far as it impinged on the traditional life and laws of the people. The Japanese were given a new constitution with a modified Diet or Parliament. Contrary to their constitutional usage which recognised a rigid separation of the executive, legislature and judiciary, MacArthur based the constitution on the principle of judicial supremacy. He forced an Anglo-American mould on the Japanese system of law which hitherto had drawn its inspiration from Europe, principally from Germany and France.

On the social plane, more especially in relation to the family and to succession laws, MacArthur drastically altered the settled pattern by abolishing the old system whereby the head of the family had enjoyed a status not unlike that of the Roman *patria potestas*. Instead of the ancient rule of primogeniture which restricted inheritance to the eldest son, who received the major part of the family property and with it the obligations of the family head, the new law required an equal division of property between the heirs. The wife's share was secured by specific provisions. These changes, though well intentioned, cut across the age-old hierarchical structure of Japanese social life and ran counter to cherished principles and beliefs. Moreover the abolition of the law of primogeniture threatened to reduce family lands and estates to microscopic, uneconomic holdings.

I had an interesting talk with Mamoru Shigemitsu, former foreign minister, who was among the signatories to Japan's unconditional surrender which took place on the battleship *Missouri*. Did he visualise a change in the constitution, I asked.

"Naturally," he replied. "It was imposed and therefore it should be changed."

He stressed that Japan was independent. "She can do what she likes," he said flatly, "even trade with China and Russia, but Japan must take care not to offend her friends." He was agreeable to accepting American aid.

I remarked on the prevailing unemployment in Japan, the figure being then placed at 700,000; although, including underemployment and part-time employment, the potential total was probably four million. Ichimida had agreed cautiously with this estimate. So did Shigemitsu.

"Yoshida," he commented, "has no policy—political or economic."

The impact of unemployment was seen in spheres other than labour—the business and professional fields. Its melancholy shadow stretched over the student world.

I spent an instructive morning at Tokyo University and sat for a while in the students' cafeteria chatting with some of the lads. In the following year, so the newspapers reckoned, about 152,000 students would pass out of the colleges, only 20 per cent of whom would secure employment.

Youth is naturally radical, but I sensed an underlying bitterness and a feeling of neglect in the conversation of these boys.

"China takes more interest in its students than Japan does," said one youngster. "At least they are assured there of employment."

They seemed, I thought, more pacifist than leftist, and were witnessing with the raw sensitivity of youth the degradation of their country and their elders. I remembered how an Indian friend had once related to me an incident of his youth when he had seen his bearded father, an ardent nationalist, beaten up by a British sergeant during a popular demonstration.

"I'll never forget the look of helplessness in his eyes," he had told me. "He was ashamed to see me witness his humiliation."

Did these Japanese boys experience the same feelings in reverse? The biblical injunction on the sins of parents visiting their children recurred to me. Japan differed from India in that it sought strength not by a liberation of the spirit but by a stiffening of the sinews, and through science reached out to a cult of strength, of blood and iron. Japan seemed little interested in humanism and the humanities. Its god was power.

And yet, moving through this lovely land, I had witnessed much gracious life and living and seen the enchantment of nature as through a glass, elfin and in miniature. The pines and cedars of Nikko and the shrines with their lacquered floors, the walls and ceilings festooned with dragons and gay with a riot of colour. The lace-like spume foaming down a waterfall at Kegon. On my way to Miyajima off the coast of Honshu I had flown in the haze of twilight over the Inland Sea and seen the mountains and hills crowd the coast line. The red-gold maples splashed the countryside near Kyoto. Colour and confusion. Light and shadow. The mist and the sun. They seemed strangely symbolic of this land of steel and cherry blossoms, of passion and docility, of garishness and grace. But too often the mist seemed to shroud the sun.

4   China to Cathay

IF THE most significant outcome of the First World War was the Soviet revolution in Russia, the emergence of a Communist government in China was the most vital consequence of the Second. In a sense the second result stemmed from the first, for, checkmated in their early attempts after the war of 1914-1918 to form workers' and soldiers' soviets in Germany, Hungary and Austria, the Bolsheviks concentrated on fostering revolutionary unrest in Asia.

The Third International or Comintern was formed under Russian auspices in 1919, and the Second Congress, which was held in the following year, saw representatives of the colonial countries, including India, China, Korea, the Dutch East Indies and Persia, participate in the discussions. "Comrades," declared Grigori Zinoviev welcoming the delegates, "we are here at a truly world congress of the Communist International. The fighting advance guard of the workers of the world are represented."

At this congress there arose the historic disagreement between Lenin and Manabendra Nath Roy, whom in later years I came to know very well. Lenin's thesis was that the Communist International and the various Communist parties should ally themselves with the nationalist movements in the colonial countries, working hand-in-hand with the "bourgeois democratic" groups. As against this, Roy felt that the revolutionary Communist crusade had nothing in common with the nationalist

movements for political independence. It should therefore have
nothing to do with the latter, but should assist exclusively the
organisation and development of the Communist movement, particularly in India.

Who says that the Reds do not compromise? As Lenin
preached, there are "compromises and compromises." In the
Marxist credo a compromise on tactics is justifiable as long as
the main objective of Red strategy is preserved. The Second Congress resolved the conflict between Lenin and Roy by a typical
compromise. It approved of both solutions, directing that while
Communist support should be extended to nationalist drives
every effort should be made to organise the working classes, to
penetrate their ranks and thus attain leadership of the revolutionary movement.

This pattern is important because it prevails. Over nearly ten
years until 1946 the Communists functioned on a dual plane in
China, ultimately achieving their objective; and it is through the
same mechanism that the Reds operate in India today, hoping
to achieve the Communist millennium by penetrating the nationalist citadels of power. Kerala is the first milestone on the
road to Delhi.

I knew Manabendra Nath Roy for nearly fifteen years until
his death in 1954. He was a massive man, physically and intellectually, and his magnificent head set on strong wide shoulders
always seemed to me as if it were carved out of old oak. He was
by then no longer a Communist, and he talked freely of his ex-
periences in Russia and Mexico, but most of all of those in
China, where he had been sent by the Communist International
in 1927 on an abortive mission which had ended in his clash
with Mikhail Borodin and his expulsion from the Comintern.

Roy's conversation lacked the grace and felicity of Nehru's;
but it had a vitality which was vibrant, and it impressed by its
rugged strength and clarity. His wit, sometimes malicious, could
often be corrosive. By temperament he was not suited to working
in harness, and his innately iconoclastic mind brought him in
conflict with others. Roy was no politician, but a political
thinker.

It is sad that in his lifetime few in his country assessed at its
true worth or appreciated accurately his enormous capacity for

analytical thinking in politics and philosophy; for he evolved ultimately his own distinctive philosophy of scientific humanism, seeing the stress on individual freedom and initiative not in contrast to Communism but as a civilised stage beyond it. Roy did much to kindle my interest in China. To exchange ideas with him after my two visits to that country was an exhilarating exercise.

I went to China for the first time as a war correspondent in December 1944 when the Japanese were engaged in making their last assault on the American airfields in the southwest. Eight years later I revisited the country, now under a Communist régime, as a member of the Government of India's cultural delegation which was led by Mrs. Vijaya Lakshmi Pandit. I can thus claim to have seen something of China under two different governments, Kuomintang and Communist.

Whereas my first visit, owing to wartime conditions, was circumscribed, being confined to Chungking and Kunming, my second took me over wide areas of the country from Canton to Mukden and through cities, towns and villages. In 1944 I had interviewed Chiang Kai-shek in Chungking; in 1952 the Indian delegation met Mao Tse-tung in Peking. On both visits I talked to a fairly representative cross section. There was another contrasting sidelight to these journeys, for while in 1944 I had gone to China as a citizen of a subject country, in 1952 I went there as a free citizen of a free country. Much had happened to India in the interval.

In wartime China the Communists' "dual plane" tactic was in operation. Chou En-lai—Chiang's "reasonable Communist"—was intermittently in Chungking and worked as a liaison between the Kuomintang and the Communists at Yenan. The united front between the Nationalists and the Communists dated from the Sian incident in December 1936 when Chang Hsueh-liang, son of the Manchurian warlord Marshal Chang Tso-lin, had kidnapped the generalissimo in a desperate effort to convince Chiang that the principal enemy were the Japanese and not the Communists.

Confronted by both, Chiang was in two minds about them. "The Japanese," he kept saying, "are a disease of the skin. The Communists are a disease of the heart."

The uneasy truce between the Kuomintang and the Communists lasted ten years, until 1946,* but even in wartime Chungking it was evident that both sides regarded it as a breathing space, as a lull before the storm which would mark the final phase. For the Communists such a tactic was in keeping with their long-term strategy.

In this intermediate period all that the Reds were concerned with was to appear reasonable and respectable, and it astonished me to see how cleverly they succeeded in doing so, particularly in the estimate of the many American correspondents in Chungking. One of the Americans who had visited the Red stronghold of Yenan assured me that Mao Tse-tung's followers were not orthodox Communists.

"They stand for agrarian democracy," he explained. "They're prepared to work with capitalist help. In some areas the rich peasants and even the landlords have a place in their economy."

In the Press Hostel at Chungking there lived or congregated many correspondents from various countries of the Allied world, among them two Russian representatives of Tass. I was friendly with both of them; and they were helpful to me, for one of them knew Chinese, and they often retailed to me the news and views of the day.

Unlike the Americans, the Russians took a realistic view of the Chinese Reds. They did not disguise from themselves or others that the present was an intermediate period for both sides, and that the national revolution must precede the social revolution. It was therefore necessary for the Communists first to capture the government and then to change the economic structure.

"Chiang is playing a waiting game," said one of the Russians. "He thinks the end of the war will deflate the Communists. It won't. The Communists will emerge with greater strength."

The Chinese Communists, with whom I spoke, were if anything more specific.

"We are not mechanical Marxists," said one of them, Pong Lee, whom I met with his German wife, who was also his inter-

---

* It was temporarily interrupted by the New Fourth Army incident of January 1941 when an armed clash took place between the Nationalist and Communist forces over the demarcation of zones of action. The Reds, wherever they won control, set up border-region governments.

preter. I was to see Pong Lee in Communist China. "We do not
want a proletarian dictatorship immediately," he explained, "for
Communism is always circumstanced by the conditions of a country. But it's nonsense to say that we are not Marxists."

One of the most instructive mornings I spent in Chungking
was with a group of Communists who included a general from
the Red Eighteenth Route Army. They plied me with questions
on India, took down elaborate notes, and in return invited questions. They were keen and lively, seemingly eager to learn and
eager also to impart what they knew. As far as I could judge,
they spoke with few reservations. The general was their spokesman.

"China," he explained, "is an agricultural country. Over 80 per
cent of our population are peasants. Industry is not developed.
There are hardly three million industrial workers. So our central
problem is how to improve the livelihood of the peasants and
how to lessen the exploitation of the landlords. What China's
peasants demand now is 'democracy.' The social revolution will
come later."

What did he mean by "democracy"?

The general was vague, but he seemed to imply a national coalition government in which the Communists were included.

"The Japanese aggression," he went on, "is against every stra-
tum of the Chinese people. So we must all unite. Just now the
Kuomintang is not co-operating with the small landlords but
only with a small number of big landlords. The burden of war
is being shifted on the peasants and small landlords."

His argument suggested that the Communists, while willing to
share political power, were not ready to usher in a social revolution; and subsequent questions and answers confirmed this impression.

"In China," said the general, "the conditions do not exist at
present for the practice of Communism. We do not copy European methods wholesale, but we try to adapt our methods to our
circumstances. At the same time we believe in the methods of
Marx and Lenin for solving our basic problems."

He complained of the Kuomintang's lukewarm fighting spirit
vis-à-vis the Japanese. "All that Chiang wants is to get arms and
save them. He knows that if he arrives at an agreement with the

Communists he will have to fight the war vigorously. So he waits
for victory while preserving his political power. For the past five
and a half years," he concluded scornfully, "Chiang and his
henchmen have been living as good neighbours with Japan."

I knew that was not true, though even in American circles one
heard the allegation that Chiang was not dedicated heart and
soul to the war against Japan. This view, of course, was repudi-
ated by Kuomintang spokesmen who vigorously countered Communist accusations by charging the Reds with precisely the same
sins of commission and omission.

I called one morning on Dr. Chen Li-Fu, head of the right-
wing C.C. clique, who was then Minister of Organisation in the
Kuomintang government. Chen, a graduate of Pittsburgh, was
grey-haired and remarkably handsome. He spoke most of the
time through an interpreter in Chinese, but as he warmed up he
broke into English which, if staccato and almost monosyllabic,
was torrential in its fluency. He quoted epigrams by Confucius
to illuminate his talk.

" 'The first principle of human relationship,' " he remarked,
citing Confucius, " 'is to be trustworthy.' "

Chen was narrow, intense, fanatical. And of the Communists
he spoke with a loathing and passion which I encountered in no
other Chinese during my stay in Chungking.

"They never fight the enemy," he said, employing the same
broad verbal sweep of the Red spokesman I had listened to.
"They are more interested in fighting the government."

Like his Communist counterparts, Chen also accused his opponents of playing for time.

I concluded that they were both playing for time, and that
each was well aware of the other's manœuvres. China was like
a coin standing on edge with each of its two faces representing
contending facets of political thought, and I wondered on which
face it would finally fall. In their idiom and ideology the Reds
and the Nationalists seemed at times curiously alike, for though
both spoke of "democracy" each visualised it as a form of pater-
nal despotism; and the idea struck me, as I reflected on China's
history, that this after all was in line with tradition, with the
father image which over the centuries has ruled Chinese thought
and conduct.

What was the political philosophy of Confucianism but a patriarchal creed which visualised the State as a large, well-knit
family owing loyalty and allegiance to its head? Confucius
thought of society as an ordinance of Heaven where the ruler expected and was entitled to his subjects' submission. By stressing
the need for benevolence and righteousness in those exercising
authority, he justified the system of benevolent despotism where
the dynasty which ruled by the Mandate of Heaven was legitimate. The teachings of Confucius' disciple Mencius echo Plato's
concept of the city-state, for according to Mencius, "without the
gentlemen there would be no one to rule the common people,
and without the common people there would be no one to feed
the gentlemen."

Chiang and Mao, in their distinctive ways, cite Confucius in
support of their own divergent political philosophies. In his
book *China's Destiny* Chiang writes, "China's philosophy of life,
developed by Confucius, amplified and propagated by Mencius,
automatically became a lofty system that is superior to any other
philosophy in the world."

Mao was also to draw from the same sources but more subtly.
On my second visit to China I had been to Ku-fow and standing
by Confucius' tomb, had heard a Communist guide describe him
as "the sage of feudal China but worthy of our esteem." The
Communists, keeping the patriarchal image, had destroyed loyalty to the family and substituted for it loyalty to the State. The
father image had become identified with Mao, and in the benignity of his Buddha-like countenance the millions of China saw the
new radiance of a benevolent despot.

China has never really known democracy as the West understands it, unless the laissez-faire preachings of Lao-tze are con-
strued as a creed of primitive democracy. While Confucius urged
absolute loyalty by the subject to a just prince who should rule
benevolently, the Taoists, echoing Lao-tse, regarded government
as intrinsically tyrannical but a necessary evil. According to their
laissez-faire faith no laws were necessary. "Govern a great State
as you would cook a small fish," adjured a Taoist sage.

Fascism had existed in China over two thousand years before
Mussolini clamped it on Italy. In the state of Ch'in, the so-called
Lord of Shang had preached to his followers, the Legists, the

need for a government of military despotism where agriculture and war constituted the prime industries. His was a doctrine of naked autocracy based on force.

Even before Christianity had established itself in the West, Confucianism had become China's predominant creed, stamping its impress on the secular life of the people and expressing itself in the concept of the Central Imperial State which, strengthened and refurbished by the T'ang dynasty in the seventh century after Christ, survived until the fall of the last Manchu emperor in 1911. Confucianism created a relationship between Heaven and the emperor, making the head of the State not merely God-appointed, as in an absolute monarchy, but the Minister of Heaven. According to this theocratic concept the emperor mod- elled himself upon the prehistoric "divine kings," combining the roles of prince and high priest. In the latter role, as the high priest of the nation, custom ordained that at the winter solstice the emperor should worship Heaven, and at the summer solstice, the Earth. The exalted conception of his office is revealed by the manner in which the emperor referred to himself as late as the nineteenth century while praying for rain during a famine: "I, Minister of Heaven, placed over mankind and responsible for keeping the world in order . . ."

China had known nothing but dynastic rule in an almost un-broken sequence from 221 B.C., when the Ch'in dynasty up-rooted the country's feudal fabric and established a centralised monarchy, until 1911, when the Manchus toppled from power. In between there ruled a succession of dynasties—Han, Sui, T'ang, Sung, Mongol and Ming—interrupted only twice in their long history of centralised rule, the first occasion being from A.D. 220 to 589 when the so-called Three Kingdoms held dis-united sway, and when internal divisions led to the infiltration of foreign elements such as the Tatars and Tibetans. The sec-ond interruption lasted for a little over fifty years from A.D. 907 to 960, and was known as the period of the Five Dynasties. But even in these troubled spells a series of dictatorships masquer-aded as dynasties.

Throughout these centuries the influence of Confucius,* who lived during the Chou dynasty, moulded the secular pattern of

* Confucius lived from 551 to 479 B.C.

the State, and from 125 B.C. until A.D. 1905 the bureaucratic rulers or mandarins who constituted the civil service had to pass an examination in the Confucian classics and philosophy. The Chinese administration was thereby impregnated with the teachings of Confucius. "Serve the parents, be loyal to the government, and establish a good name for yourself," the sage had ordained.

On my second visit to China, now Communist, I discussed with our ambassador in Peking, Sardar K. M. Panikkar, a scholar with a panoramic historical mind, the influence of Confucianism on the Communists.

"Confucianism," said Panikkar, "is no longer a State system. It was undermined with the fall of the Manchus but it survives as a cult. The Chinese have a passion for history and histrionics. By employing both, the Communists have carried their politics to the people."

"How do they do it?"

"Confucianism preached loyalty to the State and to the government. Thereby it established a liaison between the State and the family. The father image is as important to Mao as it was to the Mings and the Manchus."

"I read somewhere," I remarked, "that because of this the ruler was regarded as a king-father, the mandarins as parent-officials and the people as children-people."

"Well," said Panikkar, "I was really thinking of other analogies and examples: thought control, for instance. That isn't foreign to the Chinese. For centuries they've been taught to restrict their reading to accepted and prescribed texts. Then again the processes of public accusation, confession and self-criticism which you see today are part of the age-old Chinese pattern."

"How do you explain it?"

"Very simply. We in India think of the law as a codified system regulated and influenced by judicial decisions or case law. There has never been any such thing in China except between the fall of the Manchus and the coming of the Communists. Law, as we understand it, was in China only concerned with criminal law, which was harsh and punitive and dealt exclusively with vile criminals such as murderers, thieves, bandits and swindlers. Outside this, the State was not concerned with the law. Disputes

were settled by customary practice by associations such as merchant guilds and village clans. Family rules governed matters
like marriage, divorce and inheritance. Mao rules today. But in
certain spheres Maoism is a throwback to the Mings and the
Manchus."

Writing of the Manchus, Nehru makes a picturesque allusion:
"They had come in with the roar of a tiger to disappear like the
tail of a snake." What was to fill the void left by the ending of
dynastic rule? The Manchus had gone in 1911, but the pattern
of dynastic rule had begun to lose its lustre as far back as 1840
when the crumbling authority of the Manchus was unable to
withstand the organised onslaught of the West. India was the
prey of one imperialist power, Britain, but China became the
victim not of imperialism but of imperialisms rampant. Britain,
France, Germany, Russia and Japan fell upon the writhing
body of their enervated victim, staked their claims and extracted
their pounds of flesh. Dynastic rule came to an abrupt end, and
with it the secular authority of Confucianism. The void could
be filled only by a liberal republic, such as the Chinese intellectuals, who were influenced by French and American ideas, envisaged, or by the establishment of a new dynasty.

So China's leaders thought. Sun Yat-sen was the acknowledged
leader of the liberals, also known as the Nanking group, but
Yüan Shi-k'ai, who had worked earlier as the instrument of the
forceful Empress Dowager Tzu Hsi, cherished his own dreams of
reviving a new dynasty with himself as emperor. Yuan died in
1916 with his dreams unfulfilled.

The tragedy of Sun Yat-sen, who was to hold the centre of the
political stage for nine years from 1916, was the tragedy of a
well-intentioned man caught in the coils of an excruciatingly
difficult situation. Sun was kindly disposed toward the United
States, where he had lived for some years, and his correspond-
ence and writings reflect his regard for that country's political
ideas. As Mao Tse-tung has testified, Sun turned first to the
"Western capitalist countries" for help, but in vain. While the
Western powers at Versailles supported Japan in its claim to
Shantung, Russia in July 1918 announced its intention to renounce all her privileges in China. Despite his own inclina-

tions Sun was drawn more and more into the Soviet orbit, a process that culminated in a working alliance between the Chinese Communists and the Kuomintang in August 1922. The Chinese Communist party had been founded the year before.

Sun had never concealed his opinion that the capitalist system as it operated in the West was not suited to China, and his own ideal seems to have been a mixed economy. "It is my idea," he wrote, "to make capitalism create socialism in China so that these two economic forces of human evolution will work side by side in the civilisation of the future." While opposed politically to identification with the Communists, he agreed finally, though with initial reluctance, to association with them.

That the Reds never regarded the Kuomintang under Sun as dedicated to Communism is also clear from their own declarations, both contemporary and later. "We are not so naïve," said the Russian G. Savarov, at the 1922 Congress of the Toilers of the Far East, "as to imagine that this party [the Kuomintang] is a revolutionary Communist party. We are supporting it, we have always supported it, and will do so in the future, but, on the other hand, we cannot recognise this struggle as the struggle for the proletarian revolution." Many years later Liu Shao-ch'i, the high priest of Marxist dialectics in Communist China, described Sun's outlook as "still of a bourgeois or petty-bourgeois character."

Sun Yat-sen's Three Principles—Nationalism, Democracy and the People's Livelihood—were nearer to Lincoln than to Lenin. On succeeding to the leadership of the Kuomintang on Sun's death in 1925, Chiang Kai-shek was to nail these Principles to the party masthead while emphasising simultaneously that the Three Stages specified by Sun for achieving them had still to be fulfilled. The three stages were (1) suppression of the war lords, (2) education of the people, and (3) establishment of popular self-government.

In Chungking it was clear that Chiang, while flourishing the Three Principles as his goal and gospel, sought to employ Sun's Three Stages as an alibi for doing nothing. In a New Year's Day message heralding 1945 the Generalissimo recalled Sun Yat-sen's stipulation "that there was to be in China, first, a military period, then a period of political tutelage and then a government under a constitution." He gave a vague promise to convene a people's congress.

"It means exactly nothing," said an American correspondent, an old China hand versed in the ways of Chiang and the Kuomintang.

I interviewed the Generalissimo a fortnight later; accompanying me as interpreter was Hollington Tong, then chief of public relations, and now Taiwan's ambassador to Washington. I had been asked to submit my questions in advance, and "Holly" seemed unduly nervous that I would wander from my brief. In the anteroom, before entering the Generalissimo's chamber, "Holly" begged me to keep to my brief. I promised, because I was only interested in securing a wartime message from Chiang to the Indian people.

Chiang was standing by the fireplace as I entered the room. He wore a simple khaki tunic with no ribbons, only the gleaming brass badges on his collar denoting his rank. For fifty-seven (as he then was) I thought he looked remarkably young and well preserved. He was slim, with an erect carriage, and there was about him a hint of tautness but also of strength.

Chiang was friendly and cordial, and I was impressed by his great natural dignity and personality. Nothing in him conveyed ruthlessness, though undoubtedly it was there. As I looked at him, I found it difficult to visualise him as the epicentre of all the violence, triumphs, setbacks, bloodshed and chaos that had engulfed China since the mantle of the Kuomintang leadership had descended on him nearly twenty years earlier. In the summer of 1923 Sun had sent him to the Soviet Union for a few months to study the Red Army, and on his return Chiang had created and commanded the new military academy at Whampoa. Four years later Chiang had turned on his Communist collaborators, even while they were preparing to turn on him, and had ruthlessly liquidated them.

Chiang was a soldier, not a statesman, and had always remained so. Sung's Three Stages required first the suppression of the war lords, and Chiang had set out on his northern expedition from Canton in July 1926 vowing to defeat the war lords, to unify the Chinese nation and to restore Cathay to its place of

pristine glory. He was to fulfil some of his promises. The land
was in ferment around him. The shooting of Shanghai students
on May 30, 1925, by the foreign-controlled police of the International Settlement had lit a nationalistic fire in the mind of
the student world. The intellectuals, comprising the scholars
and students, rallied around Chiang. So did the peasants, stirred
up initially by the Communists, as did the workers of Shanghai.

Chiang's northward progress was swift, even spectacular. Early
in October the Nationalist troops captured Hankow and Wu-
chang and by the summer of 1927, with the fall of Wuhan and
Hanyang, Chiang controlled the urban core of the great Yangtze
Valley. In March 1927 his forces occupied Nanking and con-
verged on Shanghai, where authority was divided between the
Communists and the war lord Chang Tsung-chang. The Communists, gaining the upper hand with the support of the workers, paved the way for the entry of the Nationalist troops, Chiang
himself arriving at Shanghai aboard a gunboat on March 26th.

Both in Shanghai and in Moscow, the Communists underes-
timated Chiang. Only a short time before Chiang's entry into
Shanghai, Stalin in addressing some Communist workers in Moscow had spoken derisively of the Kuomintang. The session was
secret. "When the Right is of no more use to us," boasted Stalin,
"we will drive it away. At present we need the Right. . . . So
they have to be utilised to the end, squeezed like a lemon, and
then thrown away."

Trotsky, who had opposed the Stalinist line on China, was to
remark later, "The squeezed-out lemon soon seized power and
the army." It was not Stalin's last mistake on China—or on
Chiang. Within a matter of days, in April 1927, Chiang had
swooped on the unsuspecting Communists and annihilated
them. One of the few to escape was Chou En-lai.

Now in wartime Chungking the Communists and the Nationalists were together again, though their association hung un-
easily on a thin tightly drawn thread which might snap at any
moment. The elusive Chou En-lai served as a tenuous link.
Chiang did not refer to the Communists in my brief interview
with him, for he talked almost entirely of India. The Congress
party leaders were in prison at the time in what was to prove
their last term of imprisonment before independence. Though

Chiang did not mention Gandhi, he inquired solicitously after Nehru. Where was he imprisoned? How was he? Had the British policy affected India's war effort? He spoke generously of China's gratitude for India's help.

"We've been blockaded for more than two years," he remarked, "but neither the enemy nor the Himalayas have been able to prevent the passage of vital supplies."

The Generalissimo spoke of Sino-Indian goodwill.

"This is one of the most significant developments of the war," he observed. "It will live long in the minds of both peoples."

In subsequent years I have often thought of the irony with which developments since then have invested Chiang's remark. Sino-Indian goodwill continues, but Taiwan seems a great deal further away from Delhi than Peking.

I met and spoke with other prominent Chinese, Communist and Kuomintang. Gentle, mild-mannered Dr. Wang Shih-chieh, Minister for Information, had come back recently from London and talked appreciatively of Sir Stafford and Lady Cripps, both of them good friends of China. He referred to President Roosevelt.

"Roosevelt," he remarked, "appears determined to win not only the war but the peace."

I lunched with Dr. T. V. Soong, who was then the premier and acting president of the Executive Yuan. He was lively, alert and inquisitive, and through him I got my interview with Chiang.

One evening I called on Madame Sun Yat-sen, whom I was later to encounter in Communist China. She did not conceal her political feelings, and was critical of Chiang. Of India she spoke with affection.

Also outside the Kuomintang, though co-operating with it, was Dr. Sun Fo, son of the great Sun Yat-sen by his first wife. He too was opposed to Chiang, but his will did not appear to measure up to his mind. I thought him well intentioned but ineffectual.

One of the most interesting talks I had was with the smiling, diminutive Dr. Wong Wen-hao, a geologist by profession, who was then Director of the War Production Board and who was later to return to the Chinese mainland and live under the Com-

munist régime. Wong said he was not a politician, and his conversation was concerned solely with his administrative work, on
which he talked fascinatingly and with zest.

In all these conversations, whether with Communist or with
Kuomintang sympathisers, I sensed a vague feeling of restiveness
and discontent with the prevailing state of things.

Yet the shadows which even in Chungking seemed to be
gathering around Chiang were far away in the high noonday of
his career when after settling accounts with the Communists at
Shanghai he had turned to the work of reconstructing a new
China. By 1928, when the Nationalist government was firmly
installed at Nanking, Chiang held sway over more of China than
any administrator since the fall of the Manchus. In those early
years he had built roads, railways and hospitals, and until the
mid-thirties had kept China's volatile currency fairly stable by
introducing a uniform silver dollar.

The Japanese occupation of Mukden had marked the turn of
the tide; but Chiang's reluctance to act was understandable, for
the Communists and war lords threatened the rear of his fighting columns and were likely at any moment to erupt. China,
Chiang calculated, could trade space for time, and time was on
China's side. Yet the threat was not only external, for by the
mid-thirties a rot had begun to set within China's body politic.

Chiang's promised land reforms never seemed to materialise,
while corruption and nepotism waxed fast and, infecting his
own immediate circle, spread like a rash on China's ailing body.
They talked of a new dynasty in the country—the Soong dynasty. Inflation had touched dizzy heights, and a bag of peanuts
which in India cost four annas (five cents) was priced in Chungking at the official rate of exchange at eight rupees (over $1.50).
Among those trafficking in currency were minor Chinese officials
at least two of whom approached me in my room at the Press
Hostel.

"What can we do?" asked the finance minister, Dr. O. K. Yui,
helplessly. "We can't stop inflation. We can only combat it."

The dream of democracy had vanished in an oligarchic nightmare.

Chiang was a patriot, but he lacked the resilience and imagination of a statesman. He was a soldier with no ideas to offer

which could fill the vacuum created by the impact of the West, by the destruction of dynastic rule and by the crumbling of Confucian faith and doctrines. China's apparatus of intellectual self-defence had broken down. And the only idea Chiang could offer was force. For a long time the peasantry had been alienated from the Kuomintang, and the scholars and intellectuals were soon to abandon it. Deprived of these two props, the Nationalist edifice collapsed.

"Chiang will never return," a once liberal Chinese whom I had known at Kunming was to tell me in Communist Peking. "He will never be welcomed back, not even if his 'planes were to rain all the gold he has on China."

In the long history of this ancient and tortured land there have really been only three revolutions which have signified something cataclysmic, politically and socially. The first occurred in 221 B.C. when the Ch'in dynasty destroyed the country's feudal fabric and set up a centralised monarchy. In 1911 the revolt against the Manchus signalised the second revolution, which was followed by attempts to adjust the country's social and political structure to the new pattern of international influences and contacts. These failed, and China retreated within herself to generate her third great revolution when on October 1, 1949, Mao Tse-tung, standing in the yellow-tiled pavilion of the Tien An Men, or Gate of Heavenly Peace, at Peking announced the new era of Communism to the crowds milling in the great red square below him.

China has retreated into itself. To the dynastic world of ancient Cathay, loyalty to the State was loyalty to the race, bound together by the patriarchal ideas of Confucianism, content in its self-sufficiency, regarding itself as the epitome of civilisation, with the world beyond peopled by ocean devils and barbarians. Communism is the new version or variant of China's ancient faith, for Marxism has replaced Confucianism while adopting subtly its imagery and pattern. It demands unquestioning loyalty and obedience to the State, decrees belief in the new civilisation of Communism, and calls upon the individual to subordinate himself to the clan which is the party. The empire of China is identified with the realm of Communism. Beyond are the barbarians.

5   **Red Dragon**

THE thing to remember is the difference between Soviet Russia's and Communist China's revolutions, for the difference is reflected in the form and development of each.

The Russian revolution was a *coup d'état.* It began as a sudden upheaval which in the first five days swept away the monarchy and established a provisional government with the so-called bourgeois elements headed by Prince Lvov in authority. This was in March 1917. Not until two months later did the Soviet enter the government, and another two months elapsed before Kerensky became prime minister. On October 26th the Bolsheviks came into the picture with the constitution of a military revolutionary committee in Petrograd, and this was followed by the Petrograd revolution of November 7th which lit a fire enveloping Russia.

I remember hearing Nehru on his return from Moscow in July 1955 talking of these events.

"The Russians," he remarked in a conversation, "have never known democracy. When the Bolsheviks came to power nearly forty years ago, the Russians jumped from one autocracy to another—from tsarism to Communism. In fact, the Russians throughout their history have never known democracy as Western Europe understands it."

This is also true of China, but with a difference. In Peking, Panikkar* had discussed the difference with me.

* Sardar K. M. Panikkar, Indian ambassador to China from 1948 to 1952.

"The Chinese revolution," he explained, "was not an overnight affair like the Russian revolution. The Bolsheviks first came into power and then learned—by a long process of trial and error. The Russian revolution was touched off by a spark. Lenin, you remember, was imported into Russia in a sealed railway carriage—like a microbe. He'd been ten years out of Russia. Mao was never out of China before the revolution. His revolution was spread over twenty years. The pattern of Red China's rule was set at Yenan and other Communist-controlled areas long before—from the time the Communists took to the hills after the debacle of 1927. When Mao seized the government towards the end of 1949, he had a vast army of trained soldiers drawn mainly from the peasantry and skilled by experience in guerrilla fighting. He had, besides, the nucleus of an administrative cadre in the *kanpus*, or minor village officials who had grown up with the revolution. Mao had also tested out a great many ideas."

In wartime Chungking the Communists had told me something of their border-region governments. At that time (in 1944-1945) the Reds were in control of four border governments along with several other areas or pockets in Japanese-held territory which they claimed were under their influence. The main border-region government was a rectangular State south of the Great Wall with its centre at Yenan. The remaining three border regions were the Shansi-Hopei-Chahar bloc; the south Shansi, north Honan and southwest Hopei area; and a bloc in north Shantung. East and north behind the Japanese lines were guerrilla pockets extending eastward to the Yellow Sea and from the Yellow River in Honan and Hopei north into Manchuria and Mongolia.

"We control areas containing some 90 million people," declared the Communists. The Nationalists denied this.

The Communists claimed to have 650,000 well-trained regular troops aside from over two million ill-equipped guerrillas who were referred to as the People's Militia. China's Red Army numbers over four million men.

In those twenty crucial years after 1927 Mao had armed himself with men and also with ideas—some of these running counter to the tenets of orthodox Marxism. As far back as 1920, Lenin, following the dogma enshrined in *The Communist Manifesto*, had laid down that in colonial or semi-colonial countries the proletariat or urban workers must spearhead the revolution. But Lenin, like Mao, believed in adaptability and compromise. By giving land to the Russian peasants in November 1917, Lenin himself had made the Soviet revolution "irrevocable." Lenin died in 1924, and Stalin seized power. The subsequent Soviet miscalculations and misdirections on the strategy to be pursued by the Chinese Communists stemmed from Stalin's errors.

In the report which he compiled in 1927 on the possibilities for a peasant uprising in Hunan, Mao ignored the proletariat. "To give credits where they are due," he noted, "if we allot ten points to the accomplishments of the democratic revolution, then the achievements of the urban dwellers and the military units rate only three points, while the remaining seven points should go to the peasants in their rural revolution." From this line he did not depart until the revolution was accomplished twenty-two years later.

His tactics spelt an astonishing and distinctive deviation, for no one until Mao had challenged the basis of the Communist methodology in overthrowing capitalist-colonial power. Marx and Engels had enunciated the doctrine, and Lenin and Stalin had endorsed it. Mao challenged the fundamental premises of their thesis, and proved to be right. He drew his strength from the peasants, not the urban workers. He was denounced for his "peasant psychology" and his "banditry doctrine" by colleagues who swallowed wholesale the Soviet cult of proletariat leadership. Mao steadfastly refused to do this. The base of his movement was in the rural areas, not in the towns, and his weapon was not industrial unrest and strikes but the armed might and mobility of his peasant guerrillas. He did not seize power with a *coup d'état* on the Russian model. He propelled himself forward on a network of "liberated areas" which the long civil war consolidated and unified. It was the Asian variant of a European prototype. It confounded Marx and confirmed Mao.

As an Asian I was interested in discovering how far the

Chinese regarded their Communism as distinctive and how far
they acknowledged the inspiration and leadership of Moscow.
Panikkar stressed its indigenous inspiration.

"The Chinese revolution," he emphasised, "is Chinese. It has
its roots in Chinese history, for the authoritarian form of Chinese government is traditional and has existed for centuries.
Think of the glorious heights they reached under their tyrants!
Remember the Sung autocrats, the Ta'ng empress Wu and the
two Manchu emperors K'ang-hsi and Ch'ien Lung? What Mao
imported from outside was the Communist technique. Inside, he
equated Confucius with Marx."

To me it has always seemed that Mao's primary loyalty is to
Marx more than to Moscow. His basic Communism can never
be changed, but its manifestations might alter temporarily. With
Lenin he believes in the doctrine of adaptability, and is prepared always to zigzag to his target. Like Stalin he is a realist
who is ruthless.

But Mao is conscious of and takes pride in the fact that the
Communist revolution which he has led is distinctively Chinese.
By being so, it has blended and fused Chinese nationalism
with Chinese Communism in a way which Communism nowhere
else has achieved—not even in Russia.

At our first banquet in Communist China, which took place in
Canton and was given by the mayor, General Yeh Chien-ying, I
had entered into a cautious discussion on the Reds' class edifice
with the secretary-general of the local municipal executive. Communist China recognises four "friendly classes," these being the
proletariat or industrial workers; the peasants; the petty bourgeoisie or small traders; and the national bourgeoisie or capital-
ists.

The secretary-general explained that these gradations represented a passing phase. He stated frankly that the capitalist was
tolerated because his co-operation was necessary to industrialise
the country. He had experience and know-how. But when he
had served his purpose the capitalist would go. Similarly, peasant holdings were tolerated in the form of co-operatives. But
they, too, would disappear when collectivisation came and the
State acquired the land. The peasant would then be free to sell

his produce as he did now, but he would have to pay his dues to the State.

"Ours," concluded the secretary-general, "is a Chinese revolution. Therefore it had to be different."

Maoism distinguishes itself from Titoism in two ways—by remaining within the Soviet orbit and by eschewing the middle path or a third road.

"The salvoes of the October Revolution," wrote Mao, "brought us Marxism-Leninism." And elsewhere he has described Marxism-Leninism as "a universal truth which is applicable anywhere." China has applied and adapted it to its conditions and needs; and as the foremost Marxist dialectician in China, Liu Shao-ch'i, testifies, "Maoism unites the theories of Marxism-Leninism with the actual practice of the Chinese revolution."

Thus Maoism is for the moment content to operate within the ambit of Marxism and Moscow, acknowledging the inspiration of the former and following the example of the latter. "Follow the path of the Russians. This was the conclusion," Mao advised long ago.

Yet he has not always trod faithfully in the footsteps of Moscow even if he has been careful to make a show of doing so. On the other hand, unlike Tito, Mao makes no secret of the fact that he keeps within the Soviet orbit. "Internationally," he wrote in July 1949, "we belong to the anti-imperialist front headed by the U.S.S.R. and we can look only for genuine friendly aid from that front." He had led China to the same goal as Russia's but by a different road, and having reached the goal, he refused in contrast to Tito to take the middle way. Mao's means might differ from Moscow's but the ends of both are the same, and they stand or fall together. "To sit on the fence," Mao declared in the 1949 statement, "is impossible. A third road does not exist. . . . Not only in China but also in the world, without exception, one either leans to the side of imperialism or to that of socialism." Significantly Chou En-lai has capped this declaration with a prophecy. "People will be disappointed," he warns, "if they think there will ever be a Tito in China."

The tergiversations of Soviet policy in the same period are revealing. In 1931 Moscow turned its back on the Chinese Communists and in December 1932 re-established relations with Kuomintang China. Three years later the Kremlin, repudiating its ties with Chiang Kai-shek, callously sold the Chinese Eastern Railway to Japan, by then well set on its expansionist plans. As the Japanese moved deeper into Chinese territory, they caused the Russians some irritation by incursions along the Soviet border. In August 1937 the Kuomintang government at Nanking signed a treaty of non-aggression with Moscow; but four years later, in April 1941, not long before Hitler's invasion of Russia, the Kremlin endorsed the Soviet-Japanese declaration recognising the territorial integrity of Manchukuo while Japan reciprocated by recognising the People's Republic of Mongolia.

Nor did Stalin's cynical activities end here. At the Potsdam Conference he disavowed the Chinese Communists and as late as May 1945 was assuring Harry Hopkins that Chiang Kai-shek was the only leader qualified to rule China. Three months later, in August, Moscow signed a treaty of friendship and alliance with Kuomintang China. Mao was not to meet Stalin until five years later when he visited Moscow.

Meanwhile Mao's own war of "liberation" led by the peasantry trod an individual path. "The villages and the countryside will defeat the cities and the towns," he proclaimed, and later proved it. But outwardly he genuflected before Moscow even while he pursued tactics directly contrary to those decreed by the Kremlin. Since his assumption of power he has continued boldly to adapt Communism to Chinese conditions and needs, the while he continues to declare his loyalty to Moscow.

"The Chinese and Russians," remarked a European diplomat in Peking, "cannot but rely greatly on each other. The enemies of both countries are the same and their victims are identical."

Mao has no foreign supporter whom he can exploit as a counter to Russia. He depends on Moscow for military aid, for technical and industrial equipment and know-how. Yet while arming China it is unlikely that Moscow will hasten that nation's development into a military equal. When I was in China in 1952 Moscow's industrial help in the form of capital goods lagged noticeably behind its supplies of finished war materials. But the Korean War was then on.

Mao's loyalty to Moscow is unquestioned. He played down the Soviet denudation of industrial plants in Manchuria even as he played up Russian concessions on the Chinese Changchun railway. He thanked the Kremlin effusively for favours rendered, ignoring its cynical adventurism vis-à-vis the Chinese Communists in the past. He openly acknowledged the urban proletariat as the kingpin of his revolution, thereby deliberately contradicting his own ideas and actions. He chose to forget that the mandarins of Moscow had been somewhat tardy in paying him court. He had and has no alternative.

But while loyal to the Communist thesis, Mao takes pride in his Asianism and in the memory that China achieved Communism along a path that was its own.

Panikkar told me of an interview he had with Mao shortly after the Chinese leader's return from Moscow in 1950. While going on his rounds inside Russia, Mao had been shown a huge airplane plant which was producing 'planes by the minute.

The Chinese dictator turned to Panikkar in his grave, ponderous manner. He has a high thin voice, incongruous in a man of his bulk, but when he spoke it was almost wistfully.

"Not until your country and mine can do this," he remarked, "can we act decisively. Until then we must move slowly."

It was a revealing and significant remark, for it betrayed Mao's dormant feeling of Asianism and his urge to achieve equality with Russia. Even at that time, though ideologically a step behind Russia, since Peking regarded Moscow as representing a more advanced stage of socialism than China itself, Mao was careful to behave as a partner and ally rather than as a satellite and a subordinate.

"The Chinese will always be Chinese," remarked Sir Lionel Lamb, then British representative in Peking. "China's policies, internal and external, must therefore take into account not only Communist dogma but Chinese interests."

Among the Chinese this appeared to be the general attitude, and in the context it amused me that they should regard us Indians as people who, though politically independent, had still to be economically "liberated." With their natural politeness they were careful not to say this openly but they implied it artfully, though not always subtly.

"Very well," one of our delegation finally observed, "you think India is semi-colonial. You think we're still under the British influence. But do you know what we think? We think you're greatly under the influence of the Russians."

They rose to the bait.

"We do depend on Russia for advice and aid in some fields," one of them replied. "We do not conceal that. But have you ever seen a Russian order a Chinese about?"

What he said was superficially true. At Pengpu on our way to the Hwai River project we had been taken to see an exhibition of charts and pictures hung in a building which had obviously once been a Christian church. Though the altars had been removed, the Gothic windows, aisles and façade told their story. Our guide had pointed to a huge portrait of a European and explained that it was a picture of the Russian engineer who was supervising the project. Other examples occurred to me. Moreover I had been told by some veteran European residents that the Chinese dislike for "foreign devils" extended in some degree to the Russians, who were clandestinely christened "long noses."

As an Asian my interest was caught by the typically Asian argument which the Chinese employed. There was no external evidence of the Russians ordering the Chinese about. Therefore there was no overlordship. It is typical because in Asian minds colonial domination is equated with certain external manifestations such as the gunboat, "showing the flag," colour bar, rape and the bayonet. The Russians were scrupulously correct in their behaviour, and such orders as the Chinese people heard were given by Chinese individuals through Chinese voices. Over four-fifths of China's population lives on the land; probably less than twenty Chinese in every thousand have seen a Russian.

We had forgotten something we should have remembered. Throughout their history the Chinese have never dealt with other peoples as equals, and to many even under the Communist régime China remains the Middle Kingdom surrounded by barbarians. In that sense the Chinese are nearer to the Japanese

than to the Indians, whose country represents a crucible of
many racial elements and strains. In its long history India has
never shut the door on a stranger.

On the other hand, the Chinese have never known the rigid
ties of caste as India does. Chinese society consequently dis-
plays a greater mobility than either the Indian or the Japanese,
and this explains the extraordinary resilience of the Chinese people despite centuries of authoritarian tradition and rule. As
long as the emperor remained the fount of authority, the concept of the country's political unity survived as a symbol even
when it no longer functioned as a reality. In India local rather
than central loyalty had been the rule, and even the authority
of the Great Mogul had crumbled by 1750. There is another
difference. India has always welcomed trade; but China, reared
on a tradition of self-sufficiency, scoffed at foreign commerce.
From ancient days the trader has rated low in the Chinese social
hierarchy, which gives primacy to the scholar and, as an agricultural economy, respects the peasant.

The Chinese guides and interpreters who accompanied us
throughout our tour talked frequently of "Asian peace and
friendship." Even Mao, when he met our delegation and shook
hands genially with each one of us, had murmured the same
phrase.

I had seen him distantly at the May Day parade as he stood
in the yellow-tiled pavilion of the Tien An Men, and I was interested to observe him in closer proximity. He came into the
room, where we stood in a line, with the slow lumbering, un-
certain gait of a bear, and indeed there was something faintly
ursine about the flapping arms and the rounded shoulders
which seemed oddly out of place with his upright carriage. His
head was massive, and his jet-black hair worn *en brosse* crowned
a round rustic, homely face with small wide-awake eyes which
peered straight at you as he shook your hand. He smiled, all the
while looking like a bland, benign Buddha but also like a
Cheshire cat who has had his fill of cream. I sensed a strong
feline streak in him, a jumble of cruelty and charm.

Some weeks later, in a remote village in Manchuria, we
found ourselves surrounded by peasant girls who looked at us
in round-eyed wonder and asked us if it were true that we had

seen Chairman Mao. Indeed we had. Had he talked to us? Yes.
And had he shaken hands with us? Even so. Then would we
shake hands with them? Gladly we gave them their vicarious
thrill.

In Mao they saw the father image of Chinese tradition, for he
was the Benign Father, the Great Provider, and from a thousand
walls and hoardings throughout China his homely countenance
beamed on his people. Opposed though I was to the ideology of
the Communists, I felt a strange kinship with the Chinese, a
sense of "being together" which must, I reflected, stem from my
own Asian consciousness. And yet there was something which
was stylised and artificial in their constant reiteration of the
phrase "Asian peace and friendship." Asian we both were, but
the Chinese thought pattern was altogether alien to an Indian.

"Do you notice one thing?" a colleague remarked. "In India,
as in most democratic countries, the government passes a law
when it wants something done. In China it starts a movement."

He was referring to two movements which the Communists
had been conducting for some time. They were known as San
Fan, or Anti-Three, and Wu Fan, or Anti-Five, the first directed
against three major sins alleged to be infecting the party and
official ranks (these were corruption, waste and "bureaucratism"*), and the second initiated ostensibly by the business community in a mood of terrorised penitence and designed to
erase five major commercial sins. These were bribery, stealing
of government property, cheating the government, illegal specu-
lation and tax evasion.

In a way the two movements were complementary, for while
San Fan aimed at preventing officials from accepting bribes Wu
Fan aimed at preventing businessmen from corrupting the *kanpus,* or minor administrators, by offering bribes. "A Communist
cannot be corrupt, and who is corrupt cannot be a Communist,"
had been a Red axiom. Now the Reds had discovered that a
Communist no less than other men was susceptible to bribery
and to economic pressures and inducements.

The processes which characterised these campaigns were pub-

* "Bureaucratism" was defined as anything smacking of a "bourgeois pattern of conduct," and included indifference to work, ostentatious living, too
much attention to power and authority.

lic accusation, confession and self-criticism, accompanied by an orgy of brain-washing to which the accused were subjected in order to reindoctrinate and rehabilitate them. To us Indians these tactics were unnatural and repellent.

But they were not abnormal to the Chinese. As Panikkar had pointed out, public accusation, confession and self-criticism were part of an age-long pattern. They were the Chinese expression of moral and political rearmament. The Communists had developed and adapted them for their own ends. The masses were let out on a long leash.

"The identification of the Chinese people with their government is the heart of the matter," said Panikkar. "Once you understand this, you understand Communist China."

Applying this norm, it was clear that San Fan and Wu Fan were movements which represented a war in which the people were associated with the government against "the common enemy"—those elements in Liu Shao-ch'i's words who would at any moment resort to the "middle line" and compromise. It was a class war led by the working class, its immediate aim being the terrorisation of the bourgeoisie with the ultimate object of eliminating them.

And yet with what diabolical cleverness did the Communists carry the people with them in every one of their campaigns! It was so at every layer, young and old, the economic, social, political, educational, cultural and even judicial; for at the judicial level, although the judge was in fact the arbiter, the people through the process of the People's Courts and Mass Trials were led to believe that they were the final court of appeal. "The individual," as Dr. Hu Shih had remarked, "was denied even his right of silence." He was compelled to participate.

By making it appear that the people were associated with the government at all stages the Communists have achieved two things. They have identified the people with the government and, by rendering the former privy to the latter's acts, they have prevented public criticism of the régime.

Moreover, although the collective principle operates in China, everything is done to encourage, even to glorify individual performance. The number of bemedalled, beribboned labour heroes and heroines we saw testified to this. As a result the individual feels that he is not merely an impersonal unit in an inchoate structure but a vital organ in the machinery of the State and one whose contribution the government values and recognises.

"Why do you respect the Communist State?" one of our delegation asked the nonagenarian artist Chi Pai-shih,* whose memories go back to the Manchus by whom he was neglected.

"Because it respects me," was the answer.

Similar expressions of mutual respect were exchanged by Chinese and Indian spokesmen at the numerous banquets to which we were invited. From our side came innumerable references to the Chinese pilgrim Hsuen Tsang, who had visited India in the seventh century in the reign of the Emperor Harsha, and to an even earlier visitor, Fa Hsien, who was in India two centuries before in the days of Chandragupta II. The Chinese spoke continuously of "cultural interflow," of a "beautiful friendship" and of "peace and Asian friendship."

I felt that there was something familiar in the last phrase which kept recurring in their speeches and conversation. And of a sudden memory stirred. Ten years earlier the Japanese had talked of Asian Co-Prosperity when all the while they had meant Japanese prosperity. The Chinese Communists talked of "Asian friendship" but they also talked of "liberating Asia." From what? And to whom?

Two thousand miles of rugged frontier separate India from China, but the two countries face each other not only across this long mountain barrier but throughout southeast Asia. Of Asia's three most industrious peoples, the Japanese for historical reasons have functioned principally in their island home and, until the end of the Second World War, on the Chinese mainland, but throughout southeast Asia the Indians and the Chinese compete with one another economically while culturally they remain distinct and apart. There are traces of Hindu culture at Borobudur in Java and in the glories of Angkor Vat. Hinduism and Buddhism permeated these regions from India. But the Chinese intrusion has been more vigorous and assertive, and in commerce the Chinese prevail.

"It is strange," I heard Nehru remark, "that our cultural in-

* Died in September 1957 aged ninety-seven.

fluence should be mainly in the islands, while the Chinese influence is largely continental. The Chinese have vigour and vitality. So have we. But sometimes I wonder whether we have their discipline and strong spirit of co-operation."

Nehru is well aware of the irredentist urge of the Chinese for the recovery of their so-called lost territories of which even Sun Yat-sen gave an embarrassingly inclusive list. "We lost," he declared,[*] "Korea, Formosa and Peng Fu to Japan after the Sino-Japanese War, Annam to France and Burma to Britain. . . . In addition the Ryukyu islands, Siam, Borneo, Sarawak, Java, Ceylon, Nepal and Bhutan were once tributary States to China." Chiang subsequently echoed these claims, and Mao Tse-tung has reiterated them. Edgar Snow quotes him as saying, "I began to have a certain amount of political consciousness, especially after I read a pamphlet telling of the dismemberment of China . . . of Japan's occupation of Korea and Formosa, of the loss of suzerainty in Indo-China, Burma and elsewhere."

For the moment this irredentist urge is concentrated in and symbolised by the overseas Chinese for whose especial status and progress the Kuomintang was and is as equally solicitous as the Communists. I noticed this in Chungking in 1944 and again in Communist China in 1952. In the Kuomintang *China Handbook* for 1943 the number of overseas Chinese is given as a little over 8½ millions. The Communists today compute them at approximately 12 millions and, like the Kuomintang, maintain a Commission of Overseas Chinese Affairs. Before the war some three thousand educational institutions for overseas Chinese were scattered over forty-five countries in five continents, and in 1941 the number of Chinese schools in Malaya alone was over a thousand. The Kuomintang used these institutions for propagating Chinese nationalism abroad. The Communists attempt to use them equally as propaganda centres, and from their declarations it is obvious that the Reds regard the overseas Chinese as their fifth column and the nuclei of their shock brigades. If these regions were to fall to Peking, India would find itself enmeshed helplessly in the coils of the Red Dragon.

How vividly I recollect the warm handshakes, the bows, the

---

[*] Quoted in *A Documentary History of Chinese Communism* by Brandt, Schwartz and Fairbank (Cambridge, 1952).

friendly faces wreathed in smiles with which the Indian cultural delegation were greeted throughout their stay in China!
One remembers the chunky Chu Teh with his gnarled heavy
hands and wrinkled face; Liu Shao-ch'i, grey-haired and handsome, but ascetic in mien, with his gravely serene wife; and Chou
En-lai of the beetling black eyebrows whose quick smile and
laugh never concealed the wariness of his deep brown eyes. They
were friendly and always genial.

Did they really believe that we were totally unaware of their
ideas and intentions towards "semi-colonial" India as they themselves had revealed it in chapter and verse? One could not help
wondering at times.

Other memories recur—the shock on seeing Madame Sun
Yat-sen, known in Red China as Ch'ing Ling-soong, whom I had
met eight years before in Chungking. She was matronly even
then, but attractive, and I had enjoyed her English conversation
over a Chinese tea embellished with delicious wheat cakes. Now
the matron had assumed the amplitude of a matriarch and she
spoke cordially, though seemingly from a distance, in Chinese
through an interpreter. There was Kung Peng, who had been in
Chungking too, and who spoke English fluently and with grace.
She continued speaking in English, but one morning she startled
me when I went to see her at the Foreign Office in Peking by addressing me in Chinese through an interpreter whose English
was less than indifferent.

Who else? So many. Peng Chen, mayor of Peking, with whom
I discussed China one night after dinner and whom I rather
liked. Though he had a pugnacious face, he seemed to possess a
sense of humour. There were others—Chen Chien-ying, the
woman engineer, who accompanied us to the Hwai River project; and Ting Ling, the writer, short, dumpy, with her gay
plump "moon face."

They were all genial and all dedicated Communists. And at
some time or another every one of them had talked or written of
"liberating" Asia.

What do the Communists mean when they talk of "liberating"
Asia? Although today Peking expresses the friendliest sentiments
towards India, it had revealed its real designs earlier. Speaking
over a year after India achieved its independence, Liu Shao-ch'i,

writing in *Internationalism and Nationalism,** directed a call to
the Communists in Asian countries to "adopt a firm and irrecon-
cilable policy against national betrayal by the reactionary section of the bourgeoisie, especially the big bourgeoisie which has
already surrendered to imperialism. If this were not done it
would be a grave mistake." In the list of countries which Liu
characterised as "colonial and semi-colonial" were India, Burma,
Siam, the Philippines, Indonesia, Indo-China and Burma. It was
a call directed to the indigenous Reds and to the fifth columns of
the overseas Chinese to overthrow the régimes of these countries.

Since Peking's commitment to *panchshila* † in 1954 China has
been reticent on this issue, but in October 1952 Malenkov repeated the charge, pointing specifically to countries such as India, Malaya, the Philippines and Indo-China "where the movement for liberation was growing." This was five years after India
had achieved freedom. Obviously "liberation" implies being "liberated" to Communism.

Communism changes its face but never its character. When in
February 1957 Mao declared, "Let a hundred flowers blossom,
let a hundred schools of thought contend," many alleged experts
on Communism and the Kremlin saw in it a new challenge to
Moscow and its policies. Actually, Peking was throwing a lifeline
to Moscow, for Mao's new doctrine represented a middle line between Titoism (which sought to set the men of the Kremlin at
one another's throats on the issue of Stalinism) and what might
be called Molotovism (which signified a dedicated devotion to
Stalin). Since his speech to the Twentieth Party Congress in
February 1956 Khrushchev had been caught in this vise. And
from this Mao skilfully tried to extricate him without doing
damage to Marxism or to Moscow.

For obvious reasons Mao has no compelling urge to venerate
Stalin's memory, for Stalin consistently denigrated Mao and the
Chinese Communists. At the same time Mao is too loyal a Com-
munist to dismiss Stalin as of no account, for grave as Stalin's er-

---

* Published in November 1948. India achieved independence in August
1947.

† The Five Principles are: (1) mutual respect for each other's territorial
integrity and sovereignty; (2) non-aggression; (3) non-interference in each
other's internal affairs; (4) equality and mutual advantage; and (5) peaceful
co-existence and economic co-operation.

rors and deficiencies were his achievements outweighed them.
Stalin's principal error in Mao's reckoning, as developments in
Poland and Hungary proved after Khrushchev's denigration of
the dead dictator, was that Stalin insisted on ruling the satellites
from Moscow. That had never suited Mao's book, for the Chinese dictator sees Peking as a partner and ally, not as a satellite
or subordinate of Moscow.

Hence his invitation to let a hundred flowers blossom. It was
not, as some foreign observers believed, an incitement to a
free-for-all within the Communist circle. Far from it, as the
unfortunate Lo Lung-chi and Chang Po-chun of the Democratic
League discovered on challenging Maoism inside China, and as
Molotov, Malenkov, Kaganovich and others found out when
they attempted to turn on Khrushchev in Moscow.

While enunciating his new doctrine Mao made it clear that the
major basic world struggle between Communism and capitalism
should continue unabated. As between Communist and Communist he urged greater freedom of criticism—a truly Machiavellian
manœuvre as events proved, for it ended, as *Pravda* gleefully
pointed out, not in the isolation of the Communists but of the
"rightists" who had tried to undermine them. This was demon-
strated in Moscow and Peking. One outcome has been to elevate
Mao and Maoism, and with them China, in the esteem of the
Kremlin.

At the end of the Second World War Soviet Russia emerged as
the greatest single land power in Asia, a development which was
to affect the balance of power in this area. China's emergence as
a Communist State in 1949 altered still further the historical
power structure, because Russia, unlike other European countries which have penetrated Asia, has exercised a continental and
not a maritime influence. China and India border on Soviet
frontiers, and until the end of the Second World War so did
Japan. This fact is important.

If the Second World War witnessed the disappearance of European power from Asia and the end of maritime mercantilism,
it also saw the emergence of the United States as an increasingly
important factor in Sino-Soviet relations. Russia and the United
States had geographically been drawing nearer each other from
the nineteenth century when the American pioneers, going

west, reached the Pacific coast in 1844. About the same time the Russians settled in Vladivostok. In the latter half of the nineteenth century America advanced its trade across the Pacific, notably with China, and occupied the Philippines in December 1898. In Asia, meanwhile, Russia reached out to the borders of Afghanistan and India and infiltrated Manchuria. The Sino-Soviet relationship is thus of vital interest and concern to the United States, which lacks Russia's geographical advantage of being on the Asian continent. This advantage increases the danger and influence of the Soviet Union, which through China is even now seeking to "liberate" Asia.

China is well content to be Russia's ally and accomplice. In Chinese eyes India needs to be "liberated" along with the rest of Asia. Following Mao Tse-tung's success China's Communist régime has advanced to the borders of southern Asia, to the frontiers of Indo-China, Burma, Thailand and India, and later, as the Communists seeped through Tibet, to the borders of Nepal. Mao clearly regards China as the leader of Asia, and sooner or later it is certain that his present calculatedly vague references to anti-imperialism and anti-feudalism will project themselves into a move for the economic "liberation" of Asia's independent countries from the "tyranny" of capitalism and colonialism.

Like all Communists Mao excels in using the democratic vocabulary and apparatus to advance his strictly Communist ends. Inside China he interpreted Sun Yat-sen's Three Principles of nationalism, democracy and the people's livelihood as alliance with the U.S.S.R., co-operation with the Chinese Communist party and alliance with the workers and peasants. To the Kuomintang's irredentism he now gives the name of liberation, and he has not hesitated to use democracy as a cloak beneath whose cover he could achieve Communism.

This is what the democratic countries of Asia must realise and understand. With the Communists democracy is a means, not an end.

6   The Long Week End

INDIA lost its independence about the time the American colonies won their freedom. Almost coincident with the Boston Tea Party of 1773 was the Regulating Act passed by the British Parliament which appointed Warren Hastings as governor-general in Bengal, the Act itself being designed "for the better regulation of the affairs of the East India Company and of their servants in India." In 1781 Lord Cornwallis surrendered his sword to Washington at Yorktown, and five years later became governor-general in India and commander-in-chief in Bengal. The year which saw the birth of the American constitution at Philadelphia witnessed the historic impeachment of Warren Hastings by Edmund Burke.

To understand the outlook of modern Asia it is necessary to appreciate the impact which European intrusion and aggression made on the countries of this continent, notably on India, China and Japan. This impact varied in time, extent and character, and its impress was therefore different on each of the three countries.

It began with India, then infiltrated to China and Japan. The discovery of the Cape route by Bartolomeu Dias threw open the Indian Ocean to navigators from the West, and in May 1498 Vasco da Gama anchored off the port of Calicut on the southwest coast of India. Thirteen years later the establishment of the Portuguese power in Malacca enabled European ships to scour the Pacific, and in 1516 the first Portuguese adventurer, Rafael Peresterello, voyaged to the China coast in a junk. In 1542 Antônio Galvano, governor of Malacca, reached Japan.

Thus Europe's maritime supremacy enabled it to reach and in time to control the vast land mass of Asia, coming first to the Indian Ocean and from there percolating to the Pacific. From ancient days Indian ships had plied the waters of the Arabian Sea and the Indian Ocean. In the early years of the sixteenth century Affonso d'Albuquerque, sailing along the Malayan coast, noted the presence of Arab, Hindu and Chinese sailors and merchants, but their activities were restricted, being primarily commercial and coastal. India never possessed command of the seas around its shores except perhaps under the Chola dynasty.* Nor did China show any vigorous naval enterprise except for a sporadic burst under the Ming emperor Yung Lo.†

From very early days India had contact with Europe; but the impact of European trade and commerce was felt only after the discovery of the Cape route to India, following which the Portuguese, Dutch, British and French entrenched themselves with varying degrees of success and fought to consolidate their political power in rivalry with one another. From 1612, when the British established their first trade settlement at Surat, this conflict acquired a keener and with time a lethal edge. By the end of the seventeenth century Portugal's only footholds in India were at Gôa, Diu and Damão, while the Dutch were confined to Cochin and Negapatam. Thereafter Britain faced France in the Indian Ocean.

The end of the eighteenth century witnessed the withdrawal of the French from the Indian Ocean; then, having broken the back of Maratha resistance at the battle of Assaye in 1803, the East India Company became the paramount power when fifteen years later it absorbed the Maratha empire in its domains. British authority, as exercised by the company, extended in 1818 over almost the entire country from the Sutlej across the Gangetic valley to Delhi, and included the Maratha Deccan along with the coastal tracts skirting the Arabian Sea and the Bay of Bengal. Within this military triangle were a congeries of pro-

---

* The Cholas reigned from A.D. 850 to 1150.
† Yung Lo reigned from 1403 to 1424.

tected princes located mainly in the interior of the country. By 1848 the Sikhs had succumbed beyond the Sutlej, and ten years later, following the Great Rebellion, British rule was firmly established in India.

Thus India was the first Asian country to feel the initial force of Europe's commercial infiltration, and once British authority was entrenched in power it was from India as a base that Britain prised open the doors of China, the first Opium War* being provoked by the refusal of the Chinese to allow the import of opium, in which the East India Company had a lucrative traffic and trade. By 1842 the Industrial Revolution had transformed Britain's economy, and maritime supremacy helped to project England's authority into the Pacific.

From India British power radiated to other spheres of influence in Asia and beyond—to Burma, Afghanistan, to the Arab coast and the Persian Gulf, to Lhasa and Sinkiang—these wars and expeditions being financed partly or wholly from Indian revenues and being undertaken with a large leavening of Indian troops. India became a base for Britain's aggression in Asia.

Of Asia's three major countries Japan alone was untouched by the wave of European incursions. Although the Portuguese arrived in Japan in 1542, and were the first to introduce firearms into that country, their contacts were restricted mainly to trade and religion. Christianity entered Japan in the middle of the sixteenth century, being brought there from India where St. Francis Xavier had begun his mission in Gôa in 1542. Xavier introduced Christianity to Japan during a two-year stay from 1549 to 1551. In 1587 the daimio Hideyoshi ordered the banning of all Christian missionaries; and, although this policy was reversed later, Japan shortly afterwards entered on a period of isolation, virtually shutting itself off from the rest of the world for over two hundred years. The arrival of Commodore Perry's "black ships" in 1853 opened Japan to the West.

Many years ago, as a student in England, I experienced some of the deep-seated resentment which several of my Asian and Arab fellow students felt towards India. All too often British imperialism in China and Egypt had been symbolised in the figures of the Indian soldier and policeman, and to other Asians

* 1840–1842.

we seemed aiders and abettors of colonialism rampant. From them I heard many tales of the indignities to which their people had been subjected by Indians serving with British arms abroad.

Years later in Communist China I encountered the same reproach when in an unguarded moment I politely asked a Chinese woman Communist whether in her younger days she had known any Indians in the old Babylon of Shanghai.

"Yes," she replied icily, "I remember as a girl watching a Sikh policeman spitting on my father's face."

Her remark was unexpected but not unjustified, and it impressed on me the need to recognise the invidious position which India assumed in other Asian eyes as a result of its long association with the West, which exceeded that of either China or Japan, and also from the fact that apart from Indonesia India was politically dominated by a single European power longer than any other country in Asia, excluding areas like Portuguese Gôa and French Pondichéry.

How different were the colonial systems of Britain, France, Portugal and the Netherlands! I had realised this forcefully even before I visited Peking, when two years earlier, on my way from the Antipodes to India, I had halted for a brief stay in Djakarta.

"There but for the grace of God go we," was my reflection as I watched the casual, makeshift, indolent and inexperienced Indonesians at work.

Our long association with the British had given us certain advantages, but in the estimate of fellow Asians some of the stigma and slur attaching to the acts of Western imperialism were identified with us. Looking back over the years, I feel that much of this resentment derived from the belief that India was the symbol of Asian subjection and that its protracted inability to throw off the British yoke appeared in Asian eyes as a slavish yen to hug the chains that bound it. India's subjection meant the prolongation of Asia's subjection.

Often as a student in England I had heard the reproach of other Asians, particularly of Arab friends: "Why can't India with a population of over 300 million throw out a handful of Englishmen? Why must you quarrel among yourselves?" They were referring to Hindu-Muslim rivalries and antagonisms.

Their reproach was justified. Yet the protracted Indo-British association which lasted in terms of the British "presence" for three centuries and in terms of British rule for nearly two hundred years gave India a stamp distinctive from that of either China or Japan.

Racially the Caucasian strain in the Indian people springing from the Aryan invasions and surviving the intermingling of races inside the country made for greater affinity between Indian and European than subsists between the Mongoloid peoples of China and Japan and those of the West. In the Indian people are blended many racial elements—Dravidian, Indo-Aryan, Mongol, Turkish, Persian and, according to some, a filtering of Greek blood, probably a legendary legacy from the incursions of Alexander the Macedon and his general Seleucus in the fourth century B.C.* Sanskrit, Persian, Greek and Latin have a common philological origin, and it is interesting to note the claim— in view of the theory that Indian thought is heavily overlaid with religion and philosophy—that there are more terms for philosophical and religious thought in Sanskrit than there are in Greek, Latin and German combined.

Philosophy and religion are the Hindu's main intellectual preoccupations just as the development of political institutions was the central concern of the Briton. In India this concern was revealed from the early days of British authority, for even while the East India Company was busy annexing Maratha territories in the Deccan the governor-general, Lord Hastings, was peering into the future. Writing in 1818, he visualised a time "not far remote . . . when England will, on sound principles of policy, wish to relinquish domination which she has gradually and unintentionally assumed over this country."

Seventeen years later Macaulay's celebrated minute decreed a system of education in the English language and on the English pattern, and as a result the Indian intellectual was exposed increasingly to the liberal ideas of the West, more particularly to the ideas of political liberty and individual freedom. He read the speeches of Edmund Burke and the writings of Herbert Spencer, Huxley, Adam Smith and John Stuart Mill. He discov-

* Indian soldiers had fought for the Persians on Greek soil as far back as 480 B.C.

ered a new world in the ideas of Rousseau and Voltaire, of Taine, Montesquieu and Locke. Gandhi's favourite Western authors were Tolstoy and Thoreau, and from both he was to draw copiously for his own political principles and practices.

Even before Macaulay's minute there is evidence that educated Hindus could converse in English. Among the earliest to do so was the famous Hindu social reformer Ram Mohan Roy, who learned English in 1792 at the age of twenty. Roy was exceptional, although by 1818 English was in fairly wide vogue among the more cultivated Hindus. This is one reason why the Hindus, profiting by their priority in English education, scored in the matter of jobs against the Muslims, whose religious teachers encouraged a boycott of secular schools, a prejudice which they did not shed completely until 1875 when the Muslim Anglo-Oriental college, now the well-known Aligarh University, was founded. The number of Indians knowing English has never been large—it does not today exceed four million, or 1.1 per cent of the total population—but the influence of this group has been far beyond its numerical strength, and many of the ideas imbibed from Western science and literature have percolated from this top layer to a considerable proportion of the masses below.

As British rule entrenched itself, English became the language of the administration and of the law courts. Largely through the influence of the latter, educated Indians came to recognise and respect the rule of law and with it the precepts of constitutional government. Macaulay again was responsible for the introduction and application of the new legal principles enshrined in the Indian penal code which ordained the equality of all before the law in a country where the caste system had imposed rigid social layers and barriers with the Brahmin far above the lowly Sudra. This was nothing short of revolutionary.

By 1818 Britain was well on the road to becoming the workshop of the world; and the Industrial Revolution which science made possible, while it destroyed the Indian economic fabric which in turn was based on agriculture and handicrafts, infected thoughtful Indians with the spirit of scientific curiosity and infused in them a determination to master the secrets of industrial progress.

Not all of the ideas and institutions which the British introduced were alien or new to the Indian way of life. The idea of
democracy as the Western world knows and practises it had
still to develop, but its philosophical basis was laid in Europe by
the writings of Montesquieu, Rousseau and Voltaire and found
explosive expression in the slogan of liberty, fraternity and
equality which was the watchword of the French Revolution in
the last quarter of the eighteenth century. In a restricted fashion
India also knew of representative institutions and ideas.

The theocratic order, with power identified with sacerdotal
authority, prevailed in India from ancient days; but kingship
has rarely been a Brahmin preserve, being more often associated with the Kshatriyas, or warrior caste, and sometimes even
enjoyed by a Sudra. In pre-British days power rested on local
rather than on central loyalties. When the British first arrived,
Mogul rule was comparatively firm. Yet even then the pattern
of local loyalties operated over large areas of the country, particularly in peninsular India; and when by 1750 the authority of
the emperor at Delhi had for all practical purposes collapsed,
India was reduced to a mosaic of independent and warring
States. *Delhi dur ast* (Delhi is far away) ran a saying of Mogul
days, not unlike the old Chinese proverb, "Heaven is high and
the emperor is far away." In China the central concept of government survived until the 1840's when the European inter-
lopers began their penetration of the Yangtze Valley. Thereafter
the sway of the Manchus declined progressively until their
overthrow some seventy years later.

Representative government as exercised by the village
panchayat, or council, went back in India to the early Aryans;
and the *Arthashastra* written by Chanakya, also known as
Kautilya, chief minister of Chandragupta Maurya who ruled for
twenty-four years until 301 B.C., describes these ancient institutions. They have survived British rule, and continue today.

There existed in Vedic times such bodies as the *Sabha*, or
Council of Elders, and the *Samiti*, or House of the People. Law,
termed *dharma*, was sovereign, the divine right of kings or autocracy having no place in this system. The king, or *rajan*, was
elected by the *Samiti*. For centuries sayings such as *Janata
janardana* (The people are God) have been current throughout

the country, but there is no denying that the caste system which
deteriorated and acquired a thousand ramifications when the
Aryans came in contact with the Dravidians restricted these
privileges to a fairly exclusive class or hierarchy. None the less
the notion of representative institutions and government is not
new to India. British political and constitutional ideas therefore
fell on congenial soil. The Indian environment was more receptive to these ideas than the political climate of China
or Japan.

Longer exposure to Western literature, ideas and political
thought combined with the tradition of representative rule has
made the Indian more sensitive to democratic processes than
the Japanese or Chinese, in whose countries the theocratic pattern of government has always been more strongly enshrined
than in India. In the eyes of his Japanese or Chinese subjects,
the emperor was divine, and within the concept of his divinity
power—at least theoretically—coincided with authority. But in
India divinity has never hedged kingship.

Despite the deficiencies of the Hindu caste system and the
intellectual arrogance and smugness of which many accuse us,
I have always had the feeling while in Japan and China
(whether Kuomintang or Communist) that India was more genuinely democratic and tolerant than either of these countries.

The Upanishads (800-600 B.C.) breathe this spirit of freedom.

"What is the universe?" is the question.

And the answer goes, "In freedom it rises; in freedom it rests;
and into freedom it melts away."

"You might accuse us of many sins of commission and omission," an Englishman observed shortly after India attained independence in August 1947. "But at least we gave India a hundred years of peace and good government."

It was true, for that and the rule of law are among Britain's
more memorable contributions to India. The peace which the
British raj ensured enabled India and Indians to imbibe modern
ideas, to develop an international outlook, to be accustomed to
quasi-parliamentary, if not to democratic, institutions, to learn
alongside a Western people new concepts of industrial, scientific, social and political progress so that when freedom came

India found little difficulty in taking its place naturally among the free countries of the world.

Good government is no substitute for self-government, but if it was India's destiny to be ruled temporarily by a foreign power Providence was wise and benignant in choosing the British. I could therefore understand the sentiments of the Japanese politician who remarked to me in Tokyo in 1954: "If we had to have an occupying power, thank God it was America. Where would we be if it were China or Russia?"

In the latter half of the nineteenth century Japan had acquired the façade of constitutional government. The political institutions she took ready-made but trimmed them to suit her own conditions. They were imported from various countries, including Germany, France and Britain. Japan set up new institutions. What Nippon did not change was the ideas. These remained.

Of the three major Asian countries China's course was the most erratic. Following the fall of the Manchus China was torn between the factious war lords and the intellectuals, the latter imbued with the progressive political ideas of America and France. During Sun Yat-sen's lifetime the alliance between the more patriotic army elements and the liberals had brought about an uneasy truce, but the Communist challenge to the Kuomintang which began in the early twenties threatened disruption even before Sun's death. In 1927 Chiang Kai-shek's coup against the Communists signified the prelude to civil war. Chiang was a soldier, and of whatever else he might have been suspected nobody then or since has suspected him of being a democrat.

Britain, allege some British historians, conquered India in a fit of absent-mindedness. If so, the fit was remarkably sustained. None the less no fair-minded Indian, even while conscious of the deeply demoralising effect of foreign rule, can deny the material benefits which the British connection brought. It brought roads and railways, opened up the country's communications, developed its transport system and embarked on a network of irrigation projects which when India became independent gave the country rich areas of irrigated land.

Sound government was ensured by an administration con-

trolled by the *corps d'élite* of the Indian Civil Service whose
standards of competence and work were unrivalled throughout
the Commonwealth. This system gave India not only the framework of a modern government but also introduced the country
to concepts of modern administration. In the subcontinent which
is now divided into India and Pakistan are some of the world's
finest soldiers, who were trained by British methods into a highly
disciplined fighting force. While Indians under British rule were
for many years officially discouraged from developing indigenous
industries, the setting up of sizeable tariffs around 1920 enabled
several struggling industries, notably textiles, to consolidate
themselves behind a protective wall. The iron and steel industry was established despite British frowns by the courage and
foresight of J. N. Tata, founder of the House of Tata.

These developments left India when it became independent
with a workable nucleus of efficient administrators, disciplined
soldiers and a growing managerial class which together have
helped to sustain the stresses and strains of the first critical post-
independence decade. For such vital contributions India owes
Britain a debt which most Indians readily acknowledge.

Economically, China and Japan have traversed a course different from India's. In the five hundred years or more before
the sixteenth century when Europe burst the boundaries of Asia,
the only visitors from the Occident were stray missionaries or
travellers of whom the most celebrated was Marco Polo. Even
after the incursion of the West, China and Japan were virtually
closed to the "sea devils" or "barbarians" until the middle years
of the nineteenth century when the doors of both countries
were forced open—in 1842 in China with the end of the first
Opium War, and in 1853 in Japan with the arrival of Perry's
"black ships."

The reaction of the two countries to Europe's political and
economic impact was again different. Sensing that the only
chance of survival was to master European techniques, Japan
proceeded to do so with a dedicated zeal which within fifty years
was to rate it among the world's great powers. As in India and
China, the Western impact was to shake and sunder Nippon's
old economic and political structure. But whereas in India and
China this was effected by extraneous forces, in Japan it was

done by the Japanese themselves. It was a feat of inspired and
brilliant improvisation. Unfortunately, in Japan as in Europe the
Industrial Revolution which brought into being a capitalist
economy also generated a colonial appetite, and this in the end
proved Nippon's undoing. Superimposed upon the people by the
ruling caste, which found a focal point of national unity in the
emperor's divinity, the Japanese revolution was chauvinistic in
its political and economic expression. Therein lay the seeds of
life and sudden death.

China, unlike India, was the victim of several imperialisms
which simultaneously drained the country's economic resources
even while they devoured its body politic. Trade followed the
flag as the Western powers infiltrated the country, destroying
indigenous handicrafts and rearing in their stead a system of
concessions and privileges from which they extracted huge profits and providing in the process substantial fortunes to the par-
asite class of compradors, or indigenous middle men. The old
structure of commerce controlled by the emperor from Peking
collapsed and was followed by the disappearance of the Manchu dynasty. China's traditional society was undermined, leaving a void, political, economic and social, in which the country
moved like a ship cut from her moorings, derelict and bereft
even of an anchor. Unlike India, no one European power had
directly taken over the government of the country, and in the
confusion and chaos which followed the collapse of the Manchus
China had little opportunity to know or appreciate such Western doctrines as constitutional government, political liberty or
individual freedom.

What then was the unifying or cohesive factor? Although the
foundations of Confucian ideas and ideals were also shaken in
this turmoil, they were still pervasive enough to impose their
mould on the country and preserve a semblance of unity. Confucianism had withstood the influx of Buddhism, permeating it
with its spirit and stamp. In the same way Hinduism edged out
Buddhism in India where also the older religion was proof
against the infiltration of new influences. Apart from certain an-
imistic creeds Hinduism is the only religion in the world which
is confined to the boundaries of a single country. It flourishes

nowhere outside India. Over the centuries this creed has emerged as the one unifying, cohesive force in the country capable of ossifying in self-defence, as against the Islamic invader or the Christian reformer, but capable also of a resilience which draws together the Tamil in the south and the Kashmiri from the north, the Bengali in the east and the Punjabi in the west. Hinduism has preserved the unity in diversity which is India since ancient days.

"The outcome of the [Communist] struggle," Lenin wrote in March 1923, "depends in the last account on the fact that Russia, India and China comprise the gigantic majority of the population of the world." Here was an echo of the Napoleonic dictum that numbers annihilate. The observant will note the order of precedence in Lenin's litany, for India comes before China; but events have altered this gradation.

Dedicated to the democratic way of life, a legacy partly of her own tradition of representative institutions and ideas but principally the result of the prolonged impact of British notions of constitutional government, the rule of law, political liberty and individual freedom, India is the chief bulwark of democracy in the Orient. The triumph of democracy or Communism in Asia will be determined on Asian soil, not as between Russia and America but as between China and India.

"It is often difficult to know whether a man is a nationalist or a Communist," a shrewd American observer quotes Lebanon's Charles Malik as saying.

Nationalism is the Trojan horse which the Communists employ in Asia. They do so the more easily because of the curious parallel development of the Russian and Chinese revolutions, for in both countries what began as an international movement is beginning more and more to be influenced by national interests and considerations. In other words, Communism has become a potent weapon in the hands of aggressive nationalism, a sort of two-edged sword capable of exploiting nationalism and simultaneously of allowing itself to be exploited in the cause of a Nation-State. One result is that Communism can no longer claim that it alone spells hope for the workers of the world, for its basis now is neither fraternal kinship nor universal brotherhood.

"China!" exclaimed Napoleon, twirling a global map. "There lies a sleeping giant. Let him sleep, for when he wakes he will shake the world."

How right he was! For China through the centuries, until as late as 1840, was content to remain quiescent within the vast realm of its Middle Kingdom away from the "ocean devils" and "barbarians," secure and serene in its self-sufficiency. Over the years come the echoes of the Manchu emperor Ch'ien Lung's majestic rebuke to George III: "I set no value on objects strange or ingenious, and have no use for your country's manufactures. . . . It behoves you, O King, to respect my sentiments and to display even greater loyalty and submission in the future, so that, by perpetual submission to our Throne, you may secure peace and prosperity for your country thereafter. . . . Tremblingly obey and show no negligence." This was said in 1792.

Until the closing years of the fifteenth century Asia and Europe had marched in step. In the thirteenth century culture and material wealth in the leading countries of the Orient were higher than in many lands of the Occident, and Marco Polo paints an attractive picture of the court of Kublai Khan. The Mongol conquest of China in 1279 lifted the barriers between Europe and Asia, although it still left a pocket across the wastes of Siberia whence the nomadic hordes of Attila, Tamerlane and Genghiz Khan had earlier descended upon Europe and Asia. Under the Manchus, notably under K'ang Hsi and his grandson Chi'en Lung, the Mongol tribes of the north were conquered and brought to heel. Almost simultaneously Russia moved across Siberia to the borders of China, and for the first time China by way of Siberia was brought in direct geographical contact with a European nation, Russia. That fact, often overlooked, is significant.

The years between the eleventh and sixteenth centuries were not years of quiescence in India, for they saw the first organised incursions of Islam into the country. They began with Mahmud of Ghazni's sack of Somnath and ended in 1525 with the inauguration of the Mogul dynasty by Babar, descendant of the dreaded Tamerlane. There had been earlier Muslim incursions but they were of a sporadic character, dating from Mohamed ibn-Kasim's swoop on Sind in the eighth century. By the seven-

teenth century the Mogul empire extended over a considerable
area of India, reaching its zenith under Akbar who controlled
the country north of the Vindhyas and ruled over Gujarat, Bengal, Kashmir and Sind. Shortly before his death in 1603 Akbar
reached out for the Deccan States in the south, capturing Ah-
madnagar in 1600. After him came the deluge. By 1750 the writ
of the Mogul emperor had ceased to run in his domain, just as a
century later Manchu rule declined and decayed in China.

If economically and politically Asia went down under the impact of Europe, it also in time revived. Japan was the first to
bare its teeth, but in China and India too the aggressive nationalism of the West provoked an assertive counternationalism
whose fervour grew into a fever. In Asia nationalism became a pathological disease expressing itself in a cry for the expulsion of the foreigner. "Honour the emperor—expel the barbarians," was the watchword on which the Meiji Restoration was
wafted to power in Japan. In China the Communist ideology in-
voked the Confucian idiom, reconciling the Chinese to an authoritarian rule patterned on the father image of an emperor
who had ruled with a mandate from Heaven. "Quit India," was
Gandhi's peremptory cry to the British.

In a sense the British never conquered India, for their influence was restricted largely to the cities and towns and never
really permeated the villages. From immemorial days the peasant
and artisan in the village had lived apart and away from the
main stream of history, almost untouched by the successive
waves of invaders, from the Kushans and the Huns to the Muslims and the British. India lives in its villages, and the villages
are India's heart. As long as they remained untouched the old
lifeblood flowed through the country's veins. Through the centuries India has remained basically the same because of its villages
and villagers.

Gandhi, by identifying himself in his dress and manner of living with the lowly peasant, drew village India into the political
stream. Simultaneously Nehru by rationalising Gandhi to the
middle-class intellectuals in the towns and cities inflamed their
revolutionary ardour. The combination of the two produced
the distinctive Indian revolution which Gandhi led and inspired.

Revolutionaries and ardent patriots had striven long before

Gandhi lighted on the political scene, but none of them had
drawn their strength from the villager. Though Gandhi's was a
peasant revolution, it was spearheaded by the urban middle
class from which the Congress party drew its political leadership and financial funds. The Communist leaders who emerged
later also came from these urban elements.

Throughout the twenties and a large part of the thirties Soviet
Russia remained respectable in Asian eyes and in the estimate of
many Europeans and Americans. Ostensibly the Bolshevik revolution signified the overthrow of the tyranny of the tsars by individuals who were also dedicated to the freedom of colonially
oppressed peoples and to the economic betterment of the un-
derprivileged. These ideals and urges rang a bell in Asian minds
as yet unaware of the soulless despotism which Communism
cloaked. They shared this ignorance and attitude with many European intellectuals for the simple reason that Russia's was the
first Communist party to achieve power and it had still to reveal
itself as a government. Many of those who now rule India were
in that period in their susceptible twenties or thirties at a time
when not only socialism but the Soviet revolution seemed the
answer to many prayers.

If India did not embrace Marxism it was because of the effective counter-magnetism of the Mahatma whose teaching had a
strong Indian-ness about it. In China, Chiang Kai-shek had no
ideas but force to offer for filling the vacuum created by the destruction of the Manchus and the decay of Confucianism. But
the Indian atmosphere was supercharged with an Indian idea.

In India Mill had no competition from Marx until the Bolsheviks, by seizing power in Russia, made Communism not only a
political idea but an administrative reality. From that time began the challenge between Mill and Marx which still continues,
for in the opinion of many Westerners Asia remains a fertile
ground for aggressive nationalism and insidious Communism, the
one a plague, the other a cancer.

I think they are wrong. Asia's battle for nationhood has been
fought and very largely won. The real fight has still to be
waged. It is the battle between nationalism and Communism.

7   Challenge of Democracy

IN MAY 1947, a few months before Gandhi was assassinated, he was visited by the then ambassador of Kuomintang China to India. Independence was near, and also partition. Turmoil raged through the country with widespread rioting and bloodshed.

"How do you think things will shape?" asked the Chinese visitor.

Gandhi, as was his wont, paused for a moment's reflection.

"When the Ganges is in flood the water is turbid," he observed calmly. "The filth comes to the surface. When the flood subsides you see the clear blue water which soothes the eye. That is what I hope and live for. I do not wish to live to see India going barbarian. Who can predict the future? Years ago I read Joseph Butler's *The Analogy of Religion.* I remember a phrase in it—that 'the future is the result somewhat of our past.' This thought has persisted with me because it coincides with Indian belief. We are the makers of our own destiny. We can mend or mar the present, and on that will depend the future."

Though Gandhi at the time was referring to the fratricidal war between Hindus and Muslims in India, and perhaps never envisaged the equally "barbarian" threat from another form of violence, Communism, he entertained no illusions about it.

Communism was contrary to all he believed in. It was violent in deed and also in thought and word, being nourished on fear and hate, two forces which the Mahatma laboured to erase not only from the relationship of individuals but of nations. Gandhi believed in the spiritual nature of man, and for him a world or doctrine which denied the existence of God was meaningless and abnormal. Individuals were more important than governments, and he worked passionately to uphold the individual's right to freedom of opinion and action. Above all, his insistence on good means and good ends allowed for no compromise between good and evil, between truth and untruth.

"The Communists," remarked Gandhi at the end of 1946, about a year before he died, "seem to have made troublemaking their profession."

He spoke more in sorrow than in anger, for his belief in the intrinsic goodness of man did not permit him to differentiate between Communists and non-Communists as human beings.

"I have friends among them," he acknowledged. "Some of them are like sons to me. But it seems that they do not make any distinction between fair and foul, truth and falsehood. They deny the charge. But their reported acts seem to sustain it. Moreover they appear to take their instructions from Russia, which they regard as their spiritual home rather than India. I cannot countenance this dependence on an outside power. I have said that we should not depend even on Russian wheat in our present food crisis."

It is difficult to discover any latter-day statements by Gandhi which enunciate so clearly his idea of Indian independence and his attitude to Communism. The statements were made after independence; but even earlier, back in 1924, Gandhi had chided some Communist spokesmen who had sought to convert him.

"I do not know," he told them, "whether Bolshevism is for the good of Russia in the long run. But I do know that in so far as it is based on violence and denial of God it repels me. . . . I am an uncompromising opponent of violent methods even to serve the noblest of causes."

Some time before Gandhi arrived on the scene, the British government had expressed its fear of the influence which the Bolshevik revolution might exert on the politically educated Indian. Six months after the event, in April 1918, the Secretary of State for India, Mr. Edwin Montagu, and the Viceroy, Lord Chelmsford, noted their impressions in a joint report on the Indian constitutional reforms which were introduced in 1919. According to them, the Russian revolution was regarded in India as a triumph over despotism. "Notwithstanding the fact that it has since involved that unhappy country in anarchy and dismemberment it has given impetus to Indian political aspirations," they warned.

Interestingly enough, the Communist party of India was established only in 1924, three years after its prototypes were organised in China and Japan. Two reasons for this were the British occupation of India and the traditionally suspicious eye with which the raj regarded Russia, whether tsarist or Communist. Another and more vital reason was the appearance of Gandhi.

Gandhi had come to India from South Africa in January 1915, but on Gokhale's* advice he had decided to abstain from active politics for a year and to utilise the period to tour the country on a journey of discovery. At Lucknow in 1916 Nehru, then twenty-seven, met the Mahatma for the first time. The occasion was the annual session of the Congress party. Gandhi was Nehru's senior by twenty years. Over a critical period India has been blessed in its leaders, and the association of two such contrasting and widely divergent men as Gandhi and Nehru gave the revolution its stamp and character.

Without Gandhi India would in time have attained its freedom, but along a different road whose direction not even those with the hindsight of today can determine. It might have been constitutional or it might have been violent. What is certain is that it would not have been the novel and unconventional road which Gandhi taught India to tread.

Without Nehru Gandhi would probably have failed to attract the educated middle class whose modern outlook recoiled from many of the Mahatma's ideas and methods. As a political instrument non-violence seemed to them to lack an intellectual basis because violence by any rational thinking was permissible in defence of personal honour and against aggression. Mass civil disobedience was also startlingly novel, though Gandhi had employed it with some success in South Africa. By rationalising Gandhi and his ideas to the younger intellectuals Nehru gave a

* Gopal Krishna Gokhale, a highly respected, politically moderate leader who died in February 1915 at the age of forty-nine.

revolutionary ardour to the movement and simultaneously weakened the middle class prop on which the British raj relied for much of its administrative support.

Nehru proved the perfect complement to Gandhi on another plane.

"I am told," said the Mahatma when I once asked him his views on the Spanish civil war, "that I have no knowledge of two things—economics and international affairs. You must ask Jawahar." And he broke into his gay child-like, uninhibited laugh.

By insisting that nationalism was not enough and that India's struggle for freedom could only have a global significance if it was to be part of the broad stream of world progress and related to vital happenings outside the country, Nehru created a new dimension of thought and action which took the Indian intellectual outside himself. It was the objective corrective to the subjectivism which Gandhism intensified. Gandhi made India aware of itself. Nehru made Indians aware of others. He supplied the extrovert impulse to the Mahatma's introvert stress.

The doctrine of good means and good ends which Gandhi never tired of preaching has left its impress on Nehru, who since the Mahatma's death has often upheld it as one of Gandhism's most precious legacies. This alone creates a gulf between what Communism stands for and what Nehru personifies; and the gap can never be bridged, for opportunism is endemic in the Marxist mind and method which hold that the end justifies the means.

Nehru's interest in Marxism dates from his visit to Europe in March 1926. He returned there after an interval of over thirteen years, staying abroad for a year and nine months. In November 1927, a month before he left for India, Nehru paid a fleeting visit to Moscow for the tenth anniversary celebrations of the Soviet. As he writes in his autobiography, he did not then know much "about the fine points of Communism"; but Marxism with its attempt to reinterpret history by the yardstick of dialectical materialism attracted him. The heterodox has always appealed to Nehru. The rebel in Gandhi drew him to the Mahatma.

Just as Nehru found it difficult to accept some of Gandhi's

ideas and attitudes, such as his idealisation of poverty and suffering, his doctrine of wealth as a trust, his frequent stress on
the religious and spiritual aspect of the civil-disobedience movement, his attitude to machinery and modern civilisation, and
his vagueness in defining political and economic objectives, so
also Nehru recoiled from the violence, the intolerance, the regimentation, the vulgarity, the crudity and the cruelty of the
Communists.

Between Gandhi and himself, despite their differences, there
was a basic bond of understanding, appreciation and agreement.
There was and is none between him and the Communists. As is
now evident, Nehru used Gandhi's means to achieve what have
proved to be largely his own political and economic ends. He
did not do this deliberately or consciously, because at the time
he could not have foreseen the future. But there is no affinity of
either means or ends so far as Nehru and the Communists are
concerned.

Politically, like Gandhi, Nehru will allow no basic loyalty but
to India.

In India's first general elections at the end of 1951 Nehru was
heckled at one centre by a crowd of Communists carrying red
flags with the hammer and sickle.

"Why don't you go and live in the country whose flag you are
carrying?" he asked them.

"Why don't you go to New York and live with the Wall Street
imperialists?" they countered.

The incident will astonish those accustomed to regarding
Nehru as pro-Communist.

The confusion, I think, originates from the tendency of most
Westerners, particularly Americans, to see the economic counterpart of the political challenge to the free world in terms of
free enterprise versus Communism. This highly idealised state of
affairs really exists nowhere in the world, not even in the United
States where a fair sector of economic development is part of
governmental planning. Laissez faire is as dead as the dodo.

In underdeveloped countries such as India, with small capital
resources, low productivity, a rapidly increasing population and
a high degree of unemployment, the public or governmental
sector tends to bulk larger than the private sector. But this is still

far removed from the totalitarian economic system of Soviet Russia where the means of production and the instruments of control are concentrated in the hands of an omnipotent super-State, leaving no room for free enterprise of any type. Because in an underdeveloped country incapable of rapid progress the area of the public sector tends to encroach on a shrinking private sector, care must be taken to strike a balance between the two lest economic imbalance lead to an authoritarian government. In other words, democracy or political freedom can only flourish in an economic system which preserves a healthy balance of power between the public and private sectors. This is the delicate task which faces India, a situation which the West must learn to appreciate more sympathetically. What India is striving to achieve can best be described as democratic socialism with the emphasis placed equally on democracy and socialism. An underdeveloped country has no other escape route from Communism. Economically its choice is between a mixed economy and Communism. Politically its choice is between democratic socialism and Communism.

Communism belongs to the pre-democratic period because it is based on the belief that change is only possible through revolution, through the overthrow of a whole society. Democracy holds that change is possible through constitutional and peaceful processes. In so far as democracy believes in the rule of the people, by the people, for the people it approximates to nationalism of a democratic pattern. But Communism as we see it in operation in Russia and China is also increasingly governed by national considerations. This is the dilemma which faces the young independent countries of Asia, for, superficially, nationalism seems reconcilable with either Communism or democracy.

The reality is different, and it lies in the fact that nationalism to the Communist is not an end but a means. The end is international Communism based on the so-called dictatorship of the proletariat. Similarly the Communist finds no difficulty in accepting the principle of co-existence, because to him again it is a means and not an end. It is a means to lull your neighbour into somnolence before liquidating him.

To argue therefore that Communism because of its power of regimentation provides a quicker road to economic progress than democracy is to propagate a myth. In a Communist society the people, lacking as they do a compelling voice in the government, and devoid of initiative, are resigned to follow because they are in no position to inspire or lead. For them to hear is to obey. The same principle applies to the bureaucrats who, like the people, have only one right in a totalitarian State—the right to repeat the dictator's mistakes. To attempt to remedy them is only possible after the dictator's death. Stalin had to die before Khrushchev plucked up courage to denounce him. Far from demonstrating that Communism provides a short cut to progress, the history of Soviet Russia and Communist China testifies to the contrary.

Industrially Russia over the past forty years has pulled itself up by its bootstraps but at a terrible price. The price is the destruction of the peasantry and the impoverishment of the land. Where Russia copied the Western democracies, as on the industrial front, and had the aid of Western experts, machines and materials, a large proportion of them American—at least until the 1930's—the nation has prospered. It must also be remembered that this was no leap from a primitive society to the Industrial Revolution, for Russia had industrial plants even before 1914, though these did not compare with their counterparts in Western Europe. Where on the other hand Russia followed the magic of Marxism, as in agriculture, it found itself time and again floundering in a Cloud Cuckoo Land of contradictions and confusion.

"Either we choke him [the mujik] or he chokes us," said Lenin as far back as 1920.

Contempt for the peasantry was a hangover from the *Communist Manifesto* of Marx and Engels. Marx had compared the peasants to a sack of potatoes, and referred to "the idiocy of rural life." The peasants, being politically untrustworthy, had to be held on the leash of State control. Collectivisation, as Stalin in a moment of candour admitted to Churchill during the war, in effect meant mass liquidation, the liquidation of nearly 10 million peasant proprietors. This was done between 1928 and 1932.

Yet the fruits of this regimentation were neither quick nor profitable. In September 1953 the publication of the Khrushchev Report revealed that the Soviet livestock position, apart from sheep, pigs and goats, was lower even than in 1916 and was officially not expected to reach the 1928 figures before 1954. It has still to reach them.

Other revelations are equally significant. "We can no longer tolerate a situation," notes the Report, "where for over ten years milk yields in the collective farms have not exceeded 1,170 kilograms per cow."* The Report admits that in Siberia 75,000 tons of butter were produced in 1913 and 65,000 in 1952. Since 1940 the area under vegetables had fallen by 620,000 acres; and, although the area planted with potatoes had risen, the total potato harvest had dropped. Had the Soviet plan for 1955 been fulfilled—which was not the case—the total output per farmer in Russia would still be one-fifth of the American farm output.† The output per head of Britain and West Europe is substantially higher than that of America.

Nor has Soviet regimentation induced any excessive peasant attachment to the State, for the Khrushchev Report admits that of 100 million peasants barely a million are members of the Communist party. Another vital element, population, predominates. Although as in America the pressure of population on the Soviet land is not unduly high, Russia's population is growing at the rate of three million a year. This, to quote a single example, means that though the Soviet Union has less livestock than it did in 1928 it has to feed a population nearly 70 million larger, after allowing for the war toll of 14 million lives.

For Asia the rivalry between the democratic and the Communist way of life is illustrated by the economic race between India and China. In these two countries, which represent Asia's largest land masses, far-reaching governmental changes took place within two years of each other. India became independent in August 1947 and in October 1949 Mao Tse-tung inaugurated a Communist government on the Chinese mainland. The same time lag recurred in the economic sphere, for India began its

* The British average is 2,700 kilograms, and in Poland the average is between 1,600 to 1,700 kilograms.

† *Land Reform and Soviet Agriculture,* by David Mitrany (Casement Booklet).

first Five Year Plan in 1951, to be followed by China two years later.

Experience, they say, is the name men give to their mistakes, but the lessons of the Russian revolution seem to be lost on the Chinese. Like the Russians the Chinese began with the object of heavy industrialisation, although their economy, like Bolshevik Russia's, was broad-based on the land. The Marxist mould is too rigid to be broken easily.

In China as in Russia the peasant was regarded as politically unreliable even though the peasants were the spearhead of Mao's revolution. As in Russia they were the sacrificial offering in the battle for capital expansion in heavy industry. A perceptive observer of the Soviet scene* has stated the paradox cleverly. The Russian revolution of 1917, he remarks, introduced a nationalist State capitalism in the Soviet Union and inaugurated Russian capitalism. This might also be said of the Chinese revolution of 1949.

When I visited Communist China in 1952 the land reforms which had been introduced in the previous year were in the "creeping collectivisation" stage. Most of the farms were run on so-called co-operative lines.

I could not help noticing the strong sense of property which was instinct in the peasants. In a village not far from Mukden in Manchuria I came across a peasant and his wife who owned a small mud hut of two rooms and had three pigs and eighteen hens, as the woman proudly told me.

"What happens when your land is collectivised?" I asked.

The peasant shrugged his shoulders. "We shall have our share of the produce. And production will increase." But he didn't seem too happy at the prospect.

Since then the shadow of collectivisation has spread rapidly over China, and the peasants have shown signs of resistance. As with the Russian kulaks, Peking is finding it necessary to continue "a relentless struggle" against them. Symptoms of rural unrest were noticeable very early, and in July 1953 Teng Tzu-hui, vice chairman of the Committee of Financial and Economic Affairs, ruefully conceded that the government were beginning to lose

* M. R. Masani to John Scott of *Time*.

peasant support. Four years later, in May 1957, the Peking economic monthly *Chi Hua Ching Chi* published an official statement complaining of "the failure of agriculture to keep pace
with the industrial advance." In both Russia and China revolutions have been achieved with the peasants but not for the
peasants. In both countries the peasants are expendable.

Happily, India initiated its first Five Year Plan with the emphasis on agriculture, which was only natural, for nearly 80 per
cent of the country's 380 million people work on the land. Will
India succeed where both China and Russia have failed—by
achieving a revolution with the peasants and for the peasants?
Almost 60 per cent of the outlay envisaged by the Plan was on
ways and means of raising agricultural productivity, and this
was done by democratic methods such as the village community
projects (financed generously by the Ford Foundation), the
National Extension Service and the spread of co-operative enterprise. In this five-year period food-grain production went up by
20 per cent, while over 6 million acres of land were brought
under irrigation through major works and another 10 million
benefited from smaller projects. Two successive good monsoons
helped this process. The national income in this period was
raised by about 18 per cent, or by 3.8 per cent per year, which
compares favourably with the 3 per cent annual rise of Britain
and the United States.

In the agricultural sphere India, except in a few commodities
such as sugar, is ahead of China. While India's annual increase
in grain output is currently around 32 per cent, China's is 18
per cent. The corresponding figures for raw cotton are 33 per
cent (India) and 25 per cent (China). Addressing the National
People's Congress at the end of June 1957, Chou En-lai dis-
closed that 70 million people were affected by famine in China
and that the budget deficit for the previous year exceeded 700
million dollars. Chou admitted that the Red régime had over-
spent on capital production by 550 million dollars.

India's second Five Year Plan was presented to Parliament in
May 1956. This aims at laying the basis for the industrialisation
of the country, the core of the project being the achievement of
substantial increases in the production of steel, coal and power
and the enlargement of transport. These and ancillary develop-

ment schemes are calculated to require an outlay of about 12,400 million dollars, including the public and private sectors, the investment of the private sector being roughly 40 per cent of the total outlay. By Asian standards this is a considerable sum for any government to underwrite, though as Nehru graphically pointed out some time ago such an outlay spread over five years roughly represents "just eighty days' military expenditure of a great power." Nehru added: "This is in peacetime. In war it would be much more." Yet to India, and to Asia, it means the difference between Communism or democracy.

No modern State geared to a modern economy can subsist solely on an agricultural basis. Nehru, while always making it clear that only on the basis of agricultural prosperity could India make industrial progress, has stressed that the growth of industry, big and small, is essential for the growth of any modern nation. "Indeed," he once remarked, "without industrial development there cannot be any higher standard of living for our people or even enough strength in the nation for it to preserve its freedom."

Much depends on how India fares in the industrial race with China, for China is ahead of India in steel production by 58 per cent and in the output of coal by 53 per cent. If, however, our second Five Year Plan proceeds to schedule we shall probably overtake China's steel production by 1961.

In order to be able to achieve this, India will have to find ways and means of covering a four-billion dollar deficit in financial resources of which a little under half is expected to be met by foreign assistance. At the moment it is problematical whether this aid will be available in adequate volume, and soon. Against the background of India's successful first Plan and the vital issues at stake as between the free and totalitarian worlds, the reluctance of the West to extend to India the urgently needed long-term credits and aid is puzzling.

Neither in respect of her sterling balances nor of her international financial obligations has India defaulted on a single occasion. The credit of the rupee is high. According to a study compiled by the *U.S. News and World Report* in July 1957— that is, at the end of the first year of the second Plan—the rupee was more stable than the currency of all other countries in the world except that of Switzerland. While over the past ten years the American dollar went down by 20 per cent, the British pound by more than one-third and the French franc by almost two-thirds, the Indian rupee dropped only by 18 per cent. The Swiss franc depreciated by 11 per cent.

Unlike some Western democratic leaders, Nehru has consistently refused to accept the thesis that a democracy is necessarily slower in achieving economic results than a totalitarian country. Towards China his attitude is competitive.

"They [the Chinese]," he remarked on his return from China in November 1947, "can pass a law overnight if they want to. Nevertheless they go on saying that it will take them twenty years to lay the socialist basis of their society."

He said much the same thing, and more directly, to Khrushchev and Bulganin when they were in India and when they kept boasting incessantly of Russia's "wonderful achievements."

"After all," Nehru chided them, "you took forty years to get the machines running. Give us thirty years."

Nehru remarked on another occasion: "I think that the difference in the time limit is not so great as people imagine. Indeed, it need not be if the people of a democratic country are eager enough for change and are prepared to work for it."

That is why he keeps on impressing, even while some of the Western world looks askance at the second Five Year Plan, that India simply cannot afford to go more slowly. Like Gandhi he is the nation's "beloved slave driver," prodding his people to greater effort not by force but by peaceful example and persuasion. Difficulties, he insists, are meant to be surmounted.

"Our difficulties of internal and external finance," he told Parliament in July 1957, "are the difficulties of a progressing economy. These are the difficulties of a country that is moving forward. They are good difficulties—difficulties of progress and not of stagnation and inaction."

Nehru's hustle is prompted by something more than the consciousness of Red China breathing down the back of his neck. Since India's second general elections early in 1957 a Communist government has taken charge of the southern State of Kerala; Red representation has increased in the States and at the Centre.* The Communists inside India are now breathing down the back of Nehru's neck. Hence the vastly urgent need of accelerating economic progress within the country.

How does one explain the more recent Communist successes in India? Some years ago Nehru declared in a speech in Parliament that the Indian Communist party was "the most stupid among the Communist parties of the world." His contempt was justified, for if Communism has made some headway in India it is despite, and not because of, the quality of Red leadership, which is confused in outlook and generally inferior in calibre.

Communism, ironically enough, owes much to the good offices of the British, for it was among the last legacies which the raj consolidated, albeit unconsciously, and willed upon an independent India.

When the Second World War broke out, Communism in India as elsewhere was very largely on the defensive, striving to make itself respectable under the slogan of the United Front by an alliance with such radical bodies as chose to give it cover. Thus in India in the years 1937–1938 it penetrated the ranks of the Congress Socialist party, two of the joint secretaries of the party for this period actually being Communists, one of whom, the able Mr. E. M. S. Namboodripad, is now the first Communist Chief Minister of Kerala. The Reds also entered the ranks of the Congress party, the All-India Kisan Sabha, or Peasants' Union, the All-India Students Federation and the trade-union movement. Not until 1940, after the outbreak of war, did the Socialist party executive dissolve the United Front and eject the Communists.

With the Stalin-Hitler pact of August 1939 as a curtain raiser to the war, the Indian Communists after some preliminary bewilderment denounced Britain and France as "imperialist warmongers," and the British authorities thereupon put the Reds in jail. The Congress party was also opposed to the war but on the

* In the last general elections, held in 1951–1952, the Communists obtained 26 seats in India's Parliament, known as the Lok Sabha (House of the People), and a total of 161 seats in the various State Assemblies. In the 1957 elections the Reds captured 29 seats in the Lok Sabha and a total of 201 in the State Assemblies. They also more than doubled their vote in the Lok Sabha elections, polling 6,100,000 additional votes and increasing their share in the total from 5 to 9.8 per cent.

ground that India had been committed to it without prior consultation with its leaders. On June 22, 1941, the Nazi invasion of Russia induced an overnight change in the Communist
attitude. The war became a "people's war," and the Communists
were thereupon released by the British authorities who encouraged and supported them as a counterpoise to the Congress who
were still opposed to the war. There is evidence to show that a
letter from Harry Pollitt, secretary of the British Communist
party, ordering the Indian Reds to make this switchover was
delivered to the Communist leaders in detention on the orders
of Sir Reginald Maxwell, the then Home Secretary to the
Government of India. Truly imperialism—as Marx said of capitalism—provides its own gravediggers.

Thus the Indian Communists again found themselves respectable, this time under the aegis of the British government in
India. For three years until the end of the war they had a virtually open field, for from August 1942 until June 1945 the
Congress High Command were in prison, and with the Congress
immobilised the Communists were free to make headway. They
proceeded to do so, penetrating again not only the student and
labour world but the homes of the wealthy and middle-class intellectuals, the liberal fringe and similar spheres traditionally
sensitive and susceptible to cloak-and-dagger politics, particularly when played under the unfamiliar but powerful protection
of a foreign authority. On a short-term basis the British might
argue that such a policy was justifiable, but it was justifiable
only if on the long-term view its results could be controlled.
Whatever the British motivations, the results of their short-
term (and short-sighted) policy towards the Communists was to
give the Reds a long-term lease of life.

The valuable respite or rehabilitation which the British authorities provided the Reds helped the Communists to consolidate their status, but even so it does not entirely explain their
subsequent successes. The inherent weaknesses of Communist
leadership, as well as the intrinsic contradictions within that
creed, were seen later in the turnings and twistings of Red policy or policies over several years. Yet despite them the Communists seem to be edging slowly forward. How, and why?

There was first the brief post-independence honeymoon with

the Nehru government followed by the adoption of the Zhdanov line which was propounded at the so-called Southeast Asian Youth Conference at Calcutta in February 1948. This led to a trail of industrial sabotage and to terrorist excesses in Telangana, Kerala, Andhra and Bengal. Criticism of the Chinese Communists and Mao was voiced by the Indian Reds, but not long after came contrite obeisance to Peking at the behest of Moscow. The "agrarian phase" under the rural leadership of Rajeshwar Rao followed, but Rao was no Mao and in turn was dethroned. Attempts to enunciate a line of action conditioned to Indian needs, eschewing the dogma that the Chinese experiment could be transplanted intact to Indian soil, were then timidly proffered. These rested mainly on two contentions—that China's primitive communications had hampered Chiang's campaign against Mao, who had the additional advantage of coming to power with an army of seasoned veterans behind him. On the other hand, the Indian Communists faced a government with the advantage of relatively quick mobility and a trained and unquestionably loyal army. So the shifts and changes have come and gone, affected more recently by resurgent Maoism and by decaying if not decadent Stalinism. In December 1953 the Communists claimed to have 50,000 members and 25,000 candidates; but in July 1957, after the second general elections, it was claimed on their behalf that their membership had increased to 125,000 and that they hoped to double it by the end of the year.

For the Communists to have made some headway despite these deficiencies suggests the likelihood of similar counteracting deficiencies in the Indian government. These cannot be denied. The proper functioning and expression of democracy require a developed economy and equally developed political instincts and aptitudes. Such prerequisites are not easily found in an underdeveloped country. Compare this with Britain and the United States. It was Britain's peculiar good fortune that the Industrial Revolution in the last quarter of the eighteenth century almost coincided with the growth of democratic ideas in Europe. Similarly the Americans did not start from scratch, for the Pilgrim Fathers took with them to the New World sixteen hundred years of history, as the political institutions of New England prove. Despite its tradition of representative institutions, India is woefully deficient in the economic and political prerequisites of a modern democratic State. Unfortunately, we have accentuated these deficiencies by our mistakes.

It was a mistake for the Congress party to have conferred adult franchise on an electorate 80 per cent of whom are illiterate. The possession of a vote by every adult citizen does not automatically make a country democratic, for democracy lies not in possessing a vote but in knowing how to use it and in being able to use it freely according to one's individual judgement. In India adult franchise now threatens two dangers, one of which is in the process of maturing. There is a danger of it making for mobocracy, not democracy, which happily the innate and rugged good sense of the Indian people has so far prevented. The second danger is more real and imminent—that it might lead to totalitarian governments, Communist or Fascist, coming to power by democratic means. This has happened in Kerala, where a Communist government was returned to power by the electorate.

Numbers alone cannot annihilate, but numbers tutored and drilled can be effectively deployed to annihilate a democratic régime. In India, as in China, the question of unemployment is linked with the threat of a fast-growing population which averages an increase of some 12 million per year in China and about 5 million a year in India. The number of unemployed and under-employed in India is estimated at around 25 million. China's rulers confess to only about 5 million unemployed, but the number is probably much larger.

According to an eminent scientist, Dr. J. C. Ghosh, who is also a member of the Planning Committee, it will take another eighteen years before India breaks the vicious circle of poverty and growing population and climbs into an era of comparative prosperity. This would necessitate widespread family planning and a tremendous spurt in production and investment. Granted these, the target would be achieved by 1975. But considering that the present annual per capita income is in the neighbourhood of $58, the leeway to be made up is tremendous. Moreover, India's total national income is only about 6 per cent of that of the United States, while its population is more than double that of the United States.

In Nehru, as was said of Roosevelt, there is something of the lion and of the fox. World statesman though he is on the international plane, he can be very much the politician at home, even the wily politician. His foreign policy of non-alignment and his internal policy of democratic socialism are founded on sincere and deeply thought-out principles and convictions which he believes are in line with Indian conditions, tradition and thought. Yet no politician can resist the temptation of extracting some political advantage from a principle, which is, I think, the reason why Nehru in implementing his foreign policy tends to lean more often towards the Russians and the Chinese than towards the West, thereby spiking the guns of the Communists at home; while on the internal front, by emphasising socialism more than democracy, he equally neutralises his Socialist and Communist opponents.

The dangers in this tactic are obvious. It puts a premium on political equivocation at the cost, seeming or real, of moral principles. Gandhi would have supported Nehru in his policies of non-alignment and democratic socialism, but in neither case would he have compromised or even appeared to compromise with evil. On the basis of his belief that there was a spark of goodness in every man and country, he would cheerfully have negotiated with the Reds as members of the great company of the human race; but where evil reared its head, as during the Soviet butchery in Hungary or the French massacres in Algeria, the Mahatma would have raised his voice, refusing to be silent or be silenced. In the face of wrong or evil, it was not his habit to equivocate. As a result of excessive equivocation, there is little from the people's point of view to distinguish the Congress party from the Socialists, which leaves the Communists, who continue to be vocally aggressive, the only alternative to the Congress. Already the preponderant majority of the Congress party and its not infrequent resort to steamroller tactics give it a monolithic look and invest any opposition, even that of the Communists, with a democratic appearance. As long as Nehru lives the people bred on this tactic may vote for the Congress. But after he has gone the temptation to vote Communist might prove irresistible. And the danger to democracy will be enhanced by the fact that the Communists can legitimately claim to have been returned by democratic methods. In doing so, Communism will fulfil an avowed objective. It will use democracy in order to destroy democracy.

As Manabendra Nath Roy warned many years ago, "In Asia the decisive moral resistance to Communism is bound to be weak because there is no democratic tradition to defend." All the greater reason therefore why Nehru in his lifetime should dedicate his vast influence and authority in India to mobilising, organising and consolidating a "decisive moral resistance to Communism." He alone can do it, for it is in the moral tradition of India. If he fails, he will have failed not only India but, it may be, humanity.

8   Crescent Moon

FEAR and frustration leave their mark. Pakistan was born from Fear out of Frustration, and the scars it bears are the marks of its parentage. It was born, too, in travail, amid conflict and carnage, vast slaughter and suffering in a sort of Mephistophelean nightmare dank with a sense of doom. That Pakistan should have survived those terrors is a tribute to its resilience and courage, for it exhibited then and continues to exhibit a spirit of tough endeavour and a will to live.

Nobody in his senses in India would wish Pakistan anything but well. Pakistan has come to stay, and it is in India's interests that Pakistan should stay as a viable, strong State, politically stable and economically robust. A weak backward neighbour is a liability as much in the international sphere as in the social life of a community. Yet Fear and Frustration are embarrassing companions difficult to lose, and in moving constantly with them one cannot help being coloured by their outlook of gloom and grievance.

In generating this complex no party in pre-divided India can escape responsibility—neither the Hindus whose short-sighted and at times quite ungenerous and unimaginative acts alienated many Muslim friends; nor the Muslims whose free resort to violence, far from intimidating, consolidated the Hindu ranks; nor the British who, applying the Roman principle of divide and rule, unwittingly reared not one Frankenstein's monster but two who compelled them in the end to divide and quit.

Pakistan came into being from the mistakes of the Hindus and the miscalculations of the British. The ifs of history are fascinating, and if Mohamed Ali Jinnah had not taken it upon himself to lead a crusade for an Islamic Land of the Pure,* it is problematical whether Pakistan would ever have been established. On the other hand the Pakistanis might justifiably claim that the hour produced the man—which it did.

I met Jinnah for the first time when I was a student in England, where he had come to attend the Round Table Conference in London in 1930. In the following year he decided to settle down in Britain, bought a house in Hampstead and, with a view to practising before the Privy Council, acquired chambers at King's Walk. Being then actively associated with the Indian student world, I had occasion to meet Jinnah fairly frequently and got to know him well. At his invitation I often dropped in of an afternoon at his chambers and benefited greatly from his counsel and conversation. I respected and admired him and, despite political divergences, shall always do so.

He was a man of integrity. Strange though it might seem, and despite the resentment it might arouse in certain circles in India, I believe he was the most completely honest politician I have known in my experience—and I have met or known a good few in various countries of the world.

The memories and consciousness of his own hard fight for legal fame somewhat coloured his outlook. At times, talking to him and hearing him recount something of those early struggles and later victories, I had the feeling that he himself was surprised at his success, at the wonder of achievement and "arrival," of realisation, recognition and triumph. He did not suffer fools gladly—but he made many concessions to the young, and I was young then.

Perhaps the quality that drew me to him was his own youthfulness of spirit and outlook, his capacity to get into a younger man's mind and to try and understand it. To do so I have known him waste, with infinite patience and in an attempt to establish some mental rapport, many hours of his precious time. He was vain, possibly even conceited, inclined to be theatrical, to posture and pose and be pompous. He was at times even faintly

* Pakistan means Land of the Pure.

ridiculous. Yet despite his political asperities he was genuine gold. He rang true.

I remember telling him of an incident at Shafi's Indian restaurant in Gerrard Street, then a favourite haunt of the Indian colony in London. While dining there, I had heard Sir Mohamed Iqbal at the next table talking of Pakistan. I asked Jinnah what he thought of Pakistan.

He threw his head scornfully back in a characteristic gesture and chuckled. "My dear boy," he said, "don't you know that Iqbal isn't a politician? He's a poet. Poets are dreamers."

Although at that time Jinnah was aggrieved at the attitude of Gandhi and the Congress during the second Round Table Conference when an abortive attempt was made by the Indian delegates to arrive at a settlement between the Hindus and the minorities, notably the Muslims, he was still far from the parting of the ways. His attitude to the Indian student community in England was helpful and friendly and he made no differentiation between Hindu or Muslim. Rather did he strive to hold us together.

One afternoon he talked of the time when Gandhi had called on the students of India to leave their schools and colleges and to join the civil-disobedience movement. Jinnah had opposed Gandhi, arguing that this was wasteful sacrifice.

"They were my boys as much as his," Jinnah recalled, "and I told him so."

He was right. I think he was also right in his attitude during the second Round Table Conference when he worked hard to bridge the gulf between the Hindus and the Muslims and deeply deplored the occasion when with just one seat in the legislature hanging in the balance Gandhi refused to commit himself to a settlement unless the extremist Hindu leader Pandit Madan Mohan Malaviya agreed. Malaviya, of course, would not agree. It is difficult to absolve Gandhi of blame for the subsequent deepening fissure between the Hindus and the Muslims.

When Jinnah returned to India in 1934, he did so with the intention of building up the Muslim League so that in co-operation with the Congress party it could, on a basis of equality, wrest power from the British government. The stronger the League, the more powerful, he felt, would be the concerted

nationalist opposition to the government. At that time he had no
idea of organising the League as a counterpoise to the Congress.

As late as March 1937, on the eve of the elections for the provincial assemblies which under the new Government of India
Act were to enjoy provincial autonomy, Jinnah stated his plan
clearly in a speech at Delhi. "The Hindus and Muslims," he declared, "must be organised separately, and once they are organised they will understand each other better, and then we shall
not have to wait for years for an understanding. . . . I am helping 80 million people [the Muslims], and if they are more
organised they will be all the more useful for the national
struggle."

By that time I had plunged into journalism, having joined
The Times of India, which was then a British-owned organisation, and as correspondent of a number of British journals in
the United Kingdom I continued seeing Jinnah. Indeed, I saw a
fair deal of him in those years, for he had not then attained the
dizzy height of Qaid-i-Azam (Great Leader) with the Muslim
masses. He still referred with amusement and faint derision to
the idea of Pakistan.

Many talk of Jinnah's arrogance, and humility was admittedly
not his strong point. He was intellectually arrogant, but in my
personal dealings I found him always meticulously courteous—
far more courteous than many Congress party leaders who were
less distinguished and prominent. He was devoid of cant or
humbug. Events were to prove him a consummate political
tactician, but even in achieving his later aims he never stooped
to the devious.

Immediately after the 1937 elections Jinnah was hopeful that
the Congress would co-operate with the Muslim League in form-
ing coalition governments in the provinces. But it was soon evident that the Congress had other ideas. It would welcome
Muslims in the government, but only as members of the Congress party.

Jinnah was furious. "What they want to do," he exclaimed
when I saw him next, "is to suborn my Muslims from their
League loyalties with the bait of office. It's nothing but a trick
—a Hindu trick."

It was plain that his confidence in the bona fides of the Congress was shaken, and thereafter he was not prepared to take the Congress on trust.

I think the Congress, misreading the relatively poor showing of the Muslim League at the polls, made the tactical error of believing that by refusing to co-operate with the League it would drive that body into the political wilderness. It was a costly mistake, for its result was to strengthen Jinnah's hands as the foremost champion of Muslim claims and rights. Jinnah created Pakistan. But the Congress party by its sins of commission and omission helped to make it possible.

"There are only two parties in the country," Nehru declared soon after the 1937 elections, "the Congress and the British."

"No," retorted Jinnah. "There is a third—the Muslims."

From thenceforth the political cleavage between the Hindus and the Muslims grew. The resignation of the Congress ministries in November 1939 in protest against India's being committed to war without consultation with her spokesmen was another tactical blunder, for it left the field open to the Muslim League, and Jinnah cleverly capitalised on his opportunities. In March 1940 the Muslim League, meeting at Lahore, declared that Hindus and Muslims constituted two separate nations and that therefore India should be divided to contain separate homelands for each. The die was cast.

"No power on earth," declared Jinnah, "can prevent Pakistan."

The British miscalculated in believing that Jinnah, because he was now hostile to the Congress, was inclined to be friendly to the government. Hitherto the British had been accustomed to dealing with a type of Muslim leader whose antipathy to the Congress could be nurtured and encouraged by a show of official largesse and favours. But Jinnah was of a different breed. He was opposed implacably to the continuance of British rule.

"Quit India," Gandhi told the British in 1942.

"Divide and quit," said Jinnah.

About this time I had occasion to arrange an interview for a British woman correspondent with Jinnah. I asked her later how it had gone, and was amused by her reply.

"He's clever and aggressive," she remarked. "But I'd never realised he was so anti-British."

A socialist government came into power in Britain in July 1945, and not long after despatched a Cabinet Mission to India whose labours eventually culminated in the Congress heading an interim government at New Delhi. In October 1946, in the wake of widespread rioting and slaughter in Calcutta, Bombay and other centres following a call for Direct Action by Jinnah, the Muslim League entered the Central Government. If Jinnah calculated that the violence he had incited would intimidate the Hindus, he was mistaken. Its result was to close and consolidate their ranks and to induce them to accept Pakistan—but in Jinnah's own bitter words, "a moth-eaten Pakistan"—as the price of independence.

"By cutting off the head," said Nehru, "we shall get rid of the headache."

So Pakistan was born—a creature of Muslim fear and frustration, but born also of the folly and short-sightedness of the Hindus. The inauguration witnessed a two-way trail of blood as some 11,500,000 souls, Hindu, Muslim and Sikh, migrated between the two countries. India re-enacted the drama of Cain and Abel on a monstrous and gargantuan scale, with brother slaying brother in a fit of religious frenzy and hate.

As Pakistan emerged in August 1947, it was not the Pakistan visualised by early protagonists such as Choudhary Rahmat Ali, who had dreamt of a compact State covering some 520,000 square miles and stretching diagonally from Allahabad to the borders of Chitral. Jinnah had been careful never to define the concept precisely. The Lahore resolution of March 1940 mentioned only "the areas in which the Muslims are numerically in a majority as in the northwestern and eastern zones of India." These were to be "grouped to constitute independent states in which the constituent units shall be autonomous and sovereign." Despite this deliberate vagueness, there is reason to believe that at least in the early years after the Lahore resolution Jinnah and the Muslim League conceived of the Indian sub-continent as housing a confederation comprising the triple federations of Pakistan (Muslim), Hindustan (Hindu) and Rajistan (the Princes), with common arrangements for customs, communications, defence, foreign relations and the minorities.

But the rapidity of developments following the end of the war compelled an even earlier transfer of power than the British government had envisaged. Lord Mountbatten has been unfairly blamed for stampeding India and Pakistan into partition and freedom. He could hardly have done otherwise, since the alternative was anarchy.

"If Mountbatten had not transferred power when he did, there might have been no power to transfer," dryly observed the veteran C. Rajagopalachari, later governor-general of India.

In the result Pakistan had to be content with a divided Bengal in the east and a divided Punjab in the west, which was contrary to expectations, with the new State divided again into segments of East and West Pakistan separated from each other by about 1,100 miles of Indian territory. No wonder Jinnah complained bitterly of "the mutilated, truncated, moth-eaten Pakistan" which the British Plan gave him. But his own earlier reluctance to define his demand left the government with no alternative. Jinnah found himself the victim at once of his logic and politics because, though Bengal and the Punjab were both Muslim majority provinces, they contained large non-Muslim populations and on the basic principle of partition these in turn had to be divided territorially. In short, Jinnah was hoist with his own petard.

With its creation Pakistan found itself bisected into two distantly separated sectors with some 56 per cent of its 80 million population residing in the eastern zone. The situation was paradoxical; for Pakistan, demanding to be divided *from* India, found itself divided *by* India.

Distance alone does not separate the two wings, the divisive factors being many and varied. For one thing, language divides them, because Bengali is the language of the east while Urdu predominates in the west. With the capital at Karachi the centre of political gravity lies in the west, and here are concentrated to a large degree both political power and political patronage, a fact which the east resents. On its part, the east, with 23 per cent of its population non-Muslim, has plumped for joint electorates; while the west, with a microscopic non-Muslim minority, favours separate electorates. In East Pakistan the Hindus mainly constitute the landowning class, and here land reforms have been introduced, the land being parcelled out among the

Muslim peasants. On the other hand, in West Pakistan the old Muslim feudal hierarchy is left untouched and retains its estates. The east, lacking military traditions, is under-represented in the armed services and complains that it is similarly neglected in the civilian administration.

One recent plan devised to meet this situation of tension and frustration is parity which gives East Pakistan equal representation with West Pakistan in the Central Government, in overseas delegations and at various administrative levels. But this has not sufficed to extinguish the undercurrent of the east-west tension which exists on every plane of political activity. The feeling that parity has given them only nominal equality has more recently led some leaders of East Pakistan to canvass the idea of regional autonomy which would make only defence, foreign relations and currency central responsibilities, leaving East Pakistan to be autonomous in its own sector. This solution is unacceptable to the western wing.

Thus the fear-frustration complex under which Pakistan labours operates on a dual plane—externally vis-à-vis India, and internally as between the eastern and western wings. The temptation to distract attention from the latter by concentrating on the former would be irresistible to most administrations, particularly one so plagued and tormented as Pakistan's is by internal stresses and strains. There is always Kashmir. Failing Kashmir, the canal waters. Or any one of a score of other distractions—the oft-repeated but quite baseless charge of genocide against India where 40 million Muslims (the third largest number in any State, and exceeded only by Pakistan and Indonesia) reside; the allegation that the whole of the Punjab should properly belong to Pakistan; the claim to a corridor on the Polish model linking the two sectors across Indian territory.

Nehru once remarked to me during a discussion on Pakistan: "So far as Pakistan's leaders are concerned the basic problem is not Kashmir. The basic problem is India."

In other words the fundamental strategy of Pakistan's rulers is guided by the calculation that popular attention can be profitably diverted from political and economic problems at home to a bogy abroad. India is the big bad wolf—which is India's misfortune. But Pakistan is no lamb.

With all the disinterestedness, goodwill and fair-mindedness of which I might be capable I cannot in truth divest myself entirely of my Indian background in writing of Pakistan. Therefore what I write must be viewed in conjunction with that bias. Being neither a Hindu nor a Muslim but a Christian, I think I can at least claim to be free from the more acute antipathies that divide certain Hindus and Muslims.

As an Indian the sight of old and dear friends when I travel through Pakistan induces in me a sense of melancholy and frustration. The joy of meeting them is tinged by a feeling of differentness and separateness in creating which neither they nor I had any direct share and which seems, as we talk, utterly purposeless and wasteful. I am sure the feeling is reciprocated, as I am certain that on both sides and in both countries the vast mass of the people entertain nothing but the friendliest regard for each other.

How often have I heard Muslims in Lahore lament, "We miss our old Hindu and Sikh friends!" And the lament is echoed by many Hindus and Sikhs in Delhi and elsewhere. But this does not mean that there exists on either side a desire for territorial reunion. Both recognise that Pakistan has come to stay.

The bane of Pakistan is its inability to settle down as a political democracy and as a government economically and politically stable. Heaven knows that India is oppressed by its own political and economic problems; but its difficulties, as Nehru has often emphasised, are difficulties of action, not inaction; of endeavour, sometimes overambitious, but not stagnation. They are, he has said, "good difficulties, difficulties of a country that is moving forward."

During the ten years since partition and independence India has framed a constitution and held two general elections with over 160 million voters going peacefully to the polls on each occasion. India has plumped for a welfare State, has successfully accomplished its first Five Year Plan and is now engaged, though under enormous handicaps, in putting through its second Plan. Over the five years of the first Plan the per capita income of India's people increased from $53 to $58 per year, while the country's national income in the same period rose by nearly 18 per cent. This does not mean that all is lovely in the Indian paradise. Far from it. Much remains to be done. But at least some progress, political and economic, has been registered.

On the other hand Pakistan over the same ten years has not held a single general election, and it is doubtful if the first election can be held before the middle of 1958. In this period Pakistan has had five prime ministers none of whom has been responsible to an elected legislature and all of whom have owed their office either to the former governor-general or the present president. Pakistan finally adopted a constitution in 1956, six years after India. According to this constitution the government of the Islamic Republic of Pakistan is based on the Koran, its activities also conforming to Koranic principles. India's constitution is secular and forbids discrimination on grounds of race, religion and caste, although caste has still to be eradicated from the country's social system.

In Pakistan political power and wealth are concentrated in the hands of a privileged few, neither power nor wealth having percolated to the masses.

"Everything in Pakistan happens at the top. The people are never in the picture," a Pakistani journalist remarked when I was last there in April 1957. This is true of its economic life as of its politics.

Driving through Karachi in April 1957, I noticed that large housing colonies had sprung up since I was last there three years earlier. They were for the wealthier and middle-class sections of the people. Many of these spacious apartments flaunted "to let" boards which indicated that accommodation could be had at a price. Almost alongside were the squalid mud huts of the refugees—pitiful overcrowded dumps of habitation and humanity exactly as I had seen them three years ago. If anything, they seemed more destitute and dirty. I thought this typical of Pakistan, where an entrenched hierarchy far removed from the people seems busily engaged in making the rich richer and the poor poorer.

There has, for instance, been a sizeable increase in industrial production, and in 1956 production in this sector rose by 15 per cent over 1955. On the other hand agriculture, which engages nearly 80 per cent of the people and accounts for over 60 per cent of the national income, is in a sorry state. John O. Bell,

American director of the International Cooperation Administration in Pakistan, cited some figures during my last visit. According to him, in the eighteen-month period between January 1, 1956, and June 30, 1957, Pakistan had to import 1,500,000 tons of wheat and rice, which represented an outlay of about 80 crores of rupees (160 million dollars).

Agriculture supplies 90 per cent of the country's foreign-exchange earnings. Said Bell, "How can Pakistan's increasing foreign-exchange requirements be met if the products of agriculture which have been the basis for the creation of that foreign exchange are declining?"

The answer is provided partly by the foreign aid lavished on Pakistan. "But for United States help," said the blunt Major-General Iskandar Mirza, President of Pakistan, "we would have been in the soup."

Speaking at Karachi in June 1957, Mirza revealed that "so far" the United States had given Pakistan more than a billion dollars in economic and military aid. During the past six years American economic aid to Karachi has exceeded 300 million dollars; and, according to a Pakistani estimate, the country's military expenditure amounts to 4½ per cent of its national income as compared with India's 2 per cent.

In a conversation with an American correspondent* the I.C.A. director, John Bell, expressed the view that Pakistan was currently getting as much as it could absorb, and Bell doubted whether United States aid was improving American-Pakistani relations, a view which my own observations suggested. In countries such as Japan, Thailand and Pakistan, I have noticed that excessive spoon-feeding recoils psychologically on recipient and giver and is demoralising to both.

The same American correspondent reveals what a high-ranking Pakistani official said to him: "We all know we are getting aid from you. Don't keep pointing it out to us. It makes us feel as though we had sold our souls." Which some Pakistanis say, judging from the observations of the present prime minister, H. S. Suhrawardy, is exactly what they have done. It would, however, be uncharitable and untrue to believe this; for, whatever its leaders' protestations and plans, the heart of Pakistan,

* John Scott of *Time* magazine.

which is the heart of its people, is sound. But the fear and frustration from which Pakistan was born linger, and can be organised to direct a barrage of hate at India.

No responsible Indian questions America's motives in giving to Pakistan military aid which was also offered to and refused by India. Such aid is meant to be directed against Communist aggression; but this proviso, Indians also note, did not prevent the Anglo-French forces from utilising United States military equipment against Egypt in October 1956. Nor do Pakistan's leaders trouble to conceal their view against whom such aid will primarily be deployed.

The political strings which are an adjunct to this assistance were visible very early. Shortly after receipt of the aid which was first extended by Washington in February 1954, Pakistan concluded a treaty with Turkey. This was followed in November 1955 by the Baghdad Pact, initiated by Britain to include Pakistan, Turkey, Iraq and Iran as well. The Middle East Treaty Organisation served as a link in the defence chain between NATO and SEATO, Pakistan having joined the latter organisation in 1954 with a view to resisting Communist expansion in Southeast Asia and in the Far East. As Nehru charged, such arrangements brought the possibility of world war "right up to our door," and he characterised the importation of Western arms into Asia as "a reversal of the process of liberation." It was re-entering Asia militarily by the back door.

These fears have more recently been fortified by developments in West Asia (or the Middle East) and along the Persian Gulf littoral in Muscat, Oman, the Trucial States and around the Buraimi oasis which is contested by Britain and Saudi Arabia. The so-called Northern Tier States of Turkey, Iraq, Iran and Pakistan, which have a population of about 125 million among them, are designed by the West to be the democratic bulwark against Russia in the north. Ironically enough, this democratic bulwark contains not a single democratic State but is an association of virtual dictatorships. An American diplomat is said to have observed, "The only choice in the Middle East is between Communist dictatorships and anti-Communist dictatorships."

Why is it that Islam with its strong sense of social democracy, its gospel of brotherhood and equality, seems congenitally incapable of handling a system of political democracy? Islam's greatest period was in the five centuries from Mohammed's Hegira* in A.D. 622 which marks the beginning of the Muslim era. In those five hundred years while Europe slept, the Islamic peoples wielded the intellectual leadership of the world, carrying their literature, arts and sciences from Damascus, Baghdad and Cairo to the courts and cities of Europe and the East. Syrians, Persians, Turks, Berbers and Spanish Moors participated in this intellectual awakening which also took Muslim arms to Africa and Spain and challenged the naval power of the Byzantine empire. France and Constantinople were threatened, the Mediterranean ceased to be a Roman lake, and from Syria and Egypt the might of Islam spread to Persia, western Turkestan and part of the Punjab.

As suddenly as it rose, Islamic power collapsed, and from the thirteenth century onwards, except for a few flickering spurts, its strength subsided. Why? Like Christianity, Islam has had its Renaissance, but unlike Christianity it has never had its Reformation. The authoritarian strain which stems from the Muslim's reliance on the prescriptions of the Koran as interpreted by the *ulemas* (the Islamic divines or doctors) partly explains the Muslim's proneness to obey authority without question. This attitude combined with his strong sense of social democracy makes the Muslim more susceptible to Communism than the Hindu with his amorphous, normally tolerant outlook. Of my Asian student contemporaries in Europe during the thirties of this century, the majority of those who have subsequently turned Communist are Muslims.

The leader principle is strong in Islam. Turkey had its Kemal Atatürk, Iran its Reza Shah, and Egypt has its Nasser. Pakistan had its Jinnah whose word so long as he lived was law to his Muslim followers. What might have been the progress of Pakistan had Jinnah with his modern, highly rational outlook lived beyond September 1948 belongs to history's interesting speculations. He had no use for either *ulemas* or *mullahs* (learned teachers), and his forward-looking policies might have given

* Mohammed's flight to Yathrib, henceforth known as Medina en Nabi, City of the Prophet.

Pakistan a more decisive place in the politics of the Middle East.

I doubt whether there is such a thing as the Islamic spirit. Pakistan's efforts to woo the countries of the Middle East failed, and it is difficult to see any affinity between the Muslim Arabs of that region and the Muslim Bengalis of East Pakistan, the vast majority of whom are descendants of converts from Hinduism. India has closer relations with Egypt and Syria than Pakistan. I recall how when I saw Nasser in Cairo in August 1956 he bitterly denounced the attitude of Turkey, Iran and Pakistan towards the nationalisation of the Suez Canal.

"We now know who are our friends," he observed.

Much earlier, in March 1947, five months before independence came, a Middle East Mission had visited New Delhi for the first All-Asian Relations conference held in India, and had upset the Muslim League by being more than slightly lukewarm to its objective of Pakistan. Today the fissures within West Asia betray the same trend.

In Kashmir State, later to be the bone of bitter contention between India and Pakistan, Nehru shortly before independence supported the overwhelmingly Muslim-dominated National Conference against the Hindu maharaja, but Jinnah supported the maharaja against the conference. What his motivations were at the time is not clear. To an Indian, quite apart from other considerations, Pakistan's insistence on India's honouring its conditional pledge to hold a plebiscite in the State on the slogan of "Let the people decide" comes strangely from a government which has not let its own people decide on anything for the past ten years.

The facts of the Kashmir problem are indisputable. In the first place, the problem did not arise as a dispute about territory but as a complaint against aggression. It arose from India's complaint that Pakistan had committed an aggression against Jammu and Kashmir in allowing Pakistani territory to be used as a base by the frontier tribals who were provided with transport, gas, ammunition, equipment, rifles, mortars and machine guns and who were later aided by Pakistani troops and officers. At that time Jammu and Kashmir was not a no-man's land, the maharaja having acceded legally and constitutionally to India. In accepting the accession India of its own volition promised to

hold a plebiscite in Kashmir if peace and order were first restored throughout the whole of the State territory, if Pakistan
withdrew its troops from this territory, and if the displaced populations, Muslim and Hindu, returned to their respective areas.

These conditions remain to be fulfilled, and until Pakistan first
nullifies its aggression by vacating the territory it legally occu-
pies the other conditions cannot be fulfilled and the plebiscite
cannot be held. The only absolute fact in the situation is Pakistan's aggression. The only conditional fact is India's promise of
a plebiscite.

A conditional promise is a proposal, not a commitment, since
it becomes a commitment only when the conditions are fulfilled
by the other party. Moreover, in ordinary fairness, no individual
or government which makes a conditional offer can be required
to wait indefinitely on the sweet will of the other party; otherwise the latter could hold the former indefinitely to ransom.
This is what Pakistan, with the aid and connivance of its friends,
seeks to do.

Pakistan's friends want India to forget the absolute fact of
Pakistan's aggression because it happened ten years ago and because many things have occurred since then. Right. But simultaneously they want India to keep to its conditional promise of a
plebiscite, although it was also made ten years ago and although
none of the conditions have been fulfilled by Pakistan. Meanwhile many things have occurred.

Peace and tranquillity have been restored on the Indian side
of the cease-fire line, and an impressive measure of progress
and well-being. Some 40 million Muslims now reside in India
and ten million Hindus live in Pakistan. At this juncture a plebiscite in Kashmir will provoke more problems than it solves, for
once the question of accession to India or Pakistan is posed it
will cease to be a political issue and become a communal or religious issue. Pakistan has never troubled to disguise this fact. Its
propaganda on Kashmir is based on the claim that as a Muslim
majority State it belongs to Pakistan. Here are inflammatory
possibilities which on the occasion of a plebiscite will erupt, en-
gulfing in the process not only Jammu and Kashmir but the entire subcontinent, including the rest of India and Pakistan, in a
sea of blood and violence. For a plebiscite is not necessarily a

democratic expedient, since the voters in a plebiscite are faced
not with a choice between candidates or issues as in an election,
but with a loaded question which can be charged with political
or religious dynamite.

Pakistan has also sought to raise the issue of the canal waters
as part of the Kashmir dispute. This is a matter which has hung
fire for some years, a settlement having been delayed by Pakistan's reluctance to accept in principle the World Bank's proposals which divide the waters of the Indus Basin between India and Pakistan on a broad basis—India to have use of the
three eastern rivers, the Ravi, Sutlej and Beas; and Pakistan to
have use of the three western rivers, the Indus, Jhelum and
Chenab. To compensate Pakistan for the loss of waters to which
on a fair assessment it is entitled, India is required to pay for the
construction of link canals and possibly of storage facilities
which might cost anything between Rs. 60 crores (120 million
dollars) and Rs. 170 crores (340 million dollars).

India accepted these proposals in principle in 1954 when they
were first made, but Pakistan has still to do so. Meanwhile Karachi has loosed the usual spate of unfounded allegations against
India. The canal waters dispute, it alleges, is tied up with Kashmir, and India is accused of the diabolical intention of turning
Pakistan into a desert or a dust bowl. Assuming that India desires this, it cannot do so by the very nature of things.

In the first place none of these rivers except the Jhelum has its
source in Kashmir. The Sutlej rises in Tibet and so does the Indus, the remaining three rivers having their source in India. According to the World Bank's proposals Pakistan will have 80 per
cent of the available water in the Indus Basin while India will
have 20 per cent. In the Indus Basin Pakistan has approximately 30 million people to feed from 39 million acres, 21 million acres of which are irrigated land. India has to feed 25 million people from 26 million acres only five million acres of
which are irrigated. What Pakistan draws today from the three
eastern rivers allocated to India is less than 10 per cent of the
total quantity of water which Pakistan uses for irrigation. Thus
90 per cent of its water resources are even today independent
of India.

Over the past ten years India has never stopped the supply

of what are known as "historic withdrawals" of water to Pakistan—this despite the fact that Pakistan has not honoured its promise to pay for them. These historic withdrawals from the eastern rivers approximate to ten million acre-feet of water, and during the last three years Pakistan has constructed link canals capable of replacing nearly five million acre-feet, which reduces Pakistan's dependence on Indian supplies to only 5 per cent of its total requirements.

India has accepted in principle its responsibility for payment for the link canals and for the proposed storage facilities, but the quantity has to be settled. What New Delhi proposes is that its liability for these undertakings should be set off against the Rs. 300 crores (600 million dollars) of partition debt* which Pakistan allegedly owes to India.

As long as Pakistan lacks a stable government and political system, there will be these appeals to extraneous emotional incitements, to fear and hate of a neighbour, to the cry of religion in danger, such fears and frustrations being concentrated on a convenient political target such as Kashmir or the canal waters. Yet these are problems capable of solution on some basis of compromise provided a strong, stable government exists in Pakistan able to carry its people with it. Of that, unfortunately, there are no immediate signs.

* At the time of partition in August 1947 India had a public debt of Rs. 1,200 crores (2,400 million dollars). Of this, Pakistan's agreed share was Rs. 300 crores (600 million dollars), which it undertook to pay in instalments, the first being due in 1952. It has still to be paid.

9

Outer Asia

EAST of India and southwest of China lie six countries, two of them island republics, the group being known collectively as Southeast Asia. They contain nearly 180 million people—not overpopulated by Asian standards—and straddle an area between two oceans, the Indian and the Pacific. Geography which gives them strategic importance has also blessed them economically, for here is a lush tropical world with vital raw materials such as rubber, tin, petroleum, rice, sugar, tea, quinine, tobacco, hemp, tungsten and manganese.

Before the Second World War 90 per cent of the globe's rubber output came from this region, also 60 per cent of its tin, 90 per cent of its quinine, and almost the entire Manila hemp produce. Here too, with living standards on the whole higher than those prevailing in India and China, was a potentially large market for the manufactures of the pre-war Western world. With the withdrawal of Western political domination from this region, the area constitutes what might be called the pioneer fringe of South Asia and East Asia, of India, China and Japan, all three of which have left their varied impress along with the West.

I have travelled many times through this area since I went there first in the closing months of 1945, not long after the Japanese surrender in August of that year. Countries such as India and China and Japan have each their distinctive cultural and social "feel," but always it has seemed to me as I wandered through the southeast lands that here Asia looks at you through a hundred different eyes. The racial pattern of these countries is polyglot and plural, giving an impression of a sort of Asian outer world belonging to Asia but not quite of it, diffuse and amorphous in culture, hovering precariously on the rim of many civilisations, almost a ghost world stirring slowly to new life from the dreams and mirages of a confused, bewildered past. One has the impression of a million hands rubbing a million sleepy eyes.

Between Southeast Asia and the Middle East or West Asia, as it is termed in India, there are many points of similarity and contrast. Both are vulnerable areas vis-à-vis the Communist world, and both represent the "rimlands" of the democratic bloc against the continental "heartland" of Soviet Russia and of China. Both constitute important regions economically and strategically, as well as from the point of view of communications. Southeast Asia girdles an area between the Pacific and the Indian oceans and separates the Antipodes from the Asian mainland. The Middle East, situated at the crossroads of the world, forms a land bridge among three continents and is a nodal point of air communications. Its wealth is oil. The "rimland" of Southeast Asia helps to contain Communist China as it strives to reach out to the Pacific and the Indian oceans. Similarly, the Middle East enables the nations of the Atlantic Pact to bar Russia's thrust towards the warm waters of the Mediterranean and the Persian Gulf and is one of two regions of the world—the other is Central Europe—where the West can directly face Russia along a broad and fairly accessible land frontier. Both regions represent an in-between world. The Middle East does not belong to Asia, to Africa or to Europe. The southeast lands, while in Asia, are not entirely of it.

Over the Middle East, however, reigns the faith of Islam and the impress of the Arab world, whereas Southeast Asia, a plural polyglot society, carries like a palimpsest the traces of Indian, Chinese, Japanese and Western influences and presents a diversity in ethnic, linguistic and religious expressions. No racial affinity exists between the Burmese and the Indonesians, no linguistic link between the Thais and the Malays, no religious bond between the Buddhist Cambodians and the Catholic Filipinos.

Hundreds of years ago, in the early centuries of the Christian era, Hindu influences had percolated into the Philippines by way of the Malay Peninsula, Java and other adjacent islands. Many Sanskrit words occur in the language and dialects of the races inhabiting this archipelago, but basically the inhabitants are of Malay stock with a considerable admixture of Spanish and Chinese blood.

The wealthy Filipino strikes the Asian visitor as racially rootless, and his reference to the non-Christian mountain people such as the Muslim Moros in the north as "natives" sounds incongruous and absurd. Spanish rule brought Catholicism to the Filipinos. It also seems to have engendered in them a dislike for Islam, possibly a hangover from Spanish antipathy to the Moors, and this spills over into a contempt for most things Asian.

I could not help noticing during a brief stay at Manila the Filipino's tendency to rate himself as more Western than Asian. An Indian friend who was resident for some years in the islands also remarked on it.

"It's always a considerable shock to them," he observed, "to find enlightenment, progress or modernism in a fellow Asian. They can't get over the fact that a pagan country like India, with a Catholic community of only six million, has a cardinal, a prince of the Catholic Church,* and that they, a predominantly Catholic people, haven't."

The Filipinos are an emotional, highly excitable, warmhearted and friendly race. Their country reflects their mood of ease and exuberance. With its broad highways, tall buildings and sleek limousines, Manila bears witness to American influence and generosity, but there is a Latin gaiety in the garish night clubs which blend *mañana* with Manhattan.

To an Asian the Filipinos seem a marginal people living on the edge of civilisations not quite their own. The Spaniards gave them a religion and a culture of which little lingers but an admixture of rococo and baroque. America gave them democracy and mass education. The result of this is a brew which serves both as soporific and stimulant, leaving the Filipinos groping in an in-between world with no focus of national pride, few an-

* He is His Eminence Valerian **Cardinal** Gracias, Archbishop of Bombay, who was made a cardinal in 1953.

cient heroes, and a culture which seems more a hybrid graft than a genuine growth.

I have the same feeling of "differentness" whenever I travel in Thailand, although of all the Southeast Asian countries Thailand has managed to preserve a precarious independence over the years. It may be that its facility for playing off the British against the French in the latter half of the nineteenth century and thereby preserving its existence as a buffer State between the Asian domains of the two powers, though not without some territorial losses, has induced in Thailand an attitude of "differentness" and superiority towards its Asian neighbours.

During one of my visits to Thailand in the summer of 1950, I had occasion to interview Marshal Pibul Songgram, a small suave, dapper man who spoke to me blandly through an interpreter.

"Thailand," he observed, "is an oasis in a desert. Look at Burma, Indo-China and Malaya."

He did not mention India, but his manner suggested that other Asian countries might qualify for his deprecation. I remembered that when I was last in Thailand in December 1945 the marshal was in prison awaiting trial as a war criminal. I had met at that time the then prime minister, Oxford-educated Mom Rajawong Seni Pramoj, who during the war was Minister for Thailand at Washington and until the Japanese surrender the leader of the Free Thai movement outside Siam.

Seni Pramoj was pleasant and friendly. "The Thais," he remarked, "are a Chinese race with an Indian culture."

So they are, as several of their customs reveal; for Buddhism, permeating south from India to Ceylon about 240 years after the Buddha's death, spread later to Burma, Thailand and Indo-China where the Pali canon deriving from the Pali scriptures prevails. Buddhism disappeared from India after the twelfth century, but it continues to flourish in Thailand, where everywhere the saffron-clad monks add colour to the gaudy, exuberant décor of temples and shrines. The first thing an Indian notices is the namasthe, a Hindu form of greeting with folded hands, which the Siamese also observe.

None the less the Thais, after the Filipinos, are the least consciously Asian race in Southeast Asia, uninterested in the fate of

Asia or of the world, and politically and psychologically introvert enough to be interested only in themselves.

A Commonwealth diplomat who knew Thailand well stated
his views frankly. "You must recognise," he said, "that the Siamese are adept at political tightrope walking. They have a certain international finesse. I doubt what many Indians think, that
the Americans have them by the scruff of the neck. The Thais'
external politics are strictly opportunistic. Their internal politics
are personal."

An Englishman, long resident in the country, who spoke
Thai, discussed the people with more brutal candour.

"The Thais," he explained, "are an intensely practical people
who have no use for theory and are not hidebound by a sense
of moral obligation. None of them would die for an ideal. Why,
until fifteen years ago their language contained no abstract
nouns, no equivalents for qualities such as goodness, truth,
beauty. They've had to invent portmanteau words and phrases
for them."

It seems to me that whatever the cultural or political impress,
whether Indian, Chinese, Japanese or Western or all of them,
each State of this sprawling region is distinctive and in turn di-
verse within itself. The component and the parts—together and
separately—constitute a plural society. Many Asias exist in one.
In Thailand besides the Siamese are the indigenous Laos and
the ancient Ka who probably derive from the Mon-Khmer family, but apart from the local peoples are immigrant Chinese,
Indians, Cambodians, Burmese and Malays. The same racial
medley prevails in the other countries of this region.

Broadly, India's influence on these countries, extending from
the second century after Christ to about the opening years of
the fifteenth century, was cultural rather than imperialist. Apart
from a sporadic and unsuccessful attempt at imperial expansion
under the Chola dynasty in the eleventh century, the Indian
penetration was limited to culture, religion and trade. None of
the kingdoms founded by the priests, Hindu and Buddhist, and
by the traders who sailed from Indian ports was politically controlled from the homeland. India's exports were culture, commerce and religion, and the impact they made on Southeast

Asia has been likened by Western historians to the impact of Greece on the peoples of the Mediterranean.

Java, for instance, was impregnated with Hindu culture by priests and traders from Gujerat on India's west coast and from Orissa, the ancient Kalinga, on the eastern littoral. Here are relics of the Mahayana Buddhists, the most celebrated being the great shrine of Borobudur in the Vedu Valley. Rivalling Borobudur are the later group of Hindu shrines known as the Loro Jongrang, which consist of temples to Brahma, Shiva and Vishnu. The isle of Bali stands untouched by the onset of Islam in the fifteenth century.

Hindu influences also survive in Cambodia and are crystallised in the magnificent temples of Angkor Vat which were reared in the opening years of the twelfth century. Like the treasures of Ajanta in India, these remained hidden from human gaze until an itinerant foreigner stumbled on them. The spires of Angkor Vat rise in a tumult of magnificence by the banks of the Tonla Sap lake.

Reactions to this ancient cultural impact of India differ vastly in Cambodia and Indonesia. The Indonesians generally are sensitive to any mention of early Hindu culture in the sea-girt islands of their archipelago.

I remember a morning in Djakarta in 1950 when I attended a session of the provisional Indonesian Parliament to hear it addressed by the then minister of the interior, Anak Agung Gde Agung, a Hindu Shivite from Bali. Some of the words he used sounded very much like Hindi.

"What's he saying?" I asked my companion, the spade-bearded Dr. Subardjo, who has been foreign minister in more than one Indonesian cabinet.

"He's speaking in Javanese," said Subardjo, gruffly, "and Javanese is full of Sanskrit words. We had many hundred years of Hindu rule. It will take time to efface its influence."

I have often wondered whether Subardjo meant deliberately to ruffle me or whether he felt that as a Christian Indian I would not be sensitive to his remarks.

The reaction among the Cambodians in Viet-Nam was different, and talking to the local Cambodian delegate in Saigon

about the same time in 1950 I found that they were proud of
their Indian ancestry. The delegate talked with some asperity
of the Indo-Chinese.

"But what is the difference between you and them?"

"The difference between ourselves and the Indo-Chinese,"
said the Cambodian, "is the difference between the Indians and
the Chinese."

The Chinese in turn were unpopular in Indo-China, which
was sensitive to their proximity and their attempts at overlordship. Even Ho Chi-minh was careful to depreciate his reliance
on them. China's impact on the countries of Southeast Asia was
more colonial than cultural, for in Chinese eyes these lands were
peopled by the outer barbarians beyond the Middle Kingdom.
The Chinese term for Southeast Asia is Nanyang, which means
Southern Ocean; and over the past 1,500 years emigrants from
China, more particularly from Kwangtung and Fukien, have
seeped into this region, numbering now nearly twelve million.
They are located mainly in Thailand, Indonesia, Malaya and
Singapore.

The Chinese incursions, notably those of the Mongols and the
Mings, had conquest and subjugation as their aim. In the thirteenth century Kublai Khan followed the conquest of South
China by invading Burma, Cochin-China and Champa, which is
now known as Cambodia. Though concerned largely with their
northern frontier, the Mings continued the southern excursions,
the power of these thrusts waxing and waning with the internal
strength of the régime as they had done in Mongol days. By the
end of the eighteenth century the Chinese empire of the Manchus included Mongolia, Tibet and Turkestan with Burma, Annam and Korea as tributaries. Nepal was invaded in 1792. Thus
the vigour and vitality of the Chinese expressed themselves as
much in colonialism as in culture.

The sixteenth century marked the infiltration of the West,
whose pattern of rule was to be shaken by the Japanese invasion
of Southeast Asia in 1942. To the Japanese as to the Chinese
and the West this area was a colonial region of strategic value
and economic importance. It was also a potentially profitable
market for their wares. For some years Japan had grouped

Southeast Asia along with Korea, Manchuria and Formosa as part of her Asia Co-Prosperity Sphere.

In 1905 Japan's victory over Russia had stirred quiescent Asia into life, and by a curious irony Japan's defeat forty years later served again as a catalyst of Asian nationalism, no longer dormant, but awake. Though Asian countries occupied by the Japanese were repelled by the cruelties and excesses of the conquerors, the slogan of "Asia for the Asians" lit a fire which nothing could quell. Europe's day in Asia was over.

It had been a long day, for Affonso d'Albuquerque's capture of Malacca in 1511 had marked the beginning of European domination in the waters of Southeast Asia. After the Portuguese came the Spaniards who, following Magellan's discovery of the Philippines in 1521, conquered the main islands of the archipelago around 1565, remaining there—with a brief interruption of two years (1762-1764) when a British force temporarily occupied Manila—until December 1898, when at the end of the Spanish-American War the Philippines were ceded to the United States.

The Dutch followed the Spaniards, ejecting the Portuguese from Malacca and driving them out of Amboina in 1605. By about the first quarter of the seventeenth century Portuguese power in the Pacific had dwindled down to the microscopic peninsula of Macao and Timor in the Malay archipelago. In 1619 the Dutch established a factory at Djakarta, which was renamed Batavia, and from there extended their empire over Indonesia. Except for a brief interlude* during the Napoleonic war when Britain divested the Netherlands of her colonial possessions, the Dutch were to rule in Indonesia until the Japanese invasion of 1942.

From India the British infiltrated into the Pacific by way of Malacca, which was taken first in 1795 from the Dutch, restored to them in 1816, and taken again in 1824. Between 1811 and 1826 the British, as we have seen, occupied Java, returning it to the Netherlands after the Treaty of Vienna. In the course of the nineteenth century the British took Malaya and annexed Burma.

* Of fifteen years from 1811 to 1826.

Earlier in 1795 the Netherlands had ceded Ceylon to Britain. Ceylon became a Crown Colony in 1802.

In the nineteenth century the principal Western contenders for territory and dominion in Asia were Britain and France, with the latter power attempting to edge its way into the peninsula of Southeast Asia. The kingdom of Cambodia was reduced to a French protectorate in August 1863, and within the next thirty years Indo-China, comprising the three States of Viet-Nam (Tonkin, Annam, Cochin-China), along with Cambodia and Laos, became part of the French empire.

Wedged between Burma and the kingdoms of Laos and Cambodia, Thailand tapers in a thin tail south towards Malaya. Her geographical position saved her from being absorbed either by Britain or by France, since both were anxious to avoid a common boundary and each saw in Thailand's retention as an independent buffer State a solution to their common problems. This arrangement was acknowledged by the Anglo-French Convention of January 1895.

For me as an Asian the major interest of this region lay in the contrasting impact of the varied colonial administrations in its area. The British system was immeasurably more enlightened than any other, the Dutch the most rapacious, selfish and unimaginative. In India the fight for freedom with the British ended, as Nehru put it, "in dignity, grace and friendship." Whatever the shortcomings of the British régime—and it had its lapses—no fair-minded Indian would deny that it left India, and Pakistan as well, with an efficient nucleus of trained administrators and with a highly disciplined army, a layer of technical, scientific and managerial talent, and some experience of political democracy and the working of parliamentary institutions. Its literature, with its emphasis on personal and political independence and on individual liberty, opened Indian minds to the value and dignity of democratic freedom. Britain developed communications in India and built vast irrigation works. It brought the railway, the telegraph, the steamship and the 'plane. More than its material services, it contributed to the broadening and enlightenment of humanism and the human spirit, to a sense of dedicated service and a sensitivity to inequality, injustice, misery and suffering. The characteristic of British administration has always been its

deep-rooted humanity and fair-mindedness. Of all this I saw evidence in Burma and Malaya, perhaps in a different degree
from India, for the standard of British administration in India
had always been higher than in these countries. Nevertheless
the broad pattern was there, and prevailed.

How different by contrast was the condition of the Indonesians after some three hundred years of Dutch rule! The wealth
of the Indies had been developed and exploited, but entirely
for the benefit of the ruling race, who, without pity and without
imagination, had virtually converted Indonesia into a plantation
economy with the Dutch rulers as privileged planters and the
Indonesian people as dispossessed coolies devoid of rights, political or economic. The most the Indonesian aristocracy could
hope for was to serve the planters as foremen and superintend-
ents.

This state of affairs was partially remedied by the British interlude in Java between 1811 and 1826 when Stamford Raf-
fles, founder of Singapore, replaced the "indirect rule" of the
Netherlands by the more humane direct administration of the
colonial power. Until then the Dutch had been left free to exploit the country's economy alongside the political "independence" supposedly enjoyed by the local chieftains and rulers.
When Java was returned to the Dutch, the Netherlands had no
option but to continue in the letter, if not in the spirit, of Raf-
fles' reforms.

Before the British, Islamic missionary activities had developed during the first half of the seventeenth century, the movement being aided by the prestige of Turkey, then a power in the
Middle East and the Levant, and by the Mogul rulers of India, notably the Emperor Aurangzeb. Religiously this movement
represented a break-away from Hindu influences and signified
opposition to Christian missionary activities. Politically it generated, although slowly, a spirit of resistance which was to flower
in the first decade of the twentieth century in the Sarekat Islam,
a party of religious nationalism.

The Indonesians were also rigorously insulated from all progressive ideas, and until the early years of the twentieth century
they were denied access to education abroad. Islam provided the
one window on the outer world, reinforced by occasional pil-

grimages to Mecca and Medina. Only about the end of the nineteenth century did the Dutch display any great interest in the
culture and history of Indonesia; but when they did the works
of their scholars such as Nicolaas Johannes Krom, Jan Kern, Cor-
nelius van Vollenhoven and Christiaan Snouck Hurgronje, gave
the Indonesians a new vista on old glories.

In contrast to India there were very few qualified Indonesians
to replace the old colonial rulers even in the lower echelons of
the administrative services. In Djakarta in 1950 the government
offices were a riot of confusion, almost of chaos, and although
some Dutch officials were retained to help the administration
the Indonesians delighted in pointing out that they were for the
most part bypassed or ignored.

"They're the Netherlands' fifth column," an Indonesian official
remarked. "We let them sit at their desks twiddling their
thumbs."

At the time there were over 200,000 Dutchmen in the country of whom some 60,000 belonged to the Royal Netherlands Indies Army, and they were leaving at the rate of about 10,000 a
month. Some 15,000 were Dutch officials who were permitted to
stay on their old terms for two years and who had an option after
that to stay on if they so chose on Indonesian terms.

The broad situation then as now was not dissimilar—a de-
pressing commentary on Indonesian affairs. There were differences inside the government and dissensions in the armed
forces. Although the country was moving towards a unitary
pattern of government, trouble had flared up at Bandoeng
where a revolt had been incited by "Turco" Westerling, in Macassar and the South Moluccas. Corruption was rife and inflation
abounded. East Sumatra simmered with labour troubles. Commerce and trade were in Dutch hands, with more than two million Chinese well established in the retail business and also with
a share in the wholesale trade. New Guinea, or Irian, as the
Indonesians call it, was a controversial issue. Then as now there
was only one constant and dominating factor—Sukarno.

I called on him at his white palace at Djakarta and was cordially received. The showman streak is strong in Sukarno. Like
Göring, he is said to design his own uniforms, and the impecca-

ble white uniform he wore with black shoulder straps and
flashes of gold was more than faintly flamboyant. The impression was heightened by the jaunty angle of his black cap. His
manner was suave and smooth but calculated to impress. He is
able, and despite the slightly Ruritanian air which envelops
him he has decision and will. I should imagine that at any given
moment he knows his mind or is ready with the glancing apt
retort.

We talked of Irian, and I mentioned to him that according to
a Dutch official West New Guinea was ethnologically distinct
from Indonesia, being inhabited largely by Papuans and Mela-
nesians.

"Granted," said Sukarno with a smile. "But how are the Dutch
ethnologically more close to the Papuans than the Indonesians?"

In his quick, rasping, flashing repartee he reminded me of
Jinnah.

"The Dutch," he went on, "say they would welcome our co-
operation in Irian. But what sort of co-operation? They want Indonesians there as labourers. Of course I've refused their re-
quest. Why do they want Irian? Because it's economically rich—
in oil, bauxite and nickel."

He did not mention, as I thought he would, that with Java,
New Guinea forms a screen between the sprawling mainland of
Asia and the White continent of Australia.

Sukarno spoke of the need for a unitary form of government
towards which the country was then moving. He talked of East
Indonesia, which includes Bali and the Celebes, where a rebellion was brewing at Macassar.

"I believe they'll join," he remarked. "My goal is unitary government, but I'd allow provincial autonomy—particularly cultural."

What was happening in Pakistan, he asked, and commented,
"Indonesia is the largest Muslim State in the world. We have
over 65 million Muslims. Pakistan has only 55 million."*

I was with Sukarno for nearly an hour, and the showman in
him surfaced as I rose to go. He accompanied me to the door,
shook hands, suddenly clicked his heels to attention and, lifting

* This was in 1950. Since then the numbers have grown proportionately.

his right arm, shouted *"Jai Hind!"* * I was so astonished that I
forgot to shout *"Merdeka."* †

The Communists in Indonesia had launched an abortive
Putsch in August 1948 following the call for violent insurrection
and civil wars by the so-called Southeast Asian Youth conference
held in Calcutta in February of that year. Burma had erupted
in April, Malaya in June. Earlier in 1946 Tan Malaka's Trotskyites had attempted to overthrow Sukarno in favour of their
leader. The attempt failed, and in the August 1948 rising the
Trotskyites held aloof.

In 1950 there was no ostensible evidence of Communist activity, for Sukarno had crushed the Medan insurrection with an
iron hand; and although Communism was not outlawed, the
premier, Dr. Mohammad Hatta, had made it clear that he
would resist any attempt to impose it upon Indonesia by force.

I thought Hatta politically more profound than Sukarno and
emotionally more stable. He is small, bespectacled and scholarly-
looking, lacking Sukarno's mass appeal, but he has sound judgement and the ability to analyse a situation clearly. His manner
is diffident, and at times curiously negative, as of a man devoid
of confidence. Hatta has ideas but not Sukarno's ability to put
them across. And today Hatta's ideas are not Sukarno's.

"You do not see the Communists," said Hatta, "but they are
there. Communism is still alive in East Java, but it's difficult to
pin it down."

I asked him whether the Reds had mistimed their revolt in
Medan in East Sumatra. A Dutch official had told me so, add-
ing, "But they won't do it again."

Hatta smiled but evaded the question. "The Dutch," he said,
"once thought they could use the Communists against us." He
was referring to the early days shortly after the Japanese surrender when with Sukarno he was tarred as a Japanese collab-
orationist and when the Indonesian Reds had denounced the
Republic as "Japanese-controlled," characteristically changing
their attitude not long after.

Other Indonesians, less important than Hatta, agreed with
the Dutch. "The Communists of East Sumatra," said one, "mis-

---

* Means "Long live India."
† Means "Freedom," the Indonesian national cry.

took local enthusiasm for national fervour. Their rebellion was
mistimed, for it was a mistake to attack the Indonesian government when it was embarrassed by the Dutch."

In 1950 I doubt if many Indonesians visualised that the Communists would stage a political comeback within five years. No
foreign observer I encountered did, nor did I.

It was fashionable then as now in some Muslim countries to
look to Islam as a strong countervailing influence against Communism. There had been a live sense of religious unity in the
Indonesian nationalist movement, particularly in so far as it affected the peasants and workers in the outlying plantations and
rural areas. But as against this was the fact that the country's
Western-educated leaders, along with their counterparts in
other Asian countries, had been profoundly influenced by the
Soviet revolution which imparted an economic basis to their
political action and thought.

The conjunction of these two factors makes Islamic countries
peculiarly susceptible to authoritarian ideas, whether of the extreme right or left. Dictatorship is the normal political pattern
in the countries of the Middle East; and significantly both President Sukarno of Indonesia and President Iskandar Mirza of
Pakistan canvass the idea of a "controlled democracy," although
the former visualises it as inclusive of the Communists, while
the latter sees it as exclusive of the Communists but inclusive of
the armed forces. From authoritarianism of the right to authoritarianism of the left is a small step. Islam's stress on social democracy, which enjoins equality and brotherhood, renders the
transition easy; for what is Communism, asks the Muslim Red,
but equality and brotherhood as ensured by the rule of the
proletariat?

Religious nationalism is focused in three Indonesian organisations. The fanatical Dar-ul-Islam (Islamic State) movement is
largely concentrated in West Java and aims at establishing a
State on strictly Islamic lines, which it plans to do by force. It
has its own administrative machinery and army. There is the
Masjumi party which claims a following of over ten million and
which also aims at setting up an Islamic State but by constitutional means.

"We have no differences with the Dar-ul-Islam except on tac-

tics," said Dr. Mohammad Netsar, the Masjumi's parliamentary
leader.

Netsar went on to say that the Masjumi had no differences
with the veteran Sarekat Islamic, which is led by a former foreign minister who is also its founder, Hadji Agoes Salim.

Agoes Salim, an aged but lively individual with a grey goatee
and standing only five feet in his socks, spoke slightingly of the
Shivite Hindus and the Christians. At the same time he dismissed Pan-Islamism as "a Western figment" but made it clear
that he favoured an Islamic State. "Not on theocratic lines," he
added. "It is a concept opposed to Islam. Since 1919 there has
been no single theocratic State in the Middle East."

As far as I could gather, both Agoes Salim and Netsar believed that religious nationalism was a sufficiently strong
counter to Communism. I have heard the same view expressed
in Pakistan. But the recent local elections in Java* with their
Communist majorities would appear to belie this.

Indonesia has changed little over the years. The old situations
and the old arguments recur. Communism, some say, will make
small headway because of the sea, for ideas cross the sea more
slowly than they do the land, and Indonesia is a maze of islands.
I wonder. Islands no more than ideas can be insulated from the
mainland, and in Java there is widespread poverty and a growing pressure of population in an area which houses 50 million of
Indonesia's 80-odd million.

In the ultimate event economics influence politics. So long as
Asia fails to master the challenge of science and technology, it
must lag behind in the race of human advancement; for political freedom, while it can carry a country thus far, can of itself
carry it no further. Without the rich sustenance of economic
well-being, political freedom is meaningless. And without the
sinews of science economic progress is hard, if not impossible to
come by.

Indonesia has other headaches. Then as now the army was
riddled with factions led by ambitious officers. I recall a conversation with the sultan of Jogjakarta who had to resign as minister of defence in 1952 when he attempted, rightly, to reduce
the cost of the army. He was a young man who knew his mind.

* August 1957.

"What we need," he said, "is a strong central government with defence, the police and the civil administration in its hands."

His effort to bring this about led to his exit. I talked to several army officers, including the picturesque Ali Budejo, a former guerrilla leader, who was then secretary-general of the defence department. They were exhilarating characters, perhaps too exhilarating, and their raffish outlook depressed me.

I was depressed, too, by my talk with Soetan Sjahrir, who was very likable but embittered and resentful. He shrugged at the mention of Sukarno's name. "Hatta," he complained, "has bartered away our economic substance for the political shadow. The Dutch economic stranglehold survives."

The minority members of the Cabinet, such as the Hindu Shivite minister of the interior, Anak Agung Gde Agung, and the information minister, Dr. Arnold Mononutu, a Christian from the Celebes, seemed to me pathetic in their trembling anxiety to prove their national bona fides.

As I left Djakarta for Singapore, I thought sadly of Sukarno's celebrated reply to the Netherlands government when the Republic of Indonesia was hovering on the brink of the Federation. How aptly it applied to the tragic condition of the country!

"In or out?" asked The Hague.

"Neither in nor out," said Sukarno.

10   Crossroads

"WHEN the Japanese interregnum came to an end in 1945, Western rule in the region was as dead as the *ancien régime* in Germany and Italy after the rule of Napoleon." So observed a British historian* in an address to the Indian School of International Studies at New Delhi in October 1956.

The remark, directed at Southeast Asia, was exaggerated but justified. In 1945, shortly after the Japanese surrender, I visited Malaya and Burma—the first of which was to achieve freedom twelve years later and the second within two years. Away from one's country one is often apt to see it more clearly and, watching the ferment, strife and restiveness in Burma and Malaya, I realised for the first time that India's freedom was imminent and inevitable. The corollary to this realisation was to strike me during my later visits—that the Southeast lands represent the soft underbelly of Asia and that the extension of Communism in this area signifies a vital threat to India.

One other fact struck me forcefully at the time. Whereas in Burma the nationalists had come to the forefront under Aung San and his Anti-Fascist People's Freedom League (A.F.P.F.L.), which was the constitutional successor to his anti-Japanese guerrilla front, in Malaya the initiative was with the Communists, who were mostly Chinese. I mixed freely with both elements and came to know Aung San well.

* Francis G. Carnell, University Lecturer in Commonwealth Government, Oxford University.

Shortly before leaving for Southeast Asia I happened to meet Nehru in Bombay and asked him whether he would care to give a message to the A.F.P.F.L. and Aung San whom I was likely to see. He readily acceded, and with characteristic promptness wrote the message straightway and handed it to me. This proved most useful.

My first impression of Aung San was disappointing. He was on his way to address a huge meeting at the Shwe Dagon pagoda in Rangoon and, having introduced myself, I gave him Nehru's letter. He invited me to accompany him in his jeep.

Aung San's appearance took me somewhat aback. He was dressed in a crumpled, rather dirty, untidy khaki uniform which sat limply on his slight, frail frame, and his pointed ears stuck out sharply from his domed close-cropped head. There was nothing soldierly about him. He spoke English fairly well and emphasised his points with quick nervous jabs and gestures. I discovered very soon that he had a sense of humour.

"We are in the peculiar position of having an army but no government," he remarked with a wry smile.

This was true, for his guerrilla forces were still largely intact; but the then British governor, Sir Reginald Dorman-Smith, showed no great disposition to accommodate him in his cabinet.

Whether Burma's history would have taken a different course had Aung San not been assassinated shortly before the Burmese Republic was inaugurated in January 1948 nobody can say. U Nu, who as Aung San's deputy succeeded him, has proved to be a capable leader, less prickly than Aung San, with an equable disposition which invites co-operation and, despite an always smiling exterior, possessed of a will and mind of his own.

The Burmese are known as the Irish of the East; and, appropriately enough their constitution is based on the Irish model of 1937, with an elected president and two chambers— a chamber of nationalities and a chamber of deputies. I was amused by an "Irishism" perpetrated by a Burmese minister when I asked him about the constitution.

"We've drawn it from all sources," he replied. "It's half American, half Irish and the rest Burmese."

The sunny, carefree disposition of the Burmese wins friends though it might not influence people. In the coming years they were to experience much internal turmoil and trouble, with various factions, Communists, Karens and freebooters of all types, ranged against their government. "In my country," a French diplomat at Rangoon is said to have remarked, "things are serious but never disastrous. In Burma things are disastrous but never serious." At Singapore on my way to Rangoon in 1949 I discussed Burma with an American newspaperman. He was pessimistic. "The only reason it stands," he remarked, "is that it doesn't know in which direction to fall."

By mid-1950 when I visited Burma again the government had restored communications between Rangoon and Mandalay, and a relative state of order was being established slowly. U Nu was in England, but I met his deputy, General Ne Win, who was confident of stabilising conditions within three years. His guess was not far wrong, for Burma is rapidly settling down.

Like India, U Nu's government has plumped for a Socialist welfare State, and the A.F.P.F.L., dominated by the Socialists, has shown more realism in this respect than India's Congress party. Starting with a scheme for wholesale nationalisation, the government has since retraced its steps and is now engaged on a plan of "joint ventures" which are enterprises partly governmental and partly private-owned with part Burmese and part foreign capital. Rangoon has announced its readiness to accept aid without political conditions from any quarter.

Two key Socialists influential in the government are U Ba Swe and Kyaw Nyein, the latter a young forceful intellectual who is said to be the brains of A.F.P.F.L. Ba Swe is described as its strong arm, excelling in organisation. Both are actively opposed to the Communists, and Kyaw Nyein when I saw him expressed himself more toughly against the Reds than any other Burmese leader I encountered.

Burma's approach to the Communists is not unlike that of India, for while Rangoon descends heavily on Red violence inside the country its attitude to Communist China is one of wary amity. Over 300,000 Chinese reside in the country, whose long northeastern frontier abuts on the province of Yunnan, a proximity that causes dual embarrassment to Rangoon, since not only is Burma fearful of a Red trickle over the border but the establishment of the Communist régime in China has seen varied remnants of the Chinese Nationalist forces cross the frontier. Moreover Yunnan houses a so-called "Free Thai" movement whose eyes rove the Shan States covetously.

Burma, Thailand and Viet-Nam constitute the rice bowl of Asia, and each stands in dangerous proximity to China. In each is a potential fifth column of overseas Chinese, particularly in Thailand, whose twenty million inhabitants include nearly four million Chinese. Viet-Nam houses more than a million, against whom President Ngo Dinh Diem has recently deployed some restrictive measures.

"Thailand is not afraid of Communism," remarked a British diplomat in Bangkok. "Thailand is afraid of China."

Although not in actual territorial proximity with Red China— Laos and the Shan States constitute a northern wedge—Thailand's frontiers are peculiarly fluid, being penetrable by the Malays from the south, the Cambodians and Laotians on the northern and eastern fringes and the Burmese from the west. In between this multiple inflow seep the Chinese.

One realises that while the Thai government can deal effectively with the Communists inside the country, it cannot take China on singlehanded. Hence Marshal Pibul Songgram's frantic insistence at the Baguio conference which created SEATO that this military project should not only have teeth but teeth strong enough to protect Thailand from attack or invasion. The "Free Thai" movement which is based in Yunnan has the marshal's old rival, Nai Pridi Panomyong, in the background. Now both Pibul and Pridi are out of their country.

"Communism," said Pibul when I interviewed him, "is a standardised soulless philosophy. I have high regard for American, British and French values of life. Without them life is not worth living."

One could agree with much of what he said which exuded sound common sense, but what were his own values of life and those of his government? The marshal is no advertisement for democracy, and his government reeked of corruption and graft.

"Pibul," said an American sadly, "has his feet well in the gravy."

With trade largely in Chinese hands the Thais have no share in the commercial life of their country, but they are none the less happy. Thailand seems slightly unreal. The curved temple roofs with their exotic coloured tiles, the green of the paddy fields, the grotesque statuary, the saffron-robed monks slinking past soldiers in uniform, the furtive conspiratorial air in the lounges of Bangkok's hotels, all add up to an atmosphere of cloak-and-dagger and Alice in Wonderland. At any moment the March Hare might pop around the corner. This is Cloud Cuckoo Land.

"Thailand," explained the then British ambassador, Sir Geoffrey Raferty-Thompson, "is a land of princes and peasants. So long as rice and teak prices move satisfactorily both are happy. The Thais are acutely aware of the fact that nearly 20 per cent of their population is Chinese. That's what frightens them. Not Communism. China is identified today with Communism, but it would be the same so far as the Thais are concerned if Chiang and not Mao were in power in Peking."

I realised that was true, for the Kuomintang were and are as much concerned with their overseas Chinese as the Communists. And it is true not only of Thailand but of other countries in this region—of Burma where U Nu holds his Reds at bay; of Malaya where the Communists have been brought to heel; of Indo-China divided but none the less capable of tackling Communism under Diem's strong rule; of the Philippines where Magsaysay laid low the ghost of the Hukbalahaps. The only exception is Indonesia, which paradoxically enough (if the agreement between Chou En-lai and Suneria* signed during the Bandung conference of April 1955 is honoured by the Chinese) seems to have solved her Chinese problem but is embarrassed by the Communist menace. Can it be that in Indonesia the Chinese Reds have no use for their traditional Trojan horse?

Yet in all of these countries, including Indonesia, the overseas Chinese constitute a real threat. Long before the Communists came to power China drew much political inspiration and economic sustenance from her emigrants abroad. Legend more

---

* Then foreign minister of Indonesia. The agreement calls on Chinese with dual citizenship to choose between the two citizenships before two years. Those who become Indonesian citizens lose their Chinese citizenship. Those who retain it and continue to reside in Indonesia are required to "abide by the laws and customs of the State in which they reside and not to participate in political activities of the countries in which they reside."

than history ascribes the beginning of this migration to two thousand years ago, to the reign of Shih Huang Ti, founder of the centralised empire, who died in 210 B.C., but historically it is certain that from the Sung period (A.D. 960-1127) the flow of emigrants, particularly from Kwangtung and Fukien, was steady.

In 1952 while in Communist China I visited the Martyrs' Memorial in Canton which was reared in memory of seventy-two individuals who were done to death in the pre-1911 revolution. On the base of a statue of Liberty crowning the building were plaques testifying to the generous contributions from emigrant Chinese. Most of them came from the United States.

In Peking a familiar figure at official receptions was an old lady who hobbled around with the aid of a stick. She was Ho Hsiang-ning, head of the Commission of Overseas Chinese Affairs. Under the new Chinese constitution of September 1954, provision is made for the representation of overseas Chinese in the National People's Congress; and of a total of thirty seats provided for them, five are earmarked for Malaya, four for Thailand, four for Indonesia, two for Indo-China, two for the Americas, and one each for Europe, Africa, Oceania, Burma, North Borneo, the Philippines, Korea and Mongolia, India, Pakistan and Japan. The remaining seats are left for future allocation.

Communist China lays great store by these fifth columns which since the war have been active in the countries of Southeast Asia, more particularly in Malaya, where I watched them at work soon after the Japanese surrender in August 1945.

The Malayan mainland, which is now an independent unit of the British Commonwealth,* has a total population of a little over six million of whom around three million are Malays and some 2,300,000 Chinese. There are also about 720,000 Indians and Pakistanis. In the island of Singapore, which continues under British tutelage as a Crown Colony, the Chinese constitute some 970,000 in a total population of nearly 1,300,000. The Malays number around 155,000, with about 100,000 Indians and Pakistanis.

"If the Japanese hadn't conquered Malaya in 1942," re-

---

* Under the title Federation of Malaya.

marked a British businessman in Singapore, "the Chinese would have."

This was said in 1945, and the reference was to Singapore's overwhelming Chinese population. I found the general pattern in Malaya similar to that in Burma. The Malayan counterpart of the Anti-Fascist People's Freedom League was the Communist- and Chinese-dominated Malayan People's Anti-Japanese Army which by the time of my arrival at Singapore was functioning as the Three Star (Theewin Ming Tan) movement, having for its flag a red banner with three gold stars representing Malaya's three Asian races—Malays, Chinese and Indians.

Malaya differed from Burma in two respects. The Communists had a secondary role in A.F.P.F.L., but in Malaya they controlled the Three Star movement. In Burma A.F.P.F.L. was entirely Burmese, though judging from some of Aung San's remarks it might have included a microscopic number from the non-Burman minorities such as the Chins, Shans or Kachins.

I once twitted Aung San on having a minority problem much as we then had in India. His boyish face crinkled in a wide grin.

"We have friends among them," he said. "The British have theirs." At the time he was sitting cross-legged on a stool, as he sometimes did at his house, dressed incongruously in a brightly coloured lungi with a khaki shirt. And, laughing at his own remark, he nearly toppled over.

There were Communists in A.F.P.F.L., some of whom I met in Rangoon, but they played a subsidiary role in the movement. Nationalism was definitely on top in Burma, Communism to the fore in Malaya.

The Chinese at the time constituted no threat in Burma, but if Aung San's attitude to other non-Burmans such as Indians was any guide there is no doubt he would have dealt with them firmly. Indeed, the only foreign problem that existed then[*] was the problem of the Indians outnumbering the Chinese by almost five to one. In a population of 16,800,000 [†] the Indians were about a million.

Aung San spoke frankly on the Indian problem. "You must

[*] In 1945.
[†] It is now over 20,000,000.

make up your minds," he observed, "whether in Burma you are Indians or Burmese. If you regard yourselves as Indians, then all you can claim are the rights normally enjoyed by foreign people. If you regard yourselves as domiciled Burmese, you are entitled to the same rights as the people of the country. But you cannot have it both ways."

That was fair enough, and I imagine U Nu would now apply the same yardstick to the Chinese and other foreigners.

The Communists were very much to the fore in Malaya. I was at Kuala Lumpur on the Malayan mainland when the Reds made a show of formally surrendering the arms which they had received as anti-Japanese guerrillas during the war. This happened in December 1945; but, as subsequent events were to show, the Reds retained a considerable proportion of their arms and equipment which enabled them to hold out effectively for over seven years in their jungle fastness.

The Three Star movement was overwhelmingly Chinese, and the Chinese made no secret of their Communist sympathies. In the wake of the confusion that followed the Japanese surrender they had commandeered some of the best offices in Singapore. They were young for the most part, their average age being well under thirty, and they bubbled with the enthusiasm and effervescence of youth. But there was a small hard core which knew its mind and guided the movement.

I also visited some of their camps on the mainland between Johore and Kuala Lumpur where their Three Star contingents lived and drilled. I saw no Malay among them, and only three Indians, boys in their teens who doubtless found it exhilarating to wear khaki and play at soldiering.

The Communists had organised their own union, the General Labour Union which under its broad umbrella counted dock workers' organisations, transport workers' bodies and even an organisation representative of pineapple sellers. There were two strikes in Singapore while I was there, one staged by the dock labourers and the other by the transport workers. They were the prelude to the large-scale well-organised strikes which were finally to force the British authorities to move against the Communists.

Visiting Singapore five years later, I saw some of the fruits of

those early post-war years. The Communists had retreated into
the jungle of the mainland, and the war against the Chinese
"bandits" was on. There was a notable upsurge of nationalist
feeling, particularly among the Malays, but they did not appear to know quite what they wanted. Their nationalism was
articulate but nebulous. Its ultimate effect was to delay self-
government in Singapore, where the Chinese were overwhelmingly predominant, but to secure it on the mainland with
its Malay majority.

I talked with the leaders of the different sections in Singapore—with the handsome, cultured Dato Onn Bin Jaffar, president of the United Malay Nationalist Organisation, and Sardon
bin Haji Jubir, member of the legislative council.

Dato Onn was critical of what he called "the British policy of
pampering the Chinese squatters." "They benefit by breaking
the rules," he complained. "The Malays who obey the law are
the victims."

It reminded me rather of our Hindu-Muslim squabbles under
the British in India.

The Chinese who were working to get the Malays to co-
operate with them in Singapore were less forthright and more
circumspect. The only complaint I heard was from C. C. Tan,
a Chinese lawyer who headed a composite organisation, largely
of businessmen, known as the Progressive Party. He observed
sadly that no local-born Chinese or Indians were welcomed in
the army, though the Malays were being recruited.

I called on Malcolm Macdonald, the widely popular High
Commissioner, who is now British High Commissioner to India.
He thought that the "bandit" trouble might continue to fester
for a while but that it was healing slowly. "Mao Tse-tung's
triumph," he remarked, "has strengthened the hands of the Chinese Communists here," and he implied that British recognition
of Peking had had the same effect.

A remark made by an Indian resident apropos of the Indian
community in Malaya, which consists largely of estate labourers
with a thin layer of businessmen, crystallised, I thought, the
real deficiency of all the Asian communities in all the countries
of Southeast Asia.

"What we suffer from," he observed, "is the lack of an educated middle class which would provide the leaven as between labour and business. Today labour can be led by the nose while the businessman, as usual, has his feet in both camps."

The plural polyglot communities of Southeast Asia complicate a difficult situation; for if democracy means merely the rule of numbers, then the Chinese should rule in Singapore and might— so fine is the balance of numbers on the mainland—have ruled even in Malaya with the help of those Indians and Pakistanis who are Malay citizens, were it not for the cleverly devised citizenship formula which automatically disqualifies a large proportion of the Chinese. Chinese dominance would be unfair to the Malays whose country Malaya is.

In India the British raj pursued broadly a policy of "divide and rule" which intrinsic Hindu-Muslim differences rendered easy. In Malaya, at least recently, it was a policy not so much of "divide and rule" as of "balance of power," poising the Malay sultans as a conservative check on popular Malay leaders, and utilising both as a check on the Chinese, a large number of whom, though local-born,* had divided national loyalties.

Undiluted democratic rule in Malaya would undoubtedly have meant Chinese domination. In 1950 the Singapore Chinese were attempting to induce the Malays to co-operate with them and thereby preserve a national front in the hope of reaching out later for the mainland. Earlier the British through the Mac-Michael proposals had unsuccessfully tried to neutralise the Malay sultans with the purpose, as Dato Onn remarked, "of colonising Malaya." They failed. They then revised their tactics, keeping the Malays friendly by the creation on the mainland of an independent Federation (within the Commonwealth), and retaining Singapore with its Chinese majority as a Crown Colony.

Malaya has a higher standard of living than any country in Southeast Asia. Here as in Singapore a middle class is slowly emerging. Co-operation between India and Communist China is not eyed kindly, for the combination of Asia's two giants naturally revives fears of a dual domination over the countries of Southeast Asia, which with the exception of Java are far less

---

* In the Federation "local-born" means "Federation-born," not "Singapore-born," a proviso which disqualifies many Chinese.

thickly populated than India or China. I sensed this lurking fear most strongly in Thailand, but it was noticeable in varied degrees throughout the region, whose living standards are generally higher than those of India or China.

The battle of Dienbienphu was still four years away when I toured Indo-China, but its shadow lowered over that strife-torn land. I visited Saigon, Dalat, Hanoi and Haiphong, travelling by air and road. The French high commissioner was in Paris, but I spoke to several French civil and military officials, including General Marcel Alessandri, commander of the French forces in Tonkin. American and British diplomats and newspaper correspondents were most co-operative, and I learned much from conversation with scores of Indo-Chinese. I interviewed Emperor Bao Dai at Dalat, and saw the president of the council, Tran Van Hue, and his predecessor, the one-eyed Nguyen Van Long. At Hanoi I met the governor of Tonkin, Nguyen Huu Tri.

The atmosphere was drab and unreal, supercharged with so much wishful thinking on all sides that it was difficult for a visitor to see clearly through the fog of conflicting claims. Though neither the Americans nor the French seemed to realise it, the French were clearly on their way out. Their authority was confined to Saigon, Hanoi and a few towns, with a 150-mile corridor between Saigon and Cantho, and another corridor, sixty miles long, between Hanoi and Haiphong. Communications among the chief cities of Saigon, Hanoi and Hue were by air, as well as between Saigon and Bao Dai's retreat at Dalat. Tonkin in the north was the main centre of war, peopled, as in north China, by a sturdier and more active race than in the south. Hanoi bristled with pillboxes along the Red River, and there were soldiers everywhere, including the Legionnaires, among whom were many Germans and some Moroccans. Driving during the day by car from Hanoi to Haiphong, I noticed the French observation posts strung along the roadway much as Caesar's Roman towers had studded hostile Gaul.

"The French rule by day, the Viet-Minh by night," remarked my Indo-Chinese companion.

French political strategy seemed to aim at dragging the Americans deep into the mire of Indo-China by posing as the one

insurance against Communism. The Americans, though not ob-
livious to French designs, were obsessed by the thought that
the Chinese Reds were reaching out for Asia's rice bowl. The
British stood on the sidelines watching events.

"The Americans," observed a British consular official, a veteran of Indo-China, "have learned their lesson from China. Their
military aid will not be unconditional, and they might use it as
a lever to press the French to make concessions."

But the Americans were in two minds, sincerely anxious to
accelerate independence but doubtful whether Communism
could be resisted without the French.

"The British," said Ho Dung, who was Emperor Bao Dai's
representative in Saigon, "are playing their typical game of compromise. They recognise Mao Tse-tung in China and Bao Dai
here." And he added plaintively, "Why can't you do the same?"

From my talks with Tran Van Hue and the Tonkin governor
Nguyun Huu Tri, it was obvious that the Viet-Namese were
eager for India's recognition of Bao Dai. Why didn't New Delhi
do it, they asked.

I expressed my own personal view, which was that India did
not do so because recognition of Bao Dai would weaken our
ability to persuade France to make concessions. America, by
recognising Bao Dai and by extending military aid to France in
Indo-China, was unwittingly helping to perpetuate colonialism
and simultaneously weakening her own ability to bring political
pressure on the French.

An American journalist to whom I posed this dilemma agreed
with me. "The choice," he remarked, "is not between French
colonialism or Communism. What our State Department does
not realise is that colonialism at this stage can only lead to
Communism."

Many of the Indo-Chinese I met, notably in Hanoi but also
in Saigon, surprised me by their strong pro-Viet-Minh sympathies. To them Ho Chi-minh was a nationalist, not a Communist,
a greater patriot than "the creatures of France" like Bao Dai
and Tran Van Hue. As an Asian I could understand and appreciate their point of view. Nehru might have done the same in
India but for Gandhi and the enlightened foresight of the British. Not that I regarded Ho Chi-minh, then as now, as anything

but a Communist, for I remembered Manabendra Nath Roy telling me that Ho Chi-minh was among his pupils in Moscow.

I also discovered that among the junior Viet-Namese officials were many with pronounced Viet-Minh sympathies which they expressed to me with some reserve but unmistakably. On the other hand, Emperor Bao Dai surprised me by revealing himself not quite as the irresponsible playboy which the global press, Western and Communist, portrayed him as being, but as a cautious and discerning patriot.

He received me in his hunting lodge at Dalat, but I was required to send my questions in advance, and he came into the room carrying a blue folder containing his replies. They were in French which an interpreter who accompanied him translated. Bao Dai, compact and heavily built, was dressed informally in a black alpaca coat with grey trousers. On his feet were white and brown brogues and his socks were white. His manner was wary but his answers were by no means evasive. He spoke in Viet-Namese, which the interpreter translated. He agreed that the French had a surplus of arms which they were unwilling to pass on to the Viet-Namese even for the purpose of organising a rural constabulary. Although he did not say so directly, he suggested that the French had some grandiose economic schemes which they were trying to "sell" to the Americans. The primary purpose of these schemes was to buttress France's economic structure.

"I do not believe the French excuses," said the emperor.

An American diplomat had earlier told me that his government favoured the rehabilitation of the villages and the creation in them of a constabulary consisting of the peasants who would be given small arms. The Americans were evidently impressed by the success of this plan in Greece. Military aid, particularly 'planes and heavy equipment, should go to the French, but the Americans were anxious that the national Viet-Namese army should be more efficiently trained and armed.

I asked Bao Dai if he agreed with this.

"On principle, yes," he replied. "If the freed villages are armed, that would create confidence in them and support for us. It would also improve the morale of the neighboring villages which are not freed.

"I believe," went on the emperor, "that two years of Communist rule in Tonkin have turned many of the local people against Ho Chi-minh. Some 15,000 are coming monthly from their areas to ours. I have about 25,000 troops—some 7,000 in Tonkin and 8,000 apiece in Annam and Cochin-China. But I must have more aid and equipment if they are to be efficient."

"When will the French army leave?"

"They say they will leave when their purpose is served," said Bao Dai wearily.

If reports were to be credited, the emperor was indeed a playboy but a playboy with a mind of his own. In a muddled way he was a patriot and by no means a servile stooge of the French as the Communists alleged. Apart from his sybaritic tastes his main defect was lethargy. He was capable of ideas but not of initiative.

By a coincidence I happened to be in Geneva in 1954 when the Western powers were meeting Communist China's representatives to discuss Korea and Indo-China. A little earlier I had been in Colombo to cover the Colombo Powers* conference which in April 1955 was to expand into the Afro-Asian conference at Bandung. At Colombo a message had been received from Sir Anthony Eden inviting the co-operation of non-Communist Asian countries in any Indo-China settlement. The settlement came in July 1954, Viet-Nam being divided along the seventeenth parallel just north of Hue, which was once Bao Dai's capital in Annam. Laos and Cambodia were left as neutral independent territories, an arrangement which France, also recognising Viet-Nam's independence, accepted.

I thought of what the mayor of Haiphong had told me way back in 1950: "Imperialism is dead in Asia. For us France is the main enemy." And I remembered also what a Frenchman, the scholarly René de Bernal, editor of *France Asie,* had remarked in Saigon: "Politics demean men."

Bernal spoke more truly than the mayor, for imperialism was dead in Asia, but France was no longer the main enemy. It was Communism. By holding on blindly and stubbornly to Indo-China, France had weakened colonialism and simultaneously strengthened Communism. Ho Chi-minh's best allies in Viet-

* They were India, Pakistan, Burma, Ceylon and Indonesia.

Nam were the French. In the Asian countries which were freed
earlier the choice lay between nationalism and Communism. But
in Indo-China, while Communism ate like a cancer into the
body politic, the choice was between colonialism and Communism.

The Colombo conference of 1954 gave me a chance of re-
visiting Ceylon, where between 1946 and 1948 I had spent two
happy years as editor of *The Times of Ceylon.* I know its people
and politicians well, my association with it going back to the
days of the late Don Stephen Senanayake, who is now revered
as the Father of the Nation. Senanayake was a gnarled, rugged
figure of a man—they called him Jungle John in his younger
days—and with his shrewd common sense he was ideally
suited to be the leader of the more than eight million people
who form Ceylon's population.

Lanka, as Ceylon was known in ancient days, though separated from the southern tip of India by less than seventy miles
of water, belongs more appropriately to the world of Southeast
Asia. It has the same in-between air, a higher standard of
living than India and double India's per capita income. Though
not polyglot in its racial composition, Lanka has two distinct
communities—the indigenous Sinhalese, who claim an Aryan
origin, and the Tamils, who are Dravidians from southern
India. Of the latter, well over 900,000 are of Indian domicile,
descendants largely of the indentured estate labourers sent to
Ceylon in the latter half of the nineteenth century. The Indo-
Ceylon problem is concerned largely with the civic status of
these immigrants. More recently the Sinhalese, who constitute
two-thirds of the population, and the Ceylon Tamils, who total
less than a third, have been embroiled in a language controversy. While the Indo-Ceylon problem poses no threat to the
island's internal peace, the Tamil-Sinhalese language controversy is capable of being inflated to explosive proportions. Interested political groups or extremists on both sides, if they so
choose, can set the train alight.

In a sense Ceylon is India in reverse, for while in India the
Aryans drove the Dravidians south, in Ceylon a spillover of the
Dravidians in South India drove the Aryan Sinhalese south. The
Indo-Ceylon problem reflects this historical background, cre-

ating acute stresses in southern India but raising barely a ripple in the north. Mr. S. W. R. D. Bandaranaike, the present prime minister of Ceylon, once remarked, "If only the Indians in Ceylon came from anywhere but the south, we might have settled the problem." He was probably right.

Ceylon is singular in one respect. She is the only country besides Mexico that has an organised Trotskyite party split into two wings one of which supports Bandaranaike's Shri Lanka Freedom party which is now in power. Ceylon has also a small Communist party led by the attractive Pieter Keuneman, a Burgher* who was educated at Cambridge University in England.

The principal opposition party, although it was routed in the last parliamentary elections of 1956, is the United National Party (U.N.P.) founded by the late D. S. Senanayake. Because of its composition as a feudal family clan, it is sometimes referred to irreverently as the Uncle Nephew party. The last U.N.P. prime minister, Sir John Kotelawala, an exuberant extrovert who is a strong supporter of the West, once jocularly exclaimed, "In Ceylon we have a new version of Family Planning!"

Yet the winds of controversy and the cold war have not left this isle of enchantment alone. Bandaranaike's foreign policy closely follows Nehru's, and India's socialist pattern of society might be repeated in Ceylon, whose economy rests primarily on tea and rubber, two commodities sensitive to the vagaries of international commerce and trade. There is a third commercial commodity, cocoanuts. Politically Ceylon's danger lies in her comparative immaturity and inexperience, for, unlike her neighbours, India, Pakistan and Burma, freedom came to her primarily as a result of other countries' strife and struggle. Independence fell like a ripe apple in her lap.

An asset lightly won can be lightly lost. Something of the languor of the lotus eater pervades Lanka, her politicians and people. She is Shangri-La, the escapist's paradise. And escapists, alas, are too prone to ignore realities in the border world they inhabit. India bulks huge over Ceylon as China does over Southeast Asia. Both, irrespective of their political structure, might loom as menaces to smaller countries; and Asia, which has

* Burghers are Sinhalese with an admixture of Dutch blood.

seen the West reconcile colonialism with democracy, might be forgiven for being fearful of both these giants.

The test of Asian democracy will lie in the freedom which the countries of Southeast Asia will enjoy, because the so-called vacuum created by the withdrawal of the Western powers cannot be filled either by colonialism or by Communism. The same applies to the Middle East. In both areas the vacuum can be filled only by the free countries of that region. Otherwise the vacuum becomes a battleground. This means the re-establishment of colonialism and the reopening of the door to Communism. In modern Asia the continuance of colonialism can only lead to Communism. It is a lesson which the West has to learn and respect.

Southeast Asia is no stamping ground for India, for China or for the West. It is an international crossroads between Occident and Orient, between the countries bordering on the Pacific and the Indian oceans, between Asia and the Antipodes. And, like them, it has a right to be free.

11   New and Old

SCREENED from Europe by the vast land mass of Asia and Africa, and separated from the mother country which is Britain by some ten thousand miles, lies Australia with two windows opening out on the Indian and Pacific oceans. Beyond it, about twelve hundred miles to the east and situated in the South Pacific Ocean, are the three main islands known as New Zealand which "sit at the end of the world."

Australia, far removed from the Old World and the New World, also straddles a crossroads south of the equator along the world's air and shipping routes. Geologically this island continent was once part of the sprawling land mass which comprises Africa and Asia, and its topography epitomises the geological history of our globe.

In China, India and the countries of Southeast Asia reside half of the world's population. Australia, larger territorially than India, contains around nine million people, while New Zealand's population is over two million. Together, these countries of the Antipodes represent a young, numerically small people inhabiting large territorial spaces in alien waters. Australia covers an area of nearly three million square miles of which well over a million square miles are in the tropics. She is the smallest continent and the largest island in the world. Inside Australia you could squeeze thirty-two United Kingdoms, twenty-four Norways and twenty-nine New Zealands. New Zealand's north and south islands are roughly the size of Great Britain.

So long as the Western powers dominated India and Southeast Asia and controlled China, these Asian lands posed no danger to the Antipodes. But the mould of Western political power has broken in these regions and created a state of affairs which European historians liken sadly to the Balkans after the collapse of the Hapsburgs. Western rule has receded from Southeast Asia, but both the Antipodes and Southeast Asia live on the periphery of other civilisations.

Until the Second World War Australia looked to the mother country for security and support, but the war which brought Japan to New Guinea and later saw this area salvaged by the strong arm of the United States in the Pacific induced a change in military and strategic alignments. Both of Australia's main objectives—stability of the Pacific area and an adequate scheme of world security—are best ensured under American auspices.

Hence the ANZUS pact which much to Britain's chagrin drew Australia and New Zealand into a military arrangement with the United States from which Britain was excluded. The later SEATO agreement included Britain along with France, Pakistan, Thailand and the Philippines, but Australia secured a previous assurance from Mr. Dulles that SEATO would not be merged with ANZUS nor allowed to weaken the more specific provisions of the Pacific treaty.

Perhaps the most interesting talk I had in Australia when I was there shortly after Mr. Robert Menzies came to power was with old "Billy" Hughes,* who had been prime minister in the First World War and was present at Versailles. He disliked President Woodrow Wilson, and did not hesitate to say so.

"The most self-centred man I ever met," said Hughes. "I talked to him like a Dutch uncle about New Guinea. But would he listen? No. He paid no attention to my plea."

At Versailles, Hughes had urged that enemy territory in the neighbourhood of Australia should pass under Australian or British control. He wanted no new "bad neighbours" and had favoured outright annexation in the fear that if placed under international control this might permit large-scale Asian immigration to areas near Australia's coast. Hughes wanted to acquire German territory north and south of the equator, but the Japa-

* W. M. Hughes, who died in 1952 aged eighty-eight.

nese were opposed to any acquisition to the north, and in this they were supported by Britain and the United States.

"New Guinea," said Hughes, "is like a feudal lord overlooking his vassals. Countries, like trade unions, should be led."

He was scornful of the United Nations and the League. What sanctions had they? "You've got to have a wallop behind you to succeed," said "Billy."

As he grew more expansive I asked him what he thought of the white Australia policy, though I knew his views. He replied with characteristic bluntness.

"I support it on the principle that each man's home is his castle," he said. "Colour isn't involved in the question and there's no colour complex inside Australia. Why, I had Jamaican Negroes in my old Waterside Workers' Front. But each country, like each man, has a right to order its own domain. One must do things with the least offence and the most good. Bad manners are the unforgivable sin."

The strange thing about the white Australia policy is that it draws stronger support from the Labour party than from Menzies' Liberals, who approximate to the British Tories. There is something in the contention that its main motivation is economic and has less to do with epidermis.

This emerged from a conversation with Joseph Chifley, who had recently been Labour prime minister.* Chifley, a big man with a deep, grating voice, obviously of the people and exulting in it, spoke with the same frankness as Hughes.

"The reason for the white Australia policy is economic," he claimed. "We have Kanakas in Queensland and there were Chinese in the gold rush. The Indians in Fiji resort to business more than to labour, like the Maltese here. We can't afford to lower our living standards. In Australia once you are accepted as a citizen you are equal, no matter what the colour of your skin. The Labour party does not want a slave system here. The Liberals, more particularly the Country party,† would like cheap labour but they dare not say so publicly."

Both Chifley and Hughes, in defending the white Australia policy, referred to India's caste system, which was embarrassing

---

* Died in 1951 aged sixty-five.

† This represents the primary producers.

to me but none the less justified. Yet the economic excuse while plausible is not entirely convincing, for wages are strictly regulated in Australia and it would be impossible for non-white labour to accept remuneration below the prescribed level. Moreover there seems no good reason why non-white doctors, lawyers and other professionals, who are duly qualified, should not be allowed into the country on a quota basis such as the United States permits. New Zealand has about two thousand Indian settlers, a few of whom I met. They are largely traders.

Talking at Wellington to Peter Fraser,* former Labour prime minister of New Zealand, I heard him repeat almost verbatim a remark I had heard Chifley make on the wealthier Australians. Fraser was referring to his own New Zealanders "from Singapore."

"They like clapping hands for servants," he remarked, and smiled through his large glasses.

Fraser took keen interest in the Maoris, the Polynesian race described as "the Vikings of the Sunrise," who inhabited the islands of New Zealand before the British settlers came.

"I appointed the first Maori secretary of a government department," said Fraser.

The Maoris now number over 120,000. Unlike the aboriginals of Australia, who are dying out, the Maori population has grown steadily since 1896 when it was 42,000. The full-blooded aboriginals of Australia confined by "the moving frontier" to the northwest, the Northern Territory and Queensland total around 40,000. On the whole I thought that the Maoris are better looked after in New Zealand than the aboriginals in Australia, though efforts to improve the lot of these primitive people, once "driven back into the interior as if they were dogs or kangaroos," are on the upgrade.

There have been politicians among the Maoris, a few leading public figures, doctors and other professional men, farmers and teachers, and a Maori like Sir Apirana Ngata has made memorable contributions to his people's literature. On at least one river stretch in New Zealand only Maoris may fish. Their housing schemes are excellent, even enviable. Until Fraser's term as

* Died in 1950 at the age of sixty-six.

prime minister the Maoris enjoyed all social-security rights except old-age benefits. "I gave them that," said Fraser.

Some New Zealanders complain of the Maoris' shiftlessness
and indolence. Certainly they look less activated than their
white fellow citizens and they lack the staying power of the
Westerner. The Maori appears lethargic. He has not the thrift
nor the patient perseverance of the Indian settler in New Zealand.

"They are steeped and sunken in their own culture," said one
of the very few hypercritical New Zealanders I met. "They're
spoilt by social security. They now have larger families in order
to enjoy child endowment."

His view struck me as more than slightly jaundiced.

The president of the Women's Health League, a Scotswoman
who had worked among the Maoris, made an interesting comment.

"The Maoris are capable of responsibilities which devolve on
them," she remarked. "If other people take on the responsibility
they just sit back and do nothing."

The same reflection, I recalled, was often made in the old
days by some Britons on Indians. The remedy was to give them
responsibility.

To romanticise a picturesque, exotic race like the Maoris is a
temptation to which one could yield easily, for the story of this
Polynesian people who scoured the seas in their canoes search-
ing for a new homeland only to have a new civilisation descend
on them has its aura of romance and colour. What struck me as
an Indian was the genuine effort at adjustment—in social habits,
way of life, outlook and tradition—which both sides were making. Here was an example of co-existence which worked in
practice because both peoples, though reared against vastly different backgrounds, spoke the same language of the heart and
mind. It was not a question of the lamb lying down with the
wolf.

Co-existence is incompatible with Communism, for as Khrushchev, among other Reds, has proclaimed, Communism's aim is to
see that the whole world will eventually be Communist. The
lamb can lie down beside the wolf, but only in the certain

knowledge that sooner or later it will be inside it. But co-existence is compatible with democracy and should be the distin-
guishing mark of interdemocratic relations. The British Commonwealth, despite its internal differences, is a remarkable
example of democratic co-existence.

Yet colour continues to divide it, and creates an artificial frontier marking apart not only two separate civilisations but two divided worlds. With Asia resurgent it seems not only anomalous
but dangerous to proclaim a white policy in underpopulated
countries existing on the fringe of overpopulated Asian lands.
This is not to preach the policy of the Open Door but to advo-
cate a creed of tempered wisdom which, recognising the realities of the situation, will permit a freer intermingling of the
world's peoples on a basis of equality. Communism scores on
colour. Its colour consciousness does not go beyond Red.

Asian countries, now free, have had the white man as their
overlord. The superiority which science and technology gave to
the Occident the Orient is slowly mastering, and political dominance based on colour is rapidly losing its significance. As Asia
catches up with the West scientifically and technologically, a vital difference will be erased. In the atomic age the jet 'plane
and nuclear weapons have bypassed and neutralised the advantage which island countries with maritime fleets enjoyed, and
the advantage now rests with continental countries which cover
wide land spaces and are adequately populated. The United
States, Russia, China and India can claim these advantages,
though the last two countries are weighted down with various
deficiencies, chief among them being populations which outstrip
their rate of economic advance.

Australia, a huge land mass, is deficient in population, which
retards economic development and complicates defence. Since
the end of the Second World War the immigrant peoples, or the
New Australians as they are called, comprise a considerable
number of Central Europeans from the fringes of the Soviet
world. Whether in the event of another war these immigrants
would prove more reliable citizens and more vigorous soldiers
than some Asian peoples inured by contact with the white man
to co-operation, military and civilian, with the West is doubtful.
In the last war the Maori fought gallantly alongside the New

Zealander, while Indians and Pakistanis proved their mettle as soldiers on many battlefields from Burma to North Africa and beyond.

Situated as it is, Australia is in no position to regard Asians as "some lesser breed outside the law." By doing so it imperils not only its own position but that of the free world, whose strength must more and more derive from closer co-operation and association between the free peoples of the world, whether white, black, brown or yellow. Epidermis no longer connotes empire, and on the issue of colour Communism offers a challenge which the West cannot ignore.

The new world of the Antipodes must relearn something from the old worlds of the Occident and the Orient. Civilisation at one stage moved in three concentric circles representing the Indian, Chinese and Sumerian civilisations, the last based on Egypt and Mesopotamia and flowering later into the glories of Greece. Rome and Greece gave birth to Western civilisation which carries with it the imprint of Christianity, a religion cradled in the East. Later, Islam was to find a place in the cultural stream with the result that four great civilisations dominate the world today—those of the West, of Islam, the Far East and India.

The half-century between 1450 and 1500 which saw the culmination of the Renaissance in Europe marks the dividing line between the progress of Asia and the West, and as Europe forged ahead in scientific knowledge the East lagged behind. Superior knowledge brought power; but Europe, taking the wrong turn, used this knowledge to impose political domination and racial exclusiveness on the weaker peoples of Asia and Africa. The fissure dividing East and West was deepened. It was a repetition of the age-old story of right means and wrong ends.

Not until the beginning of the twentieth century did Asia awake from its long torpor. Two global wars in the first half of that century accelerated the shift of influence; and caught in the toils of the machine, the overpowering robot it had created, Europe found itself faced with the rebellion of the machine much as Lucifer rose against the God who created him. It was not and is not that the West is all materialism and the East all spiritual. It is only that the West used the means of a worthy instrument for unworthy ends. Not that the East is guiltless; for, seeing the West use its technical superiority as an instrument of domination, it is itself in danger of elevating the machine and degrading man. Both East and West are guilty of the common error of confusing means and ends. As André Rousseaux points out, "If they are to succeed, East and West must take the same road in the direction opposite from their common error."

Where does that lie? As far as Europe is concerned, the key to the answer is in Germany.

"Germany is not only the centre, it is the heart of Europe," said Dr. Hjalmar Schacht, Hitler's one-time financial adviser, when I met him in Düsseldorf in 1954.

Both Europe and Germany have travelled far since the break-up of the Roman empire saw the Latin world of the West pass into German hands as Italy, Gaul, Spain and Africa came under Teuton domain. Tacitus in writing of the West Germans— the Saxons and the Franks—in the first century after Christ foretold that the Germans had something new and valuable to give to European civilisation. Through the Saxons and the Franks grew the two medieval kingdoms of England and France; and over the long centuries from the Niebelungenlied to the Nazis, Germany, whether united or divided, submerged or triumphant, constructive or destructive, has influenced Europe not only in war, politics and action but in the realms of culture and thought, of science, music, philosophy, religion and literature.

In the latter half of the fifteenth century the invention of typography, due partly to Johann Gutenberg of Mainz, brought a tremendous revolution in the intellectual opportunities open to European man. Within fifty years of the discovery of printing some nine million printed books were in circulation as against some sixty or eighty thousand manuscripts which until then enshrined the garnered wisdom and literature of the world. Germany had always been famous for its craftsmen, whose art languished somewhat after the Reformation, giving place to music. But the names of Dürer and the Vischer family of Nuremberg rank high in the catalogue of engravings and bronzes. German literature gave to the world the thought and writings of Goethe and Schiller, of Lessing, Herder and Heine. To philosophy Germany has contributed Hegel and Kant. The Reformation began with Luther's challenge to the papacy. In every field of thought and endeavour Germany for good or ill has left her impress.

"Germany," said a member of the liberal Free Democratic party when I was last in that country, "has influenced two Russian revolutions. Peter the Great built his navy which defeated the Turks with Austrian and Prussian help. About 250 years later Germany, through the teachings of Karl Marx, ushered Communism into Russia. Thus the Germans helped Russia to turn to the West and then to turn its back on the West."

I have been in Germany more than once, having first seen it in pre-Hitler days when I was a student in England. In 1954 I visited West Germany as a member of an Indian press delegation who were guests of Dr. Adenauer's government.

Europe is no stranger to me, for I lived continuously there for seven years when I was a student at Oxford and later when I was engaged in legal studies in London. In those seven formative years until I was twenty-six I did not return to India. This period covered the last years of the tired twenties and the opening years of the twilight of the thirties before the darkness of war descended on the world. I travelled a good deal around Europe.

Not only geography but history has given Germany its pivotal place in Europe and blended in its people the qualities and deficiencies of Saxon and Frank so that the Germans over the centuries have come to acquire and represent the characteristics, elemental and advanced, conservative and heterodox, of the European civilisation which carries the imprint of both the Renaissance and the Reformation.

The German, often accused of being a robot, has also, as his capacity for recovery shows, a reservoir of resilience. He is ambivalent, and this expresses itself in a frenzy of inspired creativeness and wilful destructiveness, in the worship of Wotan and Christ, in being a sort of modern Faust always in danger of losing his soul.

Thoroughness is the mark of the Teuton, as well as obedience to the point of submissiveness; but alongside these is an unusual virility of mind and spirit. The German is sentimental but ruthless. He is industrious and methodical. Yet the proper stimuli can move him to a pitch of evangelical fervour expressing itself in extremes of thought, emotion and action.

It is curious but significant that three Germans should be the prime inspirers of the totalitarian philosophies of the twentieth century, for behind Communism, Fascism and Nazism are the shadows of Marx, Hegel and Nietzsche. The democracies which opposed and oppose them derive their inspiration from British and French sources, from Rousseau, Voltaire and Locke, from the English revolution of 1688 and the French revolution of 1789.

If it is possible to differentiate between evils, is Nazism preferable to Communism or vice versa? The question posed itself during my visit to Germany with the Indian press delegation as we listened to Germans at various levels discuss this problem.

Given the choice, an Asian, I believe, would have no hesitation. Left with no other alternative he would unhesitatingly plump for Communism, since the Nazi doctrine of race based on so-called Nordic superiority would reduce him to the position of a helot and deprive him of all self-respect as a man. Under Communism, which, whatever its other crimes and deficiencies, is devoid of a colour complex, he would not be regarded as a helot personally, though if opposed to the régime politically he would be treated as an outcaste or liquidated. But that danger also faces him under Nazism. A man places his personal self-respect above his political opinions. That is something which the West has fully to understand.

Yet I found there was much that was stimulating in the opinions expressed by the Germans. Our German hosts very kindly allowed us to make any individual contacts we chose outside our scheduled programme, and I was fortunate enough to secure interviews, among others, with Dr. Otto Dibelius, bishop of Berlin and head of the Evangelical Church in Germany; Cardinal Frings, Roman Catholic archbishop of Cologne; and Dr. Hjalmar Schacht.

"We must answer Communism with the totalitarian No, the everlasting No," said Dibelius, who looks very much like Lenin.

I asked the bishop what he thought would happen if free elections were held in East and West Berlin.

"I'll tell you," he said, "and it might surprise you. In a really

free election 7 to 10 per cent Communists would be returned by
the West and 4 to 6 per cent by the East. Why do I say this? Because they, the East Berliners, know what Communism is. We
only know what the Communists do."

The Church, he declared emphatically, would never be conquered by the State. It would always outlive the State: "Look at
the Orthodox Church in Russia. The East Berliners who support
the Communists are not Christians. They are really like the
Deutsche Christians of the Nazi period. I tell you that Communism will fail just as Nazism failed. Everybody worships or pre-
tends to worship power until it falls. In 1934 over 80 per cent of
the German people were for Hitler, but in 1945 not even 2 per
cent."

A German official remarked to me that the grip of the East
Berlin régime was stronger even than that of the Nazis under
Hitler.

"The Nazis," he observed, "were satisfied if one did not express
opinions hostile to the régime. The Communists demand more—
they want a constant confession of faith in and loyalty to the
régime."

It seemed to me a confession of Red weakness.

The same official proffered an amusing comment when he was
confronted with some luscious strawberries at lunch. I asked him
where they came from.

He laughed. "We say they come from East Berlin. They're red
outside, white within."

Cardinal Frings, who is reputed to be one of Adenauer's ad-
visers, looked like a political prelate and spoke with considerable
wariness. Having heard Dibelius, I was interested to have the
cardinal's opinion on the outcome of a free election in East
Berlin. He thought the Reds would secure 5 per cent of the votes.

"Hitler," he observed, "abolished religious schools. The Communists now say they have a right to indoctrinate children just
as the Christian churches did. It only proves that with them Communism is a religion."

While there is an inclination to deprecate Hitler as one whose
mistakes reduced the Reich to rubble, there is no apparent tendency to regard him as a criminal or a monster or to condemn or
revile him. In the eyes of most Germans he is a man who, having

stiffened their sinews and awakened their pride in being Germans, finally let his megalomania lead Germany and himself to doom. It was like Wagner.

"At the end," said Schacht when I saw him in his bank at Düsseldorf, "Hitler was mentally unbalanced. Hitler had a streak of basic moral dishonesty, and when his dishonest methods paid the ends became paramount. They blunted and blurred the means."

A former German general who had commanded a Panzer corps on the Russian front and who is now one of the top executives of a leading industrial organization confirmed this. "As the end approached, Hitler was insane."

Schacht spoke with seeming frankness on the Führer. "Do you know what was Hitler's greatest contribution to Germany?" he asked. "He stamped out class consciousness. He rallied the workers and the youth of Germany to him. Who in the end revolted against Hitler? Not the masses, but people like myself—like myself and the Prussian Junkers."

Hitler, said Schacht, had also with his help ended unemployment, bringing six million back to work. "He undoubtedly improved Germany's economy. I had a stable mark in Germany, and we expanded our trade in western and eastern Europe. Hitler was right in resisting the Versailles Treaty. I strongly supported him there."

Schacht gave an interesting explanation for Hitler's success with the workers. "He never made the mistake of treating the worker as a member of the oppressed proletariat, as the Communists did. He appealed to the worker's self-respect and patriotism as a German. By offering profitable objectives and opportunities he rallied the country's workers and youth to him. It was only when his policies became negative and ended in war that the people turned away from him."

"Why did you leave him?" I asked.

"I left him when I felt his policies were leading to war."

I remarked on the miracle of Germany's recovery. Schacht was among the last notables I interviewed in the Republic, and during the delegation's tour we had seen a great deal of the economic revival at close quarters—in the Rhineland where we had been shown around the massive plants of Demag and Krupp and the Das Kleine Wunder works at Düsseldorf, the shipyards of Hamburg, factories around Berlin, the Mercedes-Benz organisation near Stuttgart and the Bayer chemical works at Leverkusen on the outskirts of Cologne.

"Yes," nodded Schacht, "the German people's will to work made possible the miracle of Germany's economic recovery. That, and our good employer-labour relations."

It was a truly prodigious performance, and watching it I was reminded of the old *furor Teutonicus* acquiring, as it were, a new function and form. Something of a divine frenzy for creative toil and effort seemed to have seized the countrymen of Nietzsche, of Hegel and Schiller, of Hitler and Heine.

Two things made this breath-taking business initially possible —Marshall Aid and Dr. Ludwig Erhard's courageous currency reform of 1948.

"For two years," said Erhard to his people, "you will know privation and want. After that, I promise you relief—and plenty." He was right. Germany lifted herself from the gutter of Europe by her bootstraps.

Faced with the choice of a planned economy or a free market to garner the fruits of his currency reform, Erhard plumped boldly for the latter. The State, he affirmed, had the basic duty of maintaining order in the economic realm. But within the constitutional limitations and framework devised by the government all economic participants could move freely. The guiding star was free competition. In that sense the amazing economic recovery of post-war Germany is a triumph of free enterprise.

"Turn the people and the money loose and they'll make the country strong." Subsequent events abundantly justified the Erhard slogan. Rationing was removed, controls were ended, and incentives were offered to industry to plough in its profits and thereby consolidate and expand.

West Germany, with two-thirds the population of Hitler's Reich, is now Western Europe's richest country, and her riches have begun to embarrass the government. There are demands by the British and the French—the latter have revalued the franc downward—that the German mark should be revalued upward. The German reply to this is simple: "Why put a healthy man in the hospital?"

Over the past eight years Germany's labour force has been increased by six million—the same number which Schacht claimed he achieved under Hitler. Nearly 4½ million new homes have been built; the standard of living has gone up greatly, and with it the intake of food and consumer goods. In gold and dollars alone Federal Germany holds over 3½ billion dollars in the European Payments Union where France, a victor in the Second World War, is nearly two billion dollars in debt. Never has the mark been stronger.

"I do not boast," declared Adenauer during the fall elections of 1957, "but our currency is as firm as any in the world—including, yes, including the Swiss franc and the American dollar."

Schacht was right, for discipline and the will to work have largely made this miracle possible. But, looking later over the factories of Japan, I realised that the Western advantage stemming from the Industrial Revolution lies in much more than discipline and the will to work. Germany has a useful advantage in her possession of vital raw materials such as coal, lignite and potash and to a lesser extent, iron ore, though her iron mines do not produce enough ore to meet her requirements. Japan's deficiency is her lack of vital raw materials. But vis-à-vis Asia as a whole, Germany has other, equally important, assets—a wealth of industrial skills and managerial talent and a long tradition of industrial production combined with deep knowledge of the ways of machines and men. Higher standards of entrepreneur enterprise have also enabled her to pool larger reservoirs of capital which are rapidly available as developmental needs arise.

The problem of India, as also that of Asia, is one of scarcity of capital and abundance of labour. India provides an example of arrested economic growth where the government's main task is the utilisation of wasted labour or extension of the use of modern machines without creating fresh unemployment. Thus the tempo of economic progress is slower. Asia also lacks a sufficiency of industrial skills and managerial talent, one reason for this being the comparatively late arrival of the Industrial Revolution. Japan could introduce wholesale the techniques and methods of the industrial West, adapting them to her needs. But

India, which at that time was politically subject, was not economically free to do so.

Moreover India is not fortunate in her businessmen. With rare exceptions this class has been characterised more for its cupidity than for its enterprise, for its insatiable greed for quick profits rather than for any planned effort and, where necessary, sacrifice. It is doubtful if the word "sacrifice" has a place in the vocabulary of these gentlemen the majority of whom are not genuine businessmen but speculators, neither pure nor simple.

Walter Reuther, who was in India in the summer of 1956, was not exactly effusive or complimentary in his remarks on India's businessmen. As he said publicly, and also privately, they seemed to know only three ways of making bigger profits—cutting wages, increasing prices and reducing quality. With few exceptions most Indian businessmen must plead guilty to these charges. More than anyone else, they are responsible for the disastrously low place they occupy in public and governmental esteem.

In Germany the businessman, as a Gallup poll on professions showed, rated far above the politician, who was way down the list. In India the politician and the businessman would probably tie for the last place. But are politicians not scoffed at in most countries? In New Zealand's north island, which abounds in mud geysers and hot springs, our Maori guide, a woman called Rangi who is a celebrated character in the region, introduced us to the geysers with the remark, "Just like politicians—mudslinging and hot air!"

The German politicians, however, in office or opposition, impressed with their sobriety.

We were received by President Theodor Heuss, a burly white-haired, cultured man with great natural charm who recalled his conversation with our Vice President, the scholarly Dr. Radhakrishnan, on Albert Schweitzer's book on Indology. Heuss belongs to the Free Democratic party, which is liberal.

Adenauer, returned recently to power again, was then aggressively in the saddle. We saw him in the Palais Schaumburg in Bonn where he entered the room we were waiting in through a side door, stiff and straight as a ramrod, and, seating himself among us, spoke with massive sureness. It was interesting to watch the German political mind, so unlike the French or

British, at work, moving with a slow elephantine tread from established premises to cautious conclusions.

Owing to a bad motor accident in which his face was injured, Adenauer's countenance has an almost Mongol cast which is enhanced by its immobility. In Germany they sometimes refer to him as the Red Indian. He does not look you in the face as he speaks, and there is a hint of foxiness in the slanting hooded eyes. But his ability needs no embellishment. He is enormously impressive.

I was somewhat surprised that in addressing our small press delegation he should labour so much on the value of a spiritual structure, but doubtless he had been briefed on India's spirituality! He remarked that the Industrial Revolution had come too soon in Germany. He spoke of peace. "When Germany is independent she can do more for peace," he observed sombrely.

On the whole, the chancellor answered our questions directly, but he evaded two of our most important queries—on the unification of Germany and the prospects of East-West trade. "They depend on circumstances which must resolve themselves," he replied enigmatically, and his sphinx-like face grew grave and even more impassive.

"Dr. Adenauer," said Erich Ollenhauer, leader of the Social Democrats, "is lukewarm on unification. The reason for this is probably that East Germany is largely socialist. A unified Germany might not keep Dr. Adenauer in power."

A typical politician's analysis. Schacht was more emphatic. When I told him I had heard that Adenauer was lukewarm on unification, he snorted. "Much more!" he exclaimed. "Much more! He's glad about the present state of affairs."

My own impression is that every German, including Adenauer and even the Communists I met in East Berlin, is for unification, but the approach to it differs with party predilections.

Ollenhauer himself was for a unified Germany within the framework of a security system which would include East and West and have Russia as a partner in the system. This would be an influence for peace, he emphasised, but in reply to a question by one of our delegation he remarked that this did not imply that Germany would be neutral in the event of a war. "Culturally and intellectually Germany's roots are in the West."

Ollenhauer's approach seemed to me to approximate most closely to that of the British. The Americans favoured a unified Germany but only as a counterpoise against Soviet Russia. On the other hand the Russians appeared to acquiesce in a unified Germany provided it was an independent Germany which in turn was part of an independent Europe committed to neither bloc and capable of acting as a buffer between Moscow and Washington. I felt that the French disliked and feared the whole idea of unification. With Germany's entry as an equal member of the European Defence Community (E.D.C.), French fears will, if anything, be intensified; for France, like Germany, knows that a renascent Germany as a member of E.D.C. will be a force in European councils. She might well be the strongest force in Europe.

The Germans' anxiety to prove themselves good Europeans does not prevent many of them urging the restoration of normal relations with eastern Europe. Adenauer himself was tempted into a calculated indiscretion early in 1956 when in addressing an assembly of businessmen in Hamburg he made a veiled suggestion that at some stage Germany might have to think in terms of trade and co-operation with eastern Europe. This indiscretion reportedly earned the chancellor a sharp rap on the knuckles from the then United States High Commissioner Mr. James Conant, and Adenauer was busy over the next fortnight explaining that what he said was somewhat different from what it appeared to mean. But the balloon was up.

The late Dr. Karl Georg Pfleiderer, at the time a member of the Free Democratic (Liberal) party in the Bundestag who earlier had been a consular official in Russia and China, repeated the plea, which was enthusiastically received by a number of prominent businessmen. When we met him, Pfleiderer explained that the opening of trade and political relations with the East would hasten the process of German unification. In his view an independent and united Germany, though culturally in the Western world, would stand politically between the two blocs and thereby help to extend the area of peace in Europe.

This point of view has more adherents than seem apparent. As in Japan, any suggestion of trade with the countries behind the bamboo or iron curtains draws the immediate support of a

large number of big businessmen. Dr. Heinrich Brüning, a misty
memory from the Weimar Republic, emerged from his seclusion
to commend it. And it had also the warm approval of Dr.
Schacht, who as the inspirer of Hitler's *Drang nach Osten* saw
in it a vindication of his old policies.

"That was how I built the old Reich economy," he mused.

But what if the Americans withdrew their aid and left Germany exposed to the Russians, I asked.

Schacht smiled cannily. "But they can't," he affirmed, his eyes
shining behind his spectacles. It was then he said, "Germany is
not only the centre, she is the heart of Europe."

The varying reactions of the Western Allies to the spectacle of
a Germany reawakening interested me as a visitor. Many things
puzzled me, but of this I am certain: Not all the fairy godmothers will coo with delight when the sleeping giant now economically astir awakes from his political slumber.

12   The Free World

ON THE United States depend largely the answers to two vital questions: Will peace be preserved? Will liberty survive?

Until the Second World War the responsibility for preserving peace and freedom devolved on Europe or more precisely on Europe's two great democracies, Britain and France. The war laid Europe prostrate, and global hegemony is now shared between the United States, which looks out on the Atlantic and Pacific oceans to the European and Asian lands beyond, and the new power of Soviet Russia, a continental country with footholds in Europe and in Asia.

Whatever the ideological attire with which history later clothes them, wars are impelled primarily by reasons of security. Between 1787, which saw the Federal constitution of the United States emerge from the Philadelphia Convention, and the First World War (1914-1918), Europe experienced a series of conflicts, large and small, revolving around religions, thrones and empires. In the nineteenth century the Monroe Doctrine, which rested upon the support of British sea power, kept America free from hostilities; and until the Second World War American foreign policy was determined by the necessity of averting the threat of military isolation as a result of the cutting of communications in the Atlantic or the Pacific oceans. In the Atlantic America's security depended on western Europe's being under the influence of a friendly power, such as Britain. The Pacific

lifeline hinged on the maintenance of good relations with Japan
and Russia. Where the order of power in the two surrounding
oceans was not involved the United States did not intervene.
Thus it took no part in the Crimean, the Franco-Prussian, the
Sino-Japanese, the Russo-Japanese or the Balkan wars. But it
fought in both the global wars of the twentieth century.

The development of nuclear and missile warfare has altered
the strategy of diplomacy and war, creating new dimensions in
global planning and thinking. By placing at a premium those
countries such as America and Russia that cover large land areas,
it has further altered the balance of power, for with the advance
of science and the consequent development of air, rail and
motor facilities the great land masses have neutralised the advantages formerly enjoyed by the small maritime powers of Europe.

The nexus on which international security rests has changed.
Western Europe, incapable of defending itself against Soviet
Russia, is now underwritten economically and militarily by the
United States. The old basis of unassailable security on which
Europe's civilisation once reposed has vanished. Time was when
America with her doors open to immigrants from the West also
served as a lucrative market for Europe, taking, as a British
historian* writing between the two world wars noted, "her
surplus men from Europe and sending to Europe her surplus
supplies." This continues, but in a different context and on a
different scale.

Along the Pacific seaboard the withdrawal of the Western
powers from large areas of Asia has similarly placed countervailing responsibilities and burdens on the United States. Asia
has also altered economically, for the influence of science and
technological development is beginning to make its impact felt
slowly. With growing economic self-sufficiency and political independence a fresh outlook is being generated throughout this
region.

The New World coming in to redress the balance of the Old
finds itself in a situation of extraordinary delicacy and difficulty.

Asia has acquired two concepts from the West, but has ac-

* H. A. L. Fisher in *A History of Europe* (Edward Arnold & Co., London).

quired them at least a hundred years late. The concepts are
nationalism and industrialisation.

With the discovery of the Cape route to India, Europe ran
amok in Asia, which until the nineteenth century witnessed the
clash of contending Western nations for a foothold in the East.
Until then nationalism in the European sense was unknown to the
East, which, seeing it flourish among the Western conquerors,
caught the contagion in an extreme form. Asia's reply to Western imperialism was an exuberant nationalism of its own.

Thus politically Western nationalism expressed itself in the
East as imperialism, and in turn provoked aggressive nationalism. Economically it led to the destruction of indigenous handicrafts following the impact of the Western industrial system on
the old economic structure of the East. Here Asia's answer was a
cry for rapid industrialisation.

The distortion of these two concepts in Asian eyes therefore
owes not a little to the West. By an unfortunate juxtaposition
capitalism came to be regarded as a handmaid of colonialism,
for the Industrial Revolution by generating a demand for cheap
labour and cheap raw materials and for markets abroad was
the precursor to an expansion of empire. Asia recoiled from
colonialism and, along with it, from capitalism, identifying the
one with the other and seeing in both two extremes of exploitation.

The urgent compulsion to modernise itself by developing
scientific and industrial techniques poses a dilemma for Asia.
Will it achieve rapid industrialisation along the Western road
of free enterprise, which in the eyes of many of its peoples carries
the taint of capitalism? Or will it do it more effectively through
a system of organised State planning such as Soviet Russia's,
moving perilously close to the Communist way of life against
whose violence, intolerance and cruelty it also reacts?

America's attitude will mainly determine the fate of the free
world, for if the countries of Asia are to march with the democracies they will do so only as free nations resolutely resolved
never again to be hewers of wood or drawers of water. Colonialism, as the Western nations assure the world, might be dead.
But Asia notices that the corpse has a habit of stirring restively

now and again. Probably another fifty years will be required
to erase lingering doubts, and they will vanish only with a
demonstration of works and not by a proclamation of faith.

America and its people are rightly proud of the American way
of life which they identify with individual liberty and free
enterprise, but neither of these concepts is absolute and both
are influenced by the exigencies of the State and the Government. Individual liberty would be licence without the law.
Similarly, the bounds of free enterprise even in its spiritual
home are limited by the area of public administration, municipal, state, federal and international, which takes in its stride
developmental activities from housing to highways. It may surprise many that while in India the public sector at the end
of the first Five Year Plan (April 1, 1956) accounted for less
than 9 per cent of the total national investment, the corresponding figure for the United States was 18 per cent.

So far as Asia is concerned the real choice is not between free
enterprise and Communism but between a mixed economy
(with varied proportions of free enterprise and government
planning) and Communism. What India, which is Asia's largest
democracy,* is striving to achieve is democratic socialism with
the stress equally on democracy and on socialism. An underdeveloped country with small capital resources and a large population has no other alternative to Communism.† This is something which the United States must try to understand.

In the fall of 1956 I visited America and was there for the
presidential election, remaining in the country for a little over
two months. It was my first visit to that country, and I went
there with many predilections and some prejudices, for though
in the course of my professional duties I had probably read
more about America than most Indians, my attitude to the
United States was coloured by a similar background.

Until August 1947 when independence came, India saw
America mainly through British eyes, the picture being reinforced to some extent by the products of Hollywood and by
contact with or observation of the many thousands of G.I.s in

* With nearly 400 million people India is also the largest democracy in the
world.
† See Chapter VII.

India during the war. The collective impression did not flatter America.

George III lost the American colonies in the eighteenth century, but even in George V's day the Briton was wont to regard his American cousin as an ex-colonial—in Kipling's phrase "a lesser breed outside the law" with all the upstart qualities of a race brash and vulgar enough to shed the benignity of British rule. Hollywood strengthened the legend, its movies too often portraying the American as a gum-chewing loud-voiced individual, a mixture of Babbitt and Diamond Jim Brady spewing into spittoons when he was not spewing dollars on all and sundry.

The war further distorted the image, for the presence of thousands of G.I.s on Indian soil, many of them lonely, homesick, bewildered and frustrated, and inclined to find relief in riotous living and fun, did not help to improve Indo-American relations. Each saw the other at a disadvantage. The G.I.s, accustomed to thinking of India as a fabulous land peopled by maharajas and elephants, were taken aback by her poverty, misery and dirt. They were disillusioned.

In my two-month tour around the United States I met and talked to a wide cross section of the American people from President Eisenhower, who was kind enough to see me in his office at the White House, to cab drivers and shoeshine boys and a host of others, including politicians, judges, journalists, diplomats, teachers, actors, artists and businessmen.

Invariably the question asked me by the average man in the street was, "What's India like?"

To which I'd often counter, "What do you think it's like?"

Their answers impressed me, for generally they fastened on two of our primary weaknesses—poverty and the caste system. I wondered at first why they did so. Was it because the conspicuous absence of poverty in the United States high-lighted the problem in the average American's mind? Caste of a sort they have; but, paradoxical as it sounds, privilege has less place in a land of plenty such as America than it has in a land of poverty like India. I wondered too whether the massive aid disbursements, for which after all the American taxpayer pays, had brought new enlightenment and knowledge of Asia's economi-

cally underdeveloped countries. Whatever the reasons, they were
right in identifying India with these two stark drawbacks, for
poverty and caste constitute our major obstacles to stability and
unity.

It set me thinking on an allied plane. Had the average Indian's view of the American individual as basically materialistic
something to do with the Indian's own material poverty, which
in turn tempted him to sublimate it into a spirituality which he
saw as a distinctive Asian trait? Envy breeds strange fancies. It
did not take much observation in the United States to realize
how unjust were both these labels, for in themselves the terms
"spiritualistic" and "materialistic" are large generalisations, and
neither label is definitive.

Russia might portray Uncle Sam as a bloated plutocrat sitting
on his bags of gold. The gold is there—and not in Fort Knox
alone. But even assuming that the Americans are the most ruthlessly acquisitive persons on earth, are there any other people
so ruthlessly generous—and to others? In the first decade of India's freedom America's economic participation in the country's
developmental efforts totalled over one billion dollars made
available as loans and grants, in the form of commodities, and as
public and private assistance. Since the end of the Second World
War the United States has lavished on the world—Europe, Asia,
Africa, the Near East and the American republics—over 56 billion dollars in economic and military aid.

Another belief widely prevalent in India—partly a hangover
from British days—is that the average American is not cultured.

"They say America is a young country," I heard Dr. Jacques
Barzun, a leading intellectual of French parentage, remark at a
seminar at Columbia University. "The truth is, America has had
no youth."

The thesis was provocative. What Barzun meant was that
America culturally did not start from scratch, for the Pilgrim
Fathers brought a culture ready-made from Britain to the
New World—"England came over to New England and came
mature."

In other words, America has the culture but not the background. Yet this does not detract from the fact that the educated
American possesses a strong sense of tradition expressing itself

in a love for documentation and in a reverence for the treasures
of knowledge and art. Walk through the Cloisters overlooking
the Hudson in New York or through the Metropolitan Museum,
the Huntingdon Gallery or the Frick Collection and you cannot
but notice the American's intellectual curiosity and artistic alive-
ness. What if he is also gadget-minded?

The combination of the utilitarian and the artistic is characteristic of the American approach to most things—from a motor
car to, it might be, a painting. This has prompted the jibe that
in America culture has become a sort of breakfast food. But
most Americans demand that if a thing is good it must be readily available. Hence the so-called diffusion of culture which puz-
zles Europeans and Asians. For a dollar you can buy a record-
ing of Beethoven and for fifty cents a reproduction of the
Mona Lisa. Which does not signify that the average American
rates culture as cheap. What he wants is to have it handy.

True, this may make tastes and sensibilities, like fashions in
cars or clothes, streamlined and standardised. I sometimes had
the feeling that the ease with which America through her vast
resources was able to acquire the cultural and artistic glories
of other countries had led some Americans to take these treasures very much for granted. Similarly their labour-saving de-
vices, particularly as applied to standard source books sim-
plified for college reading, cumulatively encourage, one fears,
mental laziness and haziness. Perhaps this is the price one pays
for living in a highly competitive society.

The American world is explosively competitive. It is not a
question merely of keeping up with the Joneses but of over-
taking them. That is why I feel that change to an American too
often signifies progress. But, allowing for this, the American outlook represents a paradox, combining a spirit of extreme in-
dividuality with a strong sense of community. I think this again
is a relic of the pioneering spirit which brought America over
the seas and led to the trek of the covered wagons from the
east to the west. For the roots of American life repose in a
tradition of independence, the same tradition which sent the
Pilgrim Fathers questing over the seas and led Horace Greeley
to adjure young men to go West. The old pioneering spirit
lingers in an individualistic insistence on fending for oneself

while simultaneously trying to help one's neighbour. Today this
urge to help one's neighbour is projected abroad to the friendly
peoples of the free world.

On America will depend largely the preservation of peace
and the survival of freedom. It surprises me now, but for a long
time before my visit I was never sure of the bona fides of
America's protestations of peace. For this the foreigner is not
entirely to blame. One of the things that struck me inside
America was the widespread sense of psychological and, stemming from it, political insecurity, which manifests itself in a
fear or anxiety neurosis individually and communitywise. A
significant feature of modern American life is the boom in
psychiatry and psychiatrists. Nowhere in the world can one see
on entering a bookstore so many volumes, often written by eminent medical men, catering to the need for loving and being
loved. It is surprising and ironical that highly individualistic
as the average American is, he hungers for companionship and
community, and is seldom psychologically self-sufficient.

The world and his neighbour have benefited from the
American's eagerness to share and to be liked. But, viewed
from outside America, this fear or anxiety neurosis takes on a
grim, slightly sinister look. It seems suspiciously like hunting for
peace with a gun, and the very terms current in the political
vocabulary of the United States, such as "agonising reap-
praisal," "massive retaliation," and "negotiating from positions
of strength," suggest that this neurosis might at any moment
explode into war.

Dispassionate observation inside the country dispels this il-
lusion, for war is the last thing which the American people or
government desire, and peace is the one thing they cherish. Many
Indians are genuinely surprised to know that the Korean War
was never popular with the Americans, although this was proved
by the country's reaction to Eisenhower's election promise in
1952 to visit Korea if he were elected and to try to end the
war—which he did.

Nor was the desire for peace in Korea a Republican monopoly. I mentioned Korea during a conversation with Dean
Acheson and was interested in his reaction.

"The Democratic administration," he revealed, "was exploring the possibility of peace in Korea when Eisenhower made his promise to end the war if he were elected President. It became difficult for us after that to proceed with the matter, for obviously the Chinese and North Koreans would have used this as a bargaining lever to extract the best terms for themselves."

During the presidential elections of 1956 I travelled across America from east to west and back again to New York where I heard the result at a party given in the New York Times building by the genial and always friendly Arthur Hays Sulzberger.

The H-bomb tests, which Adlai Stevenson wanted the Administration to stop, and the draft, to which again Stevenson was opposed, were two important issues in the election.

I had met Stevenson earlier in India where his quick lively mind and nimble wit had impressed those who had encountered him. While not agreeing with the Republican claim that Stevenson's appeal was special and limited to America's intellectuals, or "eggheads," as they are derisively termed, I could understand it. Stevenson is more impressive in conversation than on a platform. Meeting him in Chicago during the presidential campaign, I mentioned the H-bomb.

"What I have asked for," he explained, "is the suspension of the H-bomb tests, not of atomic research. Research should go on. Eisenhower himself has said that an H-bomb test, wherever it takes place, can be detected. If Russia, for instance, were to break her undertaking and launch a test we'd know about it. And because we had kept on with our research we'd be able to make our own test and catch up. Either way we do not lose."

The draft, Stevenson argued, was obsolete, because modern warfare requires an army of trained professional soldiers with considerable experience, not mere two-year-trained draftees.

"What America needs," he remarked, "is an army of professionals, not amateurs. In that context the draft is anomalous."

But on both the H-bomb tests and the draft I had the impression that the average American preferred to trust the view of an experienced soldier like Eisenhower rather than the opinion of a lay politician like Stevenson. The voter, like Stevenson, preferred the professional to the amateur.

On the H-bomb tests Stevenson, as events proved, anticipated Eisenhower, for within less than a year the Republican administration was canvassing his idea. Yet during the presidential election the average voter seemed confident that Eisenhower, being a soldier with knowledge and experience of war, stood firmly for peace.

"I have a son who will soon be ready for the draft," said the wife of a small tradesman in an Illinois town. "Because I believe that Ike will safeguard the peace I shall vote for him. My son may be in the draft, but I know he'll never be called up to serve in a war."

The remark was typical of several others I heard on the same theme, and in varied quarters.

"Eisenhower because he is a soldier is the one man who knows the value of peace," remarked Justice Felix Frankfurter.

I had the privilege of a brief talk with the President in his office at the White House about a month before Election Day. Sherman Adams and Jim Hagerty accompanied me. The President looked very well, and his natural, friendly and informal manner puts a stranger immediately at ease. Eisenhower does not appear politically shrewd, but he seems to have an instinct for political trends and to understand the mass mind. Like the late Justice Oliver Wendell Holmes, he "might not always know the facts but he knows their significance." The overwhelming impression he gives is of a genuinely humane, fair-minded man of integrity and with the right instincts, and I could understand the goodwill and affection which the American people feel towards him.

"No President within living memory," said Walter Lippmann, "has commanded the American people's affection to the degree which Eisenhower does. Not Truman, nor Roosevelt, nor Coolidge, nor Wilson."

Watching the political and administrative systems at work in the country, it occurred to me that another reason for much of our misunderstanding of America was our ignorance of the mechanics of American politics, which differ vastly from the British parliamentary system to which many of us in India are inured. An Indian is puzzled when different personalities in the same party or administration such as Admiral Radford, Senator Knowland, Mr. Dulles and Vice President Nixon sound off in different voices. The habit is not confined to the politicians. The three services of the United States armed forces constitute highly efficient professional and technical units. Yet here again one sees the same tendency to move separately in parallel grooves, with the Navy commanders often openly at loggerheads with the Air Force chiefs while the Army agrees with neither of the other two.

Like India's Krishna Menon, America's John Foster Dulles delights in playing the combined roles of matador and bull. Being called upon in America to speak to various audiences at various places I was invariably asked my opinion of Krishna Menon, and in time I devised a technique.

"Krishna Menon," I used to say placidly, "is *our* Mr. Dulles."

It always raised a laugh and diverted the audience to another topic. I have known Menon for very many years, and know him well. He combines a masculine mind with a feminine spirit, much given to tantrums and exhibitions of pique, and is armed with an astringent tongue, verbal volubility and the tired airs and graces of a peevish prima donna. But Menon can see into and around a knotty point more clearly than most. His speech suggests an endless stream of molten lava. Yet his mind is ice-cold, razor-sharp, and capable of cutting through layers of tough tissue to the core and heart of a problem.

Dulles's "brinkmanship" has brought the United States trembling on the brink of war more than once, and with the exception of the late Senator McCarthy he has contributed more than any other American to the foreign picture of the United States as a country constantly threatening to buckle on its armour and unsheathe its sword. Mr. Dulles with his lumbering tactics does not conjure up the vision of a knight-errant rushing to the rescue of a damsel in distress. Rather does he convey the drab image of Sancho Panza ambling down a dusty road astride his pedestrian mount. Quixotry goes before him, leaving him after every encounter to emerge from a dust cloud of devious shape and texture, bewailing his friends and berating his foes.

It was John Sherman Cooper, then American ambassador to India, who introduced me to Dulles when he visited Delhi. After firmly planting a bourbon in the Secretary of State's hand and a whisky in mine, he left the two of us behind closed doors in an anteroom. Acquaintance has one advantage. It often alters preconceived notions. A less bellicose man than Dulles, who at close quarters looks a cross between a university professor and an old-fashioned family lawyer with just a touch of the church thrown in, it would be difficult to imagine. He talked to me like a Dutch uncle, regretting misunderstandings between India and the United States, particularly over Gôa, but more in sorrow than in anger. Indeed, his conversation was devoid of a hint of either anger or malice. It seemed to me very Christian.

The impression Dulles conveys is more that of a lawyer than of a politician, which explains his reputation for deviousness and for pettifogging mulishness on detail. He errs more from meticulousness than from malice. For a man who I should imagine is innately good, he is curiously insensitive to atmosphere; for while explaining America's attitude on Gôa and towards Portugal he said things which I am sure were not meant to ruffle or wound, but did. He was quite unaware of doing either.

The average American is kindly and generous, exulting in the good things of life, which he enjoys and which he identifies with the American way of life, eager to share it with others, and to like and be liked.

"God," an American friend good-humouredly remarked, "takes special care of three things—children, drunks and the United States of America." And he added: "You know why? Because all three of them have hearts of gold."

I believe he was right, and as far as the rest of the world goes the American eagerness to share and to be liked has proved a benison and a boon. Yet it is precisely here that, with all the kindliness, goodwill and generosity which inspire it, the American approach to other peoples fails. Why? Partly it is because of the old Adam in every man who resents a rich neighbour and, flowing from this, because of a feeling, basically unjustified, that the United States attempts too often to win less affluent and underdeveloped countries and peoples with charity. Such charity might be given from the best of motives—as it is. But a beggar, however tattered, feels helpless towards the man who gives him alms. Charity does not always have strings attached to it, but gratitude is invariably grudging. Helplessness breeds self-pity, which breeds resentment.

An American has expressed this Asian feeling far more clearly than most Asians could. Writing in the *Annals of the American Academy of Political and Social Science*,* Professor M. A. Line-barger observed: "The Americans believe in spiritual things but they try to buy them by material means—by dollars, by gifts, by aid. The Communists believe in material things, but they offer people something to join, something to do, something to fight. We Americans offer property; the Communists offer a reason for being alive. People who join the Communist side feel that they are needed, that the Communists want them. You couldn't join the American side if you were an Asian. There isn't anything to join."

I would not be so pessimistic as all that, but there is some truth in the professor's suggestion that to an Asian, while there is much in what the Communists offer or purport to offer—freedom from colonial rule and colour prejudice, sympathy for the dispossessed and the underdog and a feeling of being wanted for your own self—the only thing which the Americans appear to offer is the American way of life, which is beyond the average Asian's dream and which he sees no reason to defend with his life. The American approach leaves the Asian with the feeling that he is being wanted not for his own self but for America's sake—to serve as cannon fodder in order to preserve a way of life he can never attain. This combined with the Negro problem and with what seems a willingness to equivocate on certain colonial issues—to turn the blind eye on them when they are likely to embarrass one's Allies—leaves the Americans contending at a disadvantage against the Russians.

What the United States has not sufficiently appreciated is that in most Asian eyes colonialism is equated with colour. The two are intermixed. Which is why it is difficult to convince the average Asian that Soviet Russia exercises a type of imperialism and colonialism over the countries of eastern Europe. To the Asian, imperialism means the overlordship of the black, brown or yellow races by the white. The domination of a white race by another white race is generally regarded by him as the projec-tion, continuation or repetition of the wars in which European

* Of November 1951.

peoples seem to him to be almost incessantly engaged. These represent the temporary occupation of or submission to one white country by another.

A great opportunity was lost when Russian tanks and troops rode roughshod over the Hungarians in October 1956. The initial reluctance of India to condemn unequivocally the Soviet brutality in Hungary was, in my opinion, rightly criticised by the West, for the Indian attitude was inexcusable even in the context of the Anglo-French aggression on Egypt. America, bound closely to Britain and France, condemned her Allies roundly.

In a reference to the rebellion in Hungary, Nehru described it as an upsurge of nationalism, which is how the majority of the Indian public saw it, and public opinion later compelled New Delhi to retrace its steps. For the first time India saw that an upsurge of nationalism in a European country could be crushed by the might of another European country. In other words it saw Soviet colonialism in all its naked brutality and recognised it for what it was.

The opportunity to drive home the point was lost initially by the pusillanimous attitude of Delhi but also by the distraction of the Anglo-French adventure in Egypt and by the later timidity and inconsistency of American foreign policy. The French massacres in Algeria have taken a heavier toll in lives than the Soviet butchery in Hungary. Yet the State Department has been noticeably silent and lukewarm on these happenings. Why? If the alleged invitation by the Hungarian government to Russian troops to restore law and order was rightly characterised as "aggression by invitation," why was the British intervention in Muscat and Oman overlooked with a mild shrug of Uncle Sam's shoulders? It was admittedly not comparable in ferocity or brutality to the Russian action, but the principle involved was the same. The point is important since it is on such issues that Asia justifiably throws back at Washington the charge of "double talk" and "double standards."

Similarly with the Negro problem. In India the practice of untouchability, though constitutionally forbidden, continues to exist, and India is therefore in no position to cast a stone at others. Her own situation is highly vulnerable. Yet on the principle that two wrongs do not make a right, the curse of untouchability must be eradicated in India no less than the stain of anti-Negro discrimination in the United States. The oddly similar arguments used by the die-hards in America and by our orthodox elements in India struck me forcefully.

Another attitude rang a bell. In Louisville, Kentucky, where I was privileged to meet Dr. Omer Carmichael and to investigate the manner in which he and his colleagues were carrying out the desegregation experiment in their schools, I talked frankly with a number of pupils and teachers, white and coloured. At one of the desegregated schools was a woman schoolteacher from Alabama in the deep South who, while carrying out the experiment impartially, confessed that she did not believe in the equality of the Negro. I liked her frankness, though it amused me to note a similarity in her attitude and that of the old-type Briton to his Indian servant. It was feudal.

"We look after them when they're old," remarked the teacher with no trace of self-consciousness, much as if she were talking of an old dog or horse.

She was intelligent, and I respected her candour.

"But what is the real Southern attitude to the Negro?"

"Ah, there," she said, "you've got it. The Southern attitude is different from the Northern. In the South we like the Negro individually but not *en masse*. In the North they like him *en masse* but not individually."

She confirmed in an unexpected way what a bright Negro newspaper reporter, who had taken me around the coloured areas of Chicago, had said.

"In the South," he said, "a white may live next door to you but he won't have your child attend his child's school. In the North it's the other way about. The white doesn't mind desegregation in schools but he won't have a Negro neighbour. He resents Negro encroachment on his residential area."

All of which left me reflecting that things are moving slowly in the right direction as far as both America's Negroes and India's untouchables are concerned. In both countries much more needs to be done, and more quickly.

Was the white American's attitude to the Negro, I wondered, animated by the same fierce urge to preserve the American way of life whose standards in his opinion the Negroes threatened to lower? Yet the educated Negro had equally a great pride in the American way of life in which he desired only to share equally, and I confess that the spectacle one night of a Negro audience at a political meeting in Chicago's South Side singing in their deep reverberating voices "America the Beautiful" brought a lump to my throat. They *were* America, for they were part of it, just as the peoples of Asia and Africa, given equal opportunities and an equal place, would proudly share in the great human brotherhood which is democracy.

I think that in a strange way Vinoba Bhave, disciple of Gandhi and inspirer of the Bhoodan movement which he leads, a man as far removed from the material conception of the American way of life as any, touched the heart of the matter, the beauty of spirit which unconsciously but in truth animates the American way of life, when he spoke to an assembly of princes and landlords, appealing to them for gifts of land for the dispossessed peasantry.

"Follow in this at least the example of the Americans," Vinoba begged them. "They are the richest of all and they give to the whole world. . . . They do not give because they are the richest. They are the richest because they give. For riches are like the wind. If you stopped its flow, there would be no wind."

13   Yonder One World

CAN democracy work in Asia? And can it survive? Like nationalism, democracy is a concept new to the Orient. The aggressive nationalism of the West which the countries of the East saw in the image of imperialism provoked an answering and assertive nationalism in Asia. It was the West's peculiar misfortune that it presented not only nationalism in a distorted form to Eastern lands but that the concept of democracy also acquired a twisted aspect in Asian eyes, for while the Occident preached liberty, equality and fraternity at home it expressly excluded the application of these principles abroad.

In 1798 the abrogation of the charter of Holland's United East India Company in favour of the Netherlands' government in Indonesia carried a significant proviso. This stipulated that "the doctrines of liberty and equality . . . cannot be transferred to nor applied to the East Indian possessions of the State so long as the security of these possessions depends on the existing and necessary state of subordination." Thus what was good for the West was not necessarily good for the East. Here Asia saw and noted one of Europe's earliest demonstrations of "double standards" and "double talk."

The Industrial Revolution developing in the wake of the democratic ferment generated by the French Revolution unfortunately identified colonialism with capitalism. Asia noted that Europe's greed for expansionism abroad was accentuated by the hunger for new and untapped markets, for cheap labour and cheap raw materials. Colonialism appeared as the corollary of capitalism.

The cumulative result of these processes was to distort nationalism and to denigrate democracy and free enterprise in the East. To Asia colonialism and capitalism seemed to be two faces of the same coin, imperialism. And the true meaning of democracy was lost under the false veneer of nationalism perverted as imperialism.

As a result Asian revolutions were directed primarily against the West and against all that the West represented, and this makes the task of the Reds, of Soviet Russia and Communist China proportionately easier. Russia has no stain of original sin to wipe out; that stigma attaches only to the West.

Nationalism and industrialisation (with its concomitants of science and technology) arrived a hundred years late in Asia, and one reason why the Occident and the Orient appear to talk at cross purposes is that the same terms mean different things to each side. The West believes that democracy and nationalism grow together, for as the individual citizen acquires an increasing share in the government and development of his country he tends to identify democracy with nationalism. This is not necessarily the attitude of the East. Similarly, the Western democrat believes that a mixed economy permitting free enterprise subject to the limitations of governmental planning and order symbolises the true democratic State. But Asia lays greater store by organised and controlled planning.

In an underdeveloped country with an urge for quick advancement the focus is on ends, not means, and a political system which yields rapid results is generally viewed with more favour than one which promises comparatively slow returns. A hungry man finds it hard to assess the value of different political principles. Faced with the choice of deciding between a system which guarantees him freedom of opinion and another which guarantees him the right to employment, food, shelter and clothing, there is little doubt for which he would plump. For him nationalism is not necessarily identified with democracy. Rather the reverse. For democracy, lacking the ruthlessness of a dictatorship, seems in his eyes to rob nationalism or political freedom of a quick chance to acquire economic content or reality.

Manabendra Nath Roy saw this antithesis clearly and has expressed it lucidly. In an article in *Thought** in 1953 Roy wrote: "The spectacular emergence of the Communist party [in India] is mainly due to the fact that it represents a clear and persistent opposition to the party in power—politically, socially and ideologically. . . . The Communist party offers the point of crystallisation for the disillusioned and discontented. . . . In this atmosphere of despair and disillusionment, a programme promising a clean sweep of the established order has a strong appeal." In the same article Roy points out that there are two things which must be borne in mind by those concerned with devising a suitable strategy to fight Communism. These are, first, that Communism can never trade on its own; and, second, that it must have outside military assistance to succeed in its final aim. "In the north," Roy warns, "both these things may come into operation before long."

Roy was thinking of the massing of Chinese Communist troops along India's north and northeastern borders, particularly in Tibet, and his fear was justified. In this connection some significant passages occur in a statement issued by the Politbureau of the Indian Communist party in November 1951: "We cannot fail to note the fact that the Chinese Red army was surrounded and threatened with annihilation again and again until it reached Manchuria," says the statement. "There, with the industrial base in hand, the great friendly Soviet Union in the rear, the Chinese Liberation army, free from the possibility of any attack in the rear, rebuilt itself and launched the final offensive which led it to victory." The Chinese Liberation army is indeed very near. And so is "the great friendly Soviet Union in the rear."

Since then another development has taken place, for the first Communist State government in India has been established in the south in Kerala. Returned in a democratic election under a democratic constitution, it claims to be democratic, and the Red chief minister, E. M. S. Namboodripad, who once infiltrated into the Socialist party and was for a time one of its joint secretaries

* A magazine published in New Delhi.

under the United Front, blandly proclaims that his government proposes to respect the constitution and work within it. If the Reds can capture power democratically under a democratic constitution, why should they flout it? What the Communists are doing and will continue to do is to use democracy in order to destroy it. Kerala is the Indian Reds' Yenan which will lead them to Delhi, but it will all be done constitutionally. From violent revolution the Communists are shifting to a "voting revolution" enabling them to utilise a country's democratic machinery in order to capture parliamentary and political power.

Because the Socialist parties are generally weak in Asia, the value of a weapon such as the United Front is limited; but its employment on a restricted scale has its uses, particularly in India where the Reds will have to infiltrate into the Congress government at the Centre before finally capturing national power. Clearly the Indian Communists visualise this tactic, for in an interview with an American correspondent[*] a prominent Kerala Red leader[†] is quoted as saying: "I believe that first there will be a coalition government in New Delhi with perhaps a large Congress bloc." The other group in the coalition will, of course, be the Communists. Alongside this, the parliamentary machinery will be used to obtain control of the State governments.

Khrushchev in his speech to the Twentieth Party Congress in February 1956 laid down the three R's—reasonableness, reliability, respectability. Apart from Kerala in India this tactic has more recently met with spectacular success in the local Javanese elections in Indonesia where the Communist party is said to be the fourth largest in the world. The Indonesian Reds control 46 out of 257 seats in their country's parliament.

Not all Asian countries are susceptible to the same pressures, and these vary in expression and intensity, though their motivation remains rigid. Thus areas such as Formosa, South Korea, South Viet-Nam and the Philippines, which are not vulnerable to direct infiltration, can only be reached by the remote control of radio propaganda. Countries like Japan and Thailand, with close affiliations with the West, can be wooed more effectively

[*] Charles C. Lane of Associated Press.
[†] I have good reason for believing that he was Namboodripad.

by indirect methods such as the radio or by increased East-West trade.

The focal point of Red activity in Asia is represented by the six countries of India, Indonesia, Burma, Ceylon, Cambodia and Laos. Since each one of these areas is neutralist in the sense of being uncommitted to either bloc, they are more easily penetrable by various means, parliamentary and extra-parliamentary, legal and illegal. Merely because the Reds have adopted the outward cloak of reasonableness and respectability they are not deterred from resorting to illegal methods. Lenin pointed out long ago that the Communist party alone has an effective organised machinery within a country which can combine legal and illegal activities.

By proclaiming India a Welfare State and by adopting a socialistic pattern of society Nehru spiked the guns of the Socialists. Similarly, his foreign policy of non-alignment helped to keep the Communists at bay, internally and externally. But checkmated at the gate of the central citadel, the Communist party is now attempting to come in by the back door—through parliamentary elections in a country enjoying adult suffrage but with 80 per cent of its population illiterate and living a marginal existence. True, Kerala, which returned a Communist government, has the highest literacy rate in India—over 50 per cent. But with a large literate population it also combines widespread unemployment, and the combination is proverbially explosive.

Had the Socialists accepted Nehru's invitation to join his government in 1953, two years before the Avadi session of the Congress adopted a socialistic blueprint for the country, the future of democracy might have been more assured in India. For various reasons they declined. By cutting the ground from under their feet the Avadi resolution left the Socialists suspended in a vacuum, with the Communists offering the only alternate challenge to the Congress.

Kerala symbolises this challenge, placing the Congress on the defensive and encouraging the Communists to consolidate and further strengthen their position. After India's first general elections in 1952-1953 it became difficult to distinguish between the Congress and the Socialists. Following the second general elections some feel that the dividing line between the Congress

and the Communists is wearing thin. Not that the Congress
party has lost the initiative, but the confusion in Congress thinking is evident from the fact that the party has not yet made up
its mind whether or not to accept the Kerala State government
and with it the Communists as part of the democratic system
and pattern.

This confusion was reflected in a rather naïve pronouncement
by India's President, Dr. Rajendra Prasad,* whom nobody sus-
pects of even the remotest Red leanings. "Have we," asked the
President pointing at Kerala, "not got on the smallest scale an
example of the actual working of a kind of co-existence?" The
Communists seized on the declaration as an "open sesame" to further infiltration into the democratic citadel. As far as they are
concerned, Kerala is the beginning. It is the beginning of that
idyllic co-existence which in Red reckoning can end only in the
opponent's non-existence.

As the constitutional head of a democracy India's President
voices the views of the Government of India whose spokesman
he is at various ceremonies and functions. That is why the sentiments he expressed towards the Red government of Kerala dis-
turbed and dismayed democrats throughout the country. They
revealed a process of thought transference—projecting India's acceptance of co-existence in international affairs to co-existence in
national affairs—which shocked liberal public opinion by its bland
and unblushing innocence. For the net result of the President's
eloquence was to portray and present the gentlemen of Kerala
to the people of India as enlightened democrats worthy of being
included in the democratic fold.

This danger the Congress party cannot or will not see. It does
not seem to realise that for a totalitarian to be returned by democratic methods no more makes him a democrat than the possession of a vote by every adult citizen automatically makes a
country democratic. The Congress party which constitutes the
Government of India is mistaking means for ends. Nationalism,
like co-existence, signifies to the Communist not an end but a
means.

Asia's danger lies in democracy's too complacent acceptance

* In a speech in August 1957.

of Red protestations, a state of mind devastatingly exposed in
A. E. Housman's "Demise of an Imperceptive Youth":

> "The Grizzly Bear is huge and wild,
> He has devoured the infant child.
> The infant child is not aware
> It has been eaten by the bear."

In those Asian countries where Communism poses a sharp
challenge to the party in power, Red tactics are beginning to
reveal their pattern. Invited by democracy's infant child to
share its playpen, the Grizzly Bear is all amiability until the moment comes to strike and it moves in for the kill. Whatever else
the Communists are capable of, they appear to be incapable of
originality, for though their short-term tactics might change,
their long-term strategy never alters. Even within the broad
pattern their manœuvres are mannered. When the time comes
to throw off the mask of friendly co-existence, the Communists
will revert to their old policy of isolating the leaders of the op-
posing party from their followers by the familiar tactic of the
"united front from below" which requires that the Reds should
unite with the rank and file against the leaders. Then Nehru will
again be denounced as "a running dog of Western imperialism."
So will U Nu. And so might Sukarno.

Stability in Asia too often hinges on the existence of a single
leader. In India the passing of Nehru will probably see the
eventual breakup of the Congress party into two groups, right
and left. The survival of democracy will then depend on
whether the Communists or the Socialists are able to attract
the allegiance of the left group, for in an underdeveloped
country such as India democracy can only survive as a system
of democratic socialism. The alternative is Communism.

Asia cannot escape from itself as Europe did. The disloca-
tions caused by the Industrial Revolution in Britain impelled
emigration abroad where in the older Dominions such as Australia, New Zealand and to a lesser degree South Africa empty
countries with small indigenous populations offered room for
settlement and advancement. Asia's mammoth and rapidly growing populations have no such escape reservoirs, which is why the

impact of science and technology—that is, of the Industrial Revolution—must cause tremendous displacement and disorganisation unless advancement keeps pace with the rate of population
growth, which in turn must be rigorously controlled. To avail
themselves of modern industrial techniques and simultaneously
to preserve their economic and social stability the countries of
Asia must possess a sufficiency of managerial and technical talent and of financial surpluses, both of which were available
when Britain and the countries of Europe achieved their Industrial Revolution.

Lack of these prerequisites compels Asian lands to depart
from the road of traditional capitalism, which even if they
wished it is not open to them, and to plan the transformation of
their societies under some form of state direction and control.
Hence the adoption of a mixed economy which includes free
enterprise and governmental planning.

Thus the Asian picture resolves itself as a battle for the survival of peoples and ideas. Communism believes it can win
through by the process of the double squeeze, by legal and illegal methods, by persuasion and violence, by identifying nationalism with Communism and simultaneously by invoking the
examples of Russia and China, by the promise of jobs to the unemployed and the bait of dictatorial power to the politically
frustrated. Behind all this is the formidable power of the Russo-
Chinese bloc. For Communism's first and last weapon is force.

The virtue of Communism in Asian eyes is its promise of economic security; its vice consists in its denial of individual freedom. Based on force, its sanction is force, the violence incarnate
in a system motivated primarily by fear and hate. Communism
therefore can offer the new independent countries of Asia neither democracy in the form of individual freedom nor peace as
an assurance against violence, fear and hatred. But it does
seek to delude the vast, rapidly growing masses of the underdeveloped world with the promise of economic security, and
by using parliamentary instruments for the capture of political
power it assumes the garb of democracy while simultaneously
attempting to equate nationalism with Communism.

What have the democrats of Asia and the West to offer
against this? Political freedom means much to the renascent

countries of Asia, but the value of individual liberty has still to
be fully understood and respected. In Asia's eyes independence
symbolises the self-respect which for centuries it had lost with
the loss of its freedom. The nations of Europe have enjoyed
political freedom long enough to take it for granted and to elevate the value of other ideas such as democracy, free enterprise and individual freedom above it.

This difference in attitude or priorities is reflected in a recent
and curious development: while the West's stress remains on
democracy that of Asia remains on political independence. In
a compromise between the two ideas of democracy and freedom
the countries of Asia would rather compromise on democracy
than on freedom, while Western countries are inclined to do the
reverse. The phrase "controlled democracy" recurs in countries
such as Indonesia and Pakistan, while a new idea of "controlled
freedom" is enunciated, most notably as Asia sees it, by the
Eisenhower Doctrine in the Middle East. Britain operates on
much the same lines in some of the Arab States strung along the
Persian Gulf.

This development does not imply that the West seeks to re-
impose colonialism or that Asia desires to repudiate democracy.
Its significance lies in the revelation that a different order of priorities influences the two regions and governs the actions of its
peoples and rulers. No one knowing the American people, their
anti-colonial history and the political integrity of President Eisenhower would for a moment entertain the thought that the
West would rather have colonialism re-established in Asia than
Communism; for the West knows, as Asia does, that the one sure
way of establishing Communism in Asia is by re-establishing colonialism.

The Eisenhower Doctrine extends what is in effect a protective shield over the Middle East. It promises to buoy up the
stability and strength of any country in this region with economic aid and military equipment—in other words, with guns
and bread. But the offer is conditional on these countries having
no truck with the other side, with Soviet Russia or Communist
China. Left to themselves it is possible that many of these
countries, including Egypt, would rather have affiliations with
the West than with the East. But to stipulate a prior embargo

on even economic relations with one side or the other is resented
as an encroachment on political sovereignty. To Asia it appears
as an attempt to impose "controlled freedom." The double
distortion which affects the Asian and Western outlooks expresses itself in "controlled democracy" on the one side and in
"controlled freedom" on the other. Therein lies the danger to
both democracy and freedom.

However well-intentioned America's foreign policy might be—
and there is no valid reason to suppose otherwise—its application
under the magic touch of Mr. Dulles has had some unfortunate
results. In August 1956, while on my way to the United
States, I had an hour-long interview with Colonel Nasser in
Cairo. The Suez Canal nationalisation crisis was then at its
height, and a few weeks earlier Washington had gravely of-
fended Cairo by the sudden withdrawal of its offer to finance
the Aswan Dam. I did not realise the depth of Egyptian
indignation until I spoke to Nasser. His anger was directed not
so much at the refusal as at the form in which the refusal was
conveyed, reflecting, as he felt it did, on Egypt's financial credit.

"How does it help a big nation like America," he asked, "to
damage the financial credit of a small country like Egypt? What
do they hope to gain by this?"

Throughout the interview, which touched many controversial
points, Nasser had shown no evidence of excitability, but he did
when he referred to the dam. He speaks good English, with a
French accent, but at this point his English lapsed. He banged
his fist on the table. "It hurted me!" he exclaimed.

Democracy no more than Communism can survive in Asia on
guns alone. There must be bread. Political stability can be
built only on a base of economic progress and order, and the
West must recognise that politically and economically the roads
that lead to democracy need not be the same for Asia and
Europe. The different circumstances in which Asia is achieving
its Industrial Revolution call for different means, economically
implying a larger degree of State direction and control than the
West experienced or envisages. Politically nationalism having
reached Asia a hundred years late, its forms of political democracy must differ and might be distinct. The difficulty is that
though the forms of government are democratic in free Asia,

their spirit is not always democratic and in some countries is becoming increasingly authoritarian.

The spirit surely is of primary urgency. In what form it is contained is of secondary importance, provided the form is true and authentic and worthy of the spirit it enshrines. We come back to where we started, the old problem of means and ends. In achieving and preserving the end which is democracy, Asia and Europe labour under a common misconception, believing that the same means must automatically lead to the same ends, which is not true; for different means, provided they are animated by the same high spirit and resolve, can equally lead to the same ends; while similar means, deployed in a conflicting spirit, will lead to different ends.

If democracy as a political system has not worked successfully in Asia, it is not because the principles of democracy are wrong but because the political system or institutions through which Asia works it are too close to the Western mould and unsuited to Asian conditions. Asia must be left to reshape and build a true Asian form of democracy, institutionally different from that of the West but in no way departing from the principles which commonly inspire it. For the principles are basic and universal; the forms or institutions are capable of infinite variety. In Asia the principles of democracy are best expressed economically and politically as democratic socialism.

Democracy is ensured economically when the instruments of economic power are so employed and controlled as to guarantee social justice, while politically democracy is safeguarded as long as political power rests in the people and in their representatives who also participate in the functions of government. The choice in Asia is not between Communism and democracy as America and the West understand it, but between Communism and a type of democracy, such as social democracy or democratic socialism, which is better suited or adapted to Asia's needs.

The institutional forms in which such a democracy expresses itself must be left to each Asian country to determine. In India the feeling in certain socialist and liberal circles that democracy is not working successfully as a political system has led to a retreat from the present Western parliamentary forms to a grassroots search for a true democratic base in the villages. Some such emotive force has moved politicians like the American-trained socialist Jayaprakash Narayan to ally himself with the Bhoodan movement which has its roots in rural India.

Gandhi had much the same idea of democracy, for in a talk with Lois Fischer some years ago he envisaged the pyramid of India's political structure as broad-based on her villages. Like Plato's city-state Gandhi's ideal was the Indian village state with each of India's seven hundred thousand villages "organised according to the will of its citizens, all of them voting."

"Then," he said to Fischer, "there would be seven hundred thousand votes and not four hundred million. Each village, in other words, would have one vote. The villages would elect their district administrations, and the district administrations would elect the provincial administrations, and these in turn would elect a president who would be the national chief executive."

"This is very much like the Soviet system," Fischer commented.

"I did not know that," said Gandhi. "But I don't mind."

He didn't mind because the spirit of democracy mattered much more to him than its institutional forms, and the institutional forms he conceived were those which he believed were best suited to India. There is a relish of irony and of poetic justice in the thought of Asia's using Soviet institutional forms for expressing and consolidating the democratic spirit.

In assessing Asia the West must recognise that the vast majority of Asian intellectuals and leaders are both anti-capitalist and anti-Communist, much like the men and women in the Soviet satellite countries behind the iron curtain who rebel against the tyranny of the Kremlin. Neither politically, economically nor socially do the satellite countries want the clock put back by exchanging one master for another. Their attitude is curiously similar to that of Asian countries, for like them they feel that their underdeveloped and unbalanced economies can be best expanded and enlarged by a form of socialist planning, while individual freedom can again be most effectively preserved in the form of democratic socialism. Like many Asian countries they also incline to a policy of non-alignment. They want to be left in peace and to live in peace with everyone.

Here as in Asia the task of the West, if the world is to be made safe for democracy, is to help the people to help themselves; for just as Asia's hungry masses can only achieve better living standards through their own efforts aided technically and economically by the West, so also the captive peoples behind the iron curtain know that freedom must be won primarily from within. As in Asia also, the vacuum created by the withdrawal of an over-riding power in Eastern Europe can only be filled effectively not by another power stepping in but by the peoples of these regions organising themselves.

Would it, for instance, not be wiser to create a buffer belt of uncommitted States between Western Europe and the frontiers of Russia rather than to give Moscow in the event of war the advantage of erupting from the Elbe? The reunification of Germany is difficult if divorced from the context of Central Europe, but treated as part of the bigger problem it becomes less arduous to achieve. In an age of intercontinental air forces and missiles the presence of a few American divisions in Europe can hardly alter the balance of power. Sweden, which belongs neither to NATO nor to the Soviet system, is uncommitted and, like Finland, which is also uncommitted, is therefore a factor which makes for stability rather than for insecurity. The creation and extension of an uncommitted buffer belt between Russia and Western Europe must proportionately increase international security and stability, for such a belt, guaranteed by Russia and the West as part of a general European security pact, would extend the frontiers of democracy and bring nearer the One World of which many of the world's peoples dream. In order to ensure such a settlement the pact would have to commit all the signatories to immediate armed action against any State which violated the settlement.

A similar settlement in the Middle East, South Asia and the Far East, guaranteed by both the United States and Russia, would also extend the areas of democracy and peace in Asia. And as in Europe, such a settlement would be of more advantage to the West than to Russia, whose aim it is by creating tensions and keeping alive a climate of insecurity and fear to generate precisely those conditions in which Communism thrives and democracy wilts.

The satellite countries, to paraphrase Bishop Dibelius's remark, knowing what Communism is, are more allergic to the Kremlin than the free countries of Asia who only know what the Communists do. But the democratic socialism now widely discussed in Asia represents in fact not only a stage away from Communism but beyond it. It is democratic Asia's counter to Communism.

On the philosophical plane the late Manabendra Nath Roy had been working for many years on his creed of scientific humanism. This, while adopting Communist methodology through a scientific view of human nature and a rationalist interpretation of cultural and social history, offers a restatement of humanism as a challenge to Communism and other forms of institutionalism. Roy rejected both formal parliamentary democracy and an unbridled competitive economy as well as political dictatorship and economic regimentation. Stressing the freedom and initiative of the individual, he found his ideal of scientific humanism in a system of decentralised direct democracy and a co-operative economy. Along some such lines free Asia's thoughts and actions should move, and it may be that the satellite countries now behind the iron curtain will do likewise.

For if democracy is to survive, to strengthen its roots and expand, it must be allowed to nourish its spirit in different countries in different forms. Science, by annihilating space and distance, is mixing up the peoples of the world more than somewhat, and the horizons of human thought are simultaneously being more intensively and extensively enlarged. Men look at the past, present and future, and at the world, Asian, African, European and American, from a new plateau of vision, understanding and perspective. As Arnold Toynbee writes: "Our own descendants are not going to be just western like ourselves. They are going to be heirs of Confucius and Lao-Tse as well as Socrates, Plato and Plotinus; heirs of Gautama Buddha as well as Deutero-Isaiah and Jesus Christ; heirs of Zarathustra and Muhummed as well as Elijah and Elisha and Peter and Paul . . . and heirs (if still wallowing in the Serbonian bog of politics) of Lenin and Gandhi and Sun Yat Sen as well as Cromwell and George Washington and Mazzini."

Even the old concept of the African Negro as devoid of culture has changed as research and excavation have unearthed in regions in eastern Africa, in Rhodesia, Mozambique, Western Uganda and beyond the rivers of Ethiopia traces of a civilisation which existed for at least a millennium before Dr. Strydom made his appearance with his cave-man cry of *apartheid*. The frontiers of democracy are moving as enlightenment goes hand in hand with political progress and economic advance. To defend democracy we must know it.

The advantage which the Reds wield over Asia's hungry masses is that the strength of Communism lies in its promises. The strength of democracy is in its performances. Only those who have truly savoured the dignity of democratic living and known the value of individual freedom are willing to defend it with their lives. America has. So has Britain, and the countries of Western Europe. But Asia has still to savour it, and will only defend it when, adopting and working it, she at last knows it.